"This comprehensive and relevant resource provides counselors across settings with practical tips and tangible tools to foster client well-being and counselor wellness. Nonjudgmental strategies are grounded in theories and steeped in competencies. Through realistic vignettes, thought leaders illustrate how to implement techniques in an ethically and culturally appropriate manner. Counselors interested in incorporating spirituality and religion from a strengths-based perspective will find this guide indispensable for presenting concerns with people of all ages."

—**Simone Lambert, PhD, LPC, NCC**, counseling core faculty at Capella University and president of the American Counseling Association (2018–2019)

"This book is an excellent addition to any counselor's bookshelf. The table of contents reads like a who's who of the intersection of counseling and spirituality. One of the strengths of this text is that it has a balance of practitioners, who speak to the experiences in the counseling room, and of researchers, who provide a broader context for understanding. I enjoyed the reading and was challenged to expand my own beliefs about counseling."

—**Gerard Lawson, PhD**, professor of counselor education at Virginia Polytechnic Institute and past president of the American Counseling Association

"Gill and Freund provide a comprehensive resource for counselors integrating spirituality and religious issues into their clinical practices. Using critical ethical and multicultural lenses, *Spirituality and Religion in Counseling* interweaves rich case studies and practical tools that aid a counselor's ability to grow. This volume will help practitioners better understand clients' spiritual worldviews and honor the sacred in the lives of those they work with. A great addition to any professional library!"

—**Michael M. Kocet, PhD, LMHC, NCC, ACS**, professor and department chair of counselor education at the Chicago School of Professional Psychology and former board member of the Association for Spiritual, Ethical, and Religious Values in Counseling

"Gill and Freund provide a bold and essential next step in integrating spirituality and religion into the counseling process. By providing a developmental lens, case studies, and focusing on assessment and intervention skills for helping clients with spiritual and religious issues, they have moved us from the theoretical to the practical. Many of us have been waiting years for such a volume and the editors have not disappointed!"

—**Charles F. Gressard, PhD, LPC, NCC**, chancellor professor in counselor education at the College of William and Mary

Spirituality and Religion in Counseling

Spirituality and Religion in Counseling: Competency-Based Strategies for Ethical Practice provides mental health professionals and counselors in training with practical information for understanding and responding to clients' needs using a spiritual and religious framework. This work conceptualizes spiritual and faith development in a holistic way, using case examples and practical interventions to consider common issues through a variety of approaches and frameworks. This is an essential compendium of actionable strategies and solutions for counselors looking to address clients' complex spiritual and religious lives and foster meaningful faith development.

Carman S. Gill is an associate professor of mental health counseling at Florida Atlantic University and a past president of the Association for Spiritual, Ethical, and Religious Values in Counseling (ASERVIC).

Robert R. Freund is a visiting assistant professor of counseling and psychological services at the State University of New York at Oswego.

Spirituality and Religion in Counseling

Competency-Based Strategies for Ethical Practice

Edited by
Carman S. Gill and Robert R. Freund

Routledge
Taylor & Francis Group

NEW YORK AND LONDON

First published 2018
by Routledge
711 Third Avenue, New York, NY 10017

and by Routledge
2 Park Square, Milton Park, Abingdon, Oxon OX14 4RN

Routledge is an imprint of the Taylor & Francis Group, an informa business

Library of Congress Cataloging in Publication Data
Names: Gill, Carman S., editor. | Freund, Robert R., editor.
Title: Spirituality and religion in counseling : competency-based
strategies for ethical practice / edited by Carman S. Gill and
Robert R. Freund.
Description: New York, NY : Routledge,
2018. | Includes bibliographical references and index.
Identifiers: LCCN 2018004785 (print) | LCCN 2018006623 (ebook) |
ISBN 9781315211046 (eBook) | ISBN 9781138282018 (hardback) |
ISBN 9781138282025 (pbk.)
Subjects: LCSH: Counseling--Religious aspects. | Counseling
psychology.
Classification: LCC BF636.68 (ebook) | LCC BF636.68 .S65 2018
(print) | DDC 158.3--dc23
LC record available at https://lccn.loc.gov/2018004785

ISBN: 978-1-138-28201-8 (hbk)
ISBN: 978-1-138-28202-5 (pbk)
ISBN: 978-1-315-21104-6 (ebk)

Typeset in Bembo
by Taylor & Francis Books

This book is dedicated to the individuals who value the struggle for deeper spiritual intimacy across all walks of life. It is for the advocate, the seeker, the counselor, and the student. We dedicate this work to those who tap into the intrinsic longings for interconnectedness with the universe, and wish to know it better. It is for everyone, in the hope that this book will leave the world of the reader a better place.

Contents

List of Contributors   xi

About the Editors   xiii

Foreword: The Intersection of Spirituality and Counseling: History, Competencies, and an Ethical Mandate   xiv
CRAIG S. CASHWELL

Acknowledgments   xxii

Introduction: Purpose of this Book   1
CARMAN S. GILL AND ROBERT R. FREUND

PART I

Counselor Preparation and Understanding the Client in Terms of Spirituality and Religious Issues   7

1   Counselor Self-Awareness and Counselor Communication   9
STEPHANIE F. DAILEY

2   Understanding Worldview and the Impact of Spiritual Systems through Assessment: Open and Closed Faith Systems   32
CARMAN S. GILL AND ROBERT R. FREUND

3   Understanding the Development of Spirituality, Religion, and Faith in the Client's Life   51
ROBERT R. FREUND AND CARMAN S. GILL

4   Understanding the Spiritual Domain through Case Conceptualization   64
GEORGE STOUPAS, VASSILIA BINENSZTOK, AND LEN SPERRY

PART II
Theories and Interventions   **83**

  5 Spirituality and Existentialism   85
     JODI L. TANGEN AND ANDY D. FELTON

  6 Transpersonal Theory and Interventions   98
     SCOTT L. LIPP, CARMAN S. GILL, AND RYAN D. FOSTER

  7 Adler's Individual Psychology and Spirituality   116
     ROBERT R. FREUND, ANDREW Z. BAKER, AND PAUL R. PELUSO

  8 Spiritual and Religious Interventions in "Third Wave"
     Cognitive Behavioral Therapies   132
     VASSILIA BINENSZTOK, TIFFANY E. VASTARDIS, AND CARMAN S. GILL

  9 Addressing Spiritual Themes with Narrative Therapy   147
     ANDREW Z. BAKER AND ROBERT R. FREUND

 10 12-Step Spirituality   159
     KARROL-JO FOSTER

 11 Family Systems: Genograms and Socio-metric Assessments   175
     BRIAN S. CANFIELD

 12 Addressing Spiritual and Religious Themes with Play,
     Creativity, and Experiential Interventions   189
     W. BRYCE HAGEDORN, ELIZABETH PENNOCK, AND
     LAURA RENDON FINNELL

 13 Special Issues and Interventions Related to Spirituality   207
     ELIZABETH O'BRIEN AND CARMAN S. GILL

     Index   223

Contributors

Andrew Z. Baker, Ph.D., is a licensed mental health counselor and Adjunct Professor of Mental Health Counseling at Florida Atlantic University in Boca Raton, FL.

Vassilia Binensztok, M.S., is a licensed mental health counselor and doctoral candidate in Counselor Education at Florida Atlantic University in Boca Raton, FL.

Brian S. Canfield, Ed.D., is Professor of Mental Health Counseling at Florida Atlantic University in Boca Raton, FL.

Stephanie F. Dailey, Ed.D., LPC, NCC, ACS, is Assistant Professor of Counseling at Hood College in Frederick, MD.

Andy D. Felton, Ph.D., is Assistant Professor in the Rehabilitation and Counseling Department at the University of Wisconsin-Stout in Menomonie, WI.

Laura Rendon Finnell, M.S., is a licensed mental health counselor and doctoral candidate in Counselor Education at the University of Central Florida in Orlando, FL.

Karrol-Jo Foster, M.P.S., is a licensed mental health counselor, certified addictions professional and doctoral candidate in Counselor Education at Florida Atlantic University in Boca Raton, FL.

Ryan D. Foster, Ph.D., is Assistant Professor of Counseling and Clinic Coordinator at Tarleton State University in Waco, TX.

W. Bryce Hagedorn, Ph.D., is Associate Professor of Counselor Education and Program Director of Counselor Education and School Psychology at the University of Central Florida in Orlando, FL.

Scott L. Lipp, M.S., is a registered licensed mental health counselor intern and doctoral candidate in Counselor Education at Florida Atlantic University in Boca Raton, FL.

Elizabeth O'Brien, Ph.D., LPC, is Associate Professor and Counselor Education Program Director in the School of Professional Studies at the University of Tennessee at Chattanooga in Chattanooga, TN.

Paul R. Peluso, Ph.D., is Professor of Mental Health Counseling and Department Chair at Florida Atlantic University in Boca Raton, FL.

Elizabeth Pennock, M.A., is a licensed mental health counselor and doctoral candidate in Counselor Education at the University of Central Florida in Orlando, FL.

George Stoupas, Ph.D., is Associate Professor in the Human Services Department, addiction studies track, at Palm Beach State College in Lake Worth, FL.

Len Sperry, M.D., Ph.D., is Professor of Mental Health Counseling and Director of Clinical Training at Florida Atlantic University in Boca Raton, FL.

Jodi L. Tangen, Ph.D., is Assistant Professor of Counselor Education at North Dakota State University in Fargo, ND.

Tiffany E. Vastardis, M.S., is a registered mental health counseling intern and doctoral candidate in Counselor Education at Florida Atlantic University in Boca Raton, FL.

About the Editors

Carman S. Gill is currently an associate professor at Florida Atlantic University. She holds a Ph.D., a license in counseling (LPC), approved clinical supervisors credential (ACS) and a national counselor credential (NCC). She is a past president of ASERVIC and has served that organization as a past-presidents advisory board member, newsletter editor, member of the board of directors, secretary and conference committee co-chair. Dr. Gill has co-authored multiple peer-reviewed journal articles on spiritual topics including "Poor, Rural Women: The Impact of Spirituality and Religion on Wellness Across the Lifespan," "Spirituality Competency Scale: Further Analysis," "Forgive and Forget? Forgiveness As an Indicator of Wellness among Counselors-in-training," "Exploring the Spiritual Domain: Tools for Integrating Spirituality and Religion in Counseling," and "Spirituality and Religiosity: Factors Affecting Wellness for Poor, Rural Women." She has co-authored the *DSM-5 Learning Companion for Counselors*, a best-selling book on the effective use of the *DSM-5*, two book chapters on assessing spirituality, and is currently investigating the spiritual competence of counselors.

Robert R. Freund is currently a visiting assistant professor of counseling and psychological services at the State University of New York at Oswego. He holds a Ph.D. in counselor education, a licensure in counseling (LMHC), and a national counselor credential (NCC). He holds master's degrees in developmental psychology and clinical mental health counseling. In addition to teaching, he works in private practice, and has had experience working in community mental health, substance abuse, and college counseling environments. Rob currently conducts research on the therapeutic relationship in coordination with Dr. Paul Peluso in the Alliance Lab at Florida Atlantic University. He has presented at multiple conferences for the American Counseling Association and American Psychological Association. He is currently co-author on a 2017 peer-reviewed journal article on this work titled, "Predicting Dropout in Counseling Using Affect Coding of the Therapeutic Relationship: An Empirical Analysis."

Foreword: The Intersection of Spirituality and Counseling

History, Competencies, and an Ethical Mandate

Craig S. Cashwell

> "The privilege of a lifetime is to become who you truly are."
>
> —Carl Gustav Jung

In the mid-1990s, a dear friend, colleague, and frequent collaborator of mine wanted to complete his dissertation study on the integration of client religious and spiritual beliefs within the counseling process. With the support of a seasoned and talented dissertation chair who was open to the topic, he dove into the existing literature on the topic. As it turned out, though, it was a dive into a very shallow pool as there was little scholarly literature on the topic. Within just a few months, he and his chair agreed to go in a different research direction, as there simply was not enough information in the scholarly literature to support a dissertation study. Oh, how far we have come in the past 25 years!

It is not surprising, though, that the literature on the intersection of spirituality and counseling is relatively new. Historically, the relationship between the mental health professions and religion/spirituality has been tenuous and complex. In early works, Freud (1928) wrote negatively of religion as wishful illusions, a disavowal of reality, and a regression to infantile narcissism. Around the same time, however, James (1902), an American psychologist, was writing about the positive aspects of religion, viewing it as a belief in an unseen order in the universe and emphasizing the power in harmoniously adjusting to that order.

Perhaps the first therapist to write extensively about the important intersection between religion, spirituality and mental health, however, was Carl Jung, a Swiss psychiatrist and psychotherapist who split from Freud and founded analytical psychology. Jung was critical of religion for over-emphasizing the positive aspects of life and ignoring the difficulties, writing throughout his career on the importance of shadow work. At his core, however, he believed that people were longing for meaning and purpose that could not be found through a psychological perspective alone. He often spoke and wrote of the first half of life, which he believed to be largely about building a "self" or ego, and the second half of life, which he believed to be foremost about going inward and transcending the ego that had been so carefully constructed in the first half of life. In fact, Jung (1955) wrote that *every* patient in the second half of life was struggling because they had lost what the great wisdom traditions (or religions) had to offer their followers, and that their work ultimately was finding and reclaiming this perspective, which necessarily involved a de-centering of the self to serve a higher purpose. The writings of Jung heavily influenced the perspectives of many therapists, but even contemporary theorists such as Albert Ellis (2001) referred to religion as childish dependency.

There remains, then, a dynamic tension in the relationship between religion/spirituality and the mental health professions. Researchers (Cashwell et al., 2013) have found that professional counselors tend to identify as more spiritual than religious and tend to be less religious than their clients or the general population. Further, as Kurtz and Ketcham (2009) note, religion and mental health tend to know one another by caricature, that is, by the worst examples of each, such as religion that discourages treatment of severe mental health issues, encouraging instead that the problem is solely spiritual and, accordingly, that interventions need only be spiritual (i.e., "pray it away"), clergy and lay-people who shame those with a mental illness as spiritually weak, or therapists who decry religion as did Freud and Ellis, essentially shaming clients for their religious beliefs. At a practice level, supervisors uncomfortable with religious and spiritual issues mandate that supervisees avoid these topics (Ross, Suprina, and Brack, 2013) and mental health professionals, largely fearful of imposing values, avoid the topics of client religion and spirituality (Cashwell et al., 2013).

Unfortunately, this leads to fragmentation of the healing process, with some counselors refusing to address issues related to religion and spirituality, immediately referring such issues to the client's clergy member. Such compartmentalization is far from ideal, however, as it separates these two critical aspects of the individual. As a popular bumper sticker reads, "We are not human beings having a spiritual experience. We are spiritual beings having a human experience." That is, we are both human, complete with complex thoughts, emotions, behaviors, and relationships, and spiritual. To not take both the psychological and spiritual into consideration is to treat the individual sitting across from you as similarly fragmented. As a mental health professional, how can you possibly promote optimal wellness and wholeness by promoting such fragmentation?

Around the same time that my colleague was finding an insufficient base of scholarly literature to support a dissertation on the intersection of religion/spirituality and mental health, the Association for Spiritual, Ethical, and Religious Values in Counseling (ASERVIC), a division of the American Counseling Association, was convening a group of counselors and counselor educators for the first Summit on Spirituality (Cashwell and Watts, 2010). This working group established a description of spirituality and a set of competencies to guide competent and ethical practice. Initially, however, these competencies were codified only in the ASERVIC newsletter and, as such, were not archived. It was not until several years later that Miller (1999), writing of the competencies in an article published in the *Journal of Counseling and Development*, codified the competencies in an archived format and it was another several years before the competencies were examined in detail for counseling practitioners (Cashwell and Young, 2005). From 2007 to 2009, ASERVIC convened a series of meetings known as Summit II, which resulted in a revision to the competencies that remain in place today (Cashwell and Watts, 2010). The revised competencies have the advantage of being grounded in empirical research (Robertson, 2010; Robertson and Young, 2011) which has been expanded over time (Cashwell and Young, 2011; Dailey, Robertson, and Gill, 2015).

The Competencies for Addressing Spiritual and Religious Issues in Counseling provide guidelines that complement ethical standards of the profession and should be used in conjunction with evidence-based practices. The competencies were developed in six major categories aligning with the factor analytic studies of Robertson (2010) and Dailey et al. (2015) and are as follows:

Culture and Worldview

1   The professional counselor can describe the similarities and differences between spirituality and religion, including the basic beliefs of various spiritual systems, major world religions, agnosticism, and atheism.
2   The professional counselor recognizes that the client's beliefs (or absence of beliefs) about spirituality and/or religion are central to his or her worldview and can influence psychosocial functioning.

Counselor Self-Awareness

1   The professional counselor actively explores his or her own attitudes, beliefs, and values about spirituality and/or religion.
2   The professional counselor continuously evaluates the influence of his or her own spiritual and/or religious beliefs and values on the client and the counseling process.
3   The professional counselor can identify the limits of his or her understanding of the client's spiritual and/or religious perspective and is acquainted with religious and spiritual resources, including leaders, who can be avenues for consultation and to whom the counselor can refer.

Human and Spiritual Development

1   The professional counselor can describe and apply various models of spiritual and/or religious development and their relationship to human development.

Communication

1   The professional counselor responds to client communications about spirituality and/or religion with acceptance and sensitivity.
2   The professional counselor uses spiritual and/or religious concepts that are consistent with the client's spiritual and/or religious perspectives and that are acceptable to the client.
3   The professional counselor can recognize spiritual and/or religious themes in client communication and is able to address these with the client when they are therapeutically relevant.

Assessment

1   During the intake and assessment processes, the professional counselor strives to understand a client's spiritual and/or religious perspective by gathering information from the client and/or other sources.

Diagnosis and Treatment

1   When making a diagnosis, the professional counselor recognizes that the client's spiritual and/or religious perspectives can a) enhance well-being; b) contribute to client problems; and/or c) exacerbate symptoms.
2   The professional counselor sets goals with the client that are consistent with the client's spiritual and/or religious perspectives.
3   The professional counselor is able to a) modify therapeutic techniques to include a client's spiritual and/or religious perspectives, and b) utilize spiritual and/or religious practices as techniques when appropriate and acceptable to a client's viewpoint.
4   The professional counselor can therapeutically apply theory and current research supporting the inclusion of a client's spiritual and/or religious perspectives and practices.

These competencies are aspirational as no therapist can master all of these areas, yet it is incumbent on the ethical practitioner to be working toward increased knowledge, skills, and self-awareness to best support those they serve. Why are these competencies and the ethical and intentional attention to the intersection of religion/spirituality and counseling so critical? The answer is multi-faceted:

1   Many clients identify as religious and spiritual – Researchers have shown that 86 percent of the U.S. population endorses a belief in the Divine and more than 80 percent report a specific religious affiliation (Gallup, 2015). Additionally, one of the fastest growing groups in the U.S. is those who identify as spiritual but not religious.

2   There is a clear ethical mandate within all mental health professions to not impose our values on the client. While client autonomy is a core value for mental health professionals, this is simple and straightforward only within the walls of the ivory tower of academia. In the therapy room, it is complex and nuanced and every counselor, if they are honest, can list multiple clients and presenting issues that test their capacity to not impose personal values.

3   Relatedly, there is great variance in beliefs not only across major religious and spiritual traditions, but also *within* traditions. That is, the label with which someone identifies (Wiccan, Buddhist, Christian) tells you little about the actual beliefs of the individual. Accordingly, a thorough assessment is necessary to understand the unique worldview of the individual client sitting across from you.

4   Within the counseling profession specifically, two core areas of training are *social and cultural diversity* and *human growth and development*. Religious and spiritual beliefs, rituals, and experiences are a vital aspect of a client's culture (Fukuyama, Siahpoush, and Sevig, 2005), one that intersects with other aspects of culture to constitute personal identity (Foster and Holden, 2011). Further, many spiritual and faith development models provide detailed information both on the developmental process and how to support/cultivate optimal client development (Foster and Holden, 2011), a cornerstone of the counseling profession (Myers and Sweeney, 2005). Culture and development are addressed in more detail in Chapters 2 and 3 of this text, respectively.

The competencies are aspirational and counselors who work diligently through study, consultation, and supervision will become more adept at implementing these competencies with clients. Two over-arching concepts from the multicultural counseling literature, *broaching* and *cultural humility*, provide important context to the competencies. *Broaching* has been defined as a "consistent and ongoing attitude of openness with a genuine commitment by the counselor to continually invite the client to explore issues of diversity" (Day-Vines et al., 2007, p. 402). Applied to religion, this *attitude* of openness and curiosity, rather than an expert stance, is critical to the application of the spirituality competencies. Similarly, *cultural humility* refers to the "ability to maintain an interpersonal stance that is other-oriented (or open to the other) in relation to aspects of cultural identity that are most important to the client" (Hook et al., 2013, p. 354). Note that both definitions include *open* or *openness*. It is this stance of curious consultant, not of expert or enlightened guru that is most helpful to clients.

It seems critical to highlight at the close of this introduction, however, that while the competencies are aspirational, failure to act within established best practices, including the competencies, broaching, and cultural humility, can do great damage to the therapeutic relationship, process and, indeed, the client. Consider the following scenarios:

- A novice therapist who recently attended a day-long workshop on the integration of spirituality in counseling uses a spiritually oriented intervention in a session with a client without providing context to the client or getting the client's permission. The client, a devout atheist, is angry by this but passively goes along. She does not return to counseling after that session.

- A devoutly religious client tells her story in the first session, one of depression and struggle. She speaks often of her religious faith and the belief that God is strengthening her through her personal struggles and teaching her to rely more fully on Him. The counselor, who defines himself as more spiritual than religious, does not attend to this part of her story and, instead, implements a treatment plan based on strategic planning and individual empowerment. The client tries to get her counselor to respond to the spiritual aspect of her experience, but he continues to ignore this part of her narrative.

- A client tells her counselor that she started meditating about three months prior, and has started hearing a voice both during meditation and outside of her practice. The counselor excuses herself and consults with her supervisor. Together, they enter the counseling room to discuss voluntary commitment. The client is shaken by this, believing the voice to be the voice of God that she now hears more directly, and refuses to agree to voluntary commitment. Without any further evaluation (which would have revealed that she remains highly functional in her life and that the "voice" is encouraging greater love, compassion, and self-compassion), the counselor files paperwork to have her evaluated for involuntary commitment. The client is evaluated and released later that evening. She does not return to see her counselor. Throughout her life, there are numerous times she might have benefitted from personal counseling, but her view of counseling is so negative from this experience, she never again seeks professional help.

Variations on these scenarios play out all too frequently in counseling rooms around the country. Counselors impose worldviews (scenario 1), dismiss client's religion and spirituality, either overtly or covertly by ignoring this content (scenario 2), and either elevate pathology to a spiritual experience or, as in the case of scenario 3, pathologize a spiritual experience.

It is in all this context, then, that *Spirituality and Religion in Counseling: Competency-Based Strategies for Ethical Practice*, is a much-needed text for the counseling field. This book is grounded in the established competencies, but is uniquely focused on the integration of spirituality and religion in counseling through the lens of practice skills and major counseling theories. In that regard, it is a critical read for the counseling practitioner who is serious about the competent and ethical integration of spirituality and religion in the counseling process.

References

Cashwell, C. S., and Watts, R. E. (2010). The new ASERVIC competencies for addressing spiritual and religious issues in counseling. *Counseling and Values*, 55, 2–5.

Cashwell, C. S., and Young, J. S. (Eds.) (2005). *Integrating spirituality in counseling: A guide to competent practice*. Alexandria, VA: American Counseling Association.

Cashwell, C. S., and Young, J. S. (Eds.) (2011). *Integrating spirituality in counseling: A guide to competent practice* (2nd ed.). Alexandria, VA: American Counseling Association.

Cashwell, C. S., Young, J. S., Fulton, C., Willis, B. T., Giordano, A. L., Wyatt, L. L., Crockett, J., Tate, B. N., and Welch, M. (2013). Clinical behaviors for addressing religious/spiritual issues: Do we "Practice What We Preach"? *Counseling and Values*, 58, 45–58.

Dailey, S. F., Robertson, L. A., and Gill, C. S. (2015). Spiritual competency scale: Further analysis. *Measurement and Evaluation in Counseling and Development*, 48, 15–29.

Day-Vines, N., Wood, S. M., Grothaus, T., Craigen, L., Holman, A., Dotson-Blake, K., and Douglass, M. J. (2007). Broaching the subjects of race, ethnicity, and culture during the counseling process. *Journal of Counseling and Development*, 85, 401–409.

Ellis, A. (2001). *Overcoming destructive beliefs, feelings, and behaviors: New directions for Rational Emotive behavior therapy*. Amherst, NY: Prometheus.

Foster, R. D., and Holden, J. M. (2011). Human and spiritual development and transformation. In C. S. Cashwell and J. S. Young (Eds.), *Integrating spirituality and religion into counseling: A guide to competent practice* (2nd ed., pp. 97–118). Alexandria, VA: American Counseling Association.

Freud, S. (1928). *The future of an illusion*. New York: Liveright.

Fukuyama, M. A., Siahpoush, F., and Sevig, T. D. (2005). Religion and spirituality in a cultural context. In C. S. Cashwell and J. S. Young (Eds.), *Integrating spirituality and religion into counseling: A guide to competent practice* (pp. 123–142). Alexandria, VA: American Counseling Association.

Gallup, G. (2015). *Religion: Historical Trends*. Princeton, NJ: Author. Retrieved from http://www.gallup.com/poll/1690/Religion.aspx?utm_source=how%20many%20people%20believe%20in%20God?&utm_medium=search&utm_campaign=tiles.

Hook, J. N., Davis, D. E., Owen, J., Worthington, Jr., E. L., and Utsey, S. O. (2013). Cultural humility: Measuring openness to culturally diverse clients. *Journal of Counseling Psychology*, 60(3), 353–366. doi:10.1037/a0032595.

James, W. (1902/2016). *The varieties of religious experience*. Charleston, SC: CreateSpace.

Jung, C. G. (1955). *Modern man in search of a soul*. San Diego, CA: Harcourt.

Kurtz, E., and Ketcham, K. (2009). *The spirituality of imperfection: Storytelling and the search for meaning*. New York: Bantam.

Miller, G. A. (1999). The development of the spiritual focus in counseling and counselor education. *Journal of Counseling and Development*, 77, 498–501.

Myers, J. E., and Sweeney, T. J. (2005). *Counseling for wellness: Theory, research, and practice*. Alexandria, VA: American Counseling Association.

Robertson, L. (2010). The spiritual competency scale. *Counseling and Values*, 55, 6–24.

Robertson, L. (2011). The revised ASERVIC spiritual competencies. In C. S. Cashwell and J. S. Young (Eds.), *Integrating spirituality and religion into counseling: A guide to competent practice* (2nd ed., pp. 25–42). Alexandria, VA: American Counseling Association.

Robertson, L. A., and Young, M. E. (2011). The revised ASERVIC Spiritual Competencies. In C. S. Cashwell and J. S. Young (Eds.), *Integrating religion and spirituality in counseling: A guide to competent practice* (2nd ed., pp. 25–42). Alexandria, VA: American Counseling Association.

Ross, D. K., Suprina, J. S., and Brack, G. (2013). The spirituality in supervision model (SACRED): An emerging model for a meta-synthesis of the literature. *Practitioner Scholar: Journal of Counseling and Professional Psychology, 2*, 68–83.

Acknowledgments

We would like to acknowledge those without whom the quality of this book would be greatly diminished and those without whom this book would not have been possible. First, we are very grateful for the hard work of all the chapter authors who agreed to share their time and expertise. This book would not have been possible without your efforts. We would like to thank the students who worked on this project, in particular, Tiffany Vastardis and Scott Lipp, both of whom willingly contributed extra effort toward this project. We look forward to great things from you both. We would like to thank colleagues who happily added extra support when asked, including Paul Peluso and Ryan Foster. Finally, where would we be without our dear family? Carman would like to specifically acknowledge and thank Robert and Dorothy Botkin, Rob Ambridge, Mark, Roberta, and Debbie for their support and love. She also acknowledges the support from Rev. Dean Kurpjuweit. Rob would like to acknowledge and thank his wife Jenny, his little daughter Claire, Andrew Baker, and Patricia Diaz, as well as Jim Bitter, for his training and expertise in Adlerian theory.

Introduction
Purpose of this Book

Carman S. Gill and Robert R. Freund

The purpose of this book is to aid psychotherapists, counselors, counselors in training and counselor educators in working with clients within the spiritual and religious domains. Nearly all clients are engaged in or have experience with these domains and, because of this reality, it is unethical not to attend to this aspect of their world. In the foreword for this book, Craig Cashwell describes ASERVIC's spiritual competencies. In preparing this book, we fully embraced these competencies and we used them as a scaffold for delivering our content. The literature and research surrounding these competencies continues to indicate a need for concrete information regarding the practical components related to integrating spiritual and religious aspects into counseling theories and interventions. Whereas practitioners appear proficient with self-awareness, intake assessment and diagnosis, there are gaps in the steps that follow. It is our intention to provide a useful resource for ethical, and spiritual, therapeutic practice.

When attempting to develop spiritual competency in clinical practice, many well-intentioned counselors focus exclusively on religion, and feel as if they need to have an in-depth understanding of specific religions and belief systems. As an intellectual task, this presents a daunting challenge. If someone were to become intimately familiar with the major faith traditions and variations of spiritual practice, he or she would likely need to attend a seminary or divinity school. Even if the task were accomplished, the well-meaning counselor would still be at risk for gross overgeneralization if he or she overlooked the individual differences in client's experiences of spirituality and religion. Since a vast majority of counselors do not take this approach to working with client spirituality, the counselor may instead rely on a cursory knowledge of major faiths and his or her own personal experiences. The resulting clinical practice does not inspire significant confidence in that counselor's ability to be truly useful in the spiritual realm, and yet, this is often the approach that is used in the classroom or in therapy.

Developing spiritual and religious competency is, in many ways, similar to education in engineering and technology fields. Today's fast pace of progress and innovation makes it nearly impossible for a novice engineering student to develop an effective, static knowledge base; by the time he or she graduates, much of the knowledge has already become obsolete! Engineering education then takes a *skills-based* approach to training students. Rather than merely teaching content, educators teach students how to learn and gain the knowledge needed to keep pace with a rapidly changing field. The resulting graduate engineers are fluid, versatile, and possess dynamic knowledge.

We believe that the same concept must necessarily apply to spiritual experiences. To attempt to provide adequate detail about all possible spiritual and religious systems would be overwhelming and inadequate, to say the least. We also consider it culturally insensitive to encapsulate our clients' spiritual experiences with generalities. For example, Christianity is often portrayed as teaching believers to follow a strict moral code. However, this does not account for the range of teaching, authority, and practice (e.g. fundamentalist Christianity vs. universalist Unitarian Christianity). Instead, we feel it is better for a counselor to learn a set of assessment and intervention skills that allow him to understand the dynamics of a client's spiritual experience. This also honors the subjective, post-modernistic nature of that individual's spiritual reality.

Organization of this Book

Conceptualizing religion and spirituality within the treatment planning process, with an appropriate developmental lens, is crucial to positive counseling outcomes. Further, understanding the integration of religious and spiritual aspects (the extent to which it is positive or negative) provides the key to appropriate theory and intervention selection. In this book, we follow the ASERVIC competencies, focusing heavily on the final four, which include diagnosis and treatment of client issues within the spiritual domain. In Section I, the first four chapters cover competencies 1–10 and the authors demonstrate competent counselor integration through detailed case studies. In Chapter 1, Stephanie Dailey provides an in-depth discussion of counselor self-awareness and communication. Chapter 2 describes culture and worldview, defines spirituality and religion, and explores belief systems in terms of a continuum of open to closed systems, as well as examining the specifics of spiritual assessment in the counseling process. In Chapter 3, we discuss development of faith, religion, and spirituality across the lifespan and Chapter 4 describes how to formulate a case conceptualization with spiritual and religious aspects fully integrated.

In Chapters 5–13, we give full attention to the impact of spiritual and religious aspects on client well-being. Here, the authors describe specific theories, issues and/or techniques aimed at ameliorating impairing symptoms and increasing holistic wellness. In Chapter 5, Tangen and Felton describe existentialism, the connection with spiritual and religious issues, appropriate interventions and a case study. Chapter 6 includes information about transpersonal psychology. The authors explore the meaning and history of transpersonal psychology, as well as the connections with spirituality, interventions and a case study. Adlerian theory is the focus of Chapter 7 and the authors express ideas pertinent to the spiritual and religious domains, as well as exploring interventions and illustrating these using a case study.

In Chapter 8, popular Third-Wave Cognitive-Behavioral Theories (CBT) are described, including Mindfulness-Based Cognitive-Behavioral Therapy (MBCT), Dialectical Behavioral Therapy (DBT), and Acceptance and Commitment Therapy (ACT). Along with the description of each, integration into the spiritual is elucidated, interventions are explored and we provide a case study for integration. Narrative Therapy is the focus of Chapter 9, in which authors expound on this theory and provides an integration with spiritual and religious concerns, as well as providing interventions and a case study. In Chapter 10, KJ Foster illuminates the history and efficacy of 12 Step Spirituality, describes integration into counseling within the spiritual domain and gives specific interventions, as well as an integrated case study based in this theory.

Chapters 11 through 13 vary from the previous theory-based chapters as the focus turns more toward special issues noted in spiritual and religious counseling. Chapter 11 focuses on family systems in terms of socio-metric assessments. Brian Canfield describes integration of spirituality and religion with the family system and provides multiple assessments, using a case example. In Chapter 12, Hagedorn, Pennock, and Finnell address spiritual and religious themes as they arise in counseling, using play, creativity, and experiential interventions. They explore integration using a case study. Chapter 13 includes special issues such as spiritual bypass, forgiveness and shame as well as expressive arts and creative interventions for addressing these special issues. As with all chapters, a case study is used to clarify the material.

Client Profiles and Chapter Case Studies

In order to preserve the practical spirit of the project, we have included five client profiles that authors have referenced in each chapter. Our goal in doing this has been to allow the reader to get a sense of application with a theory or concept in the relevant spiritual domain. These profiles are entirely fictitious, and are not based on any real-world or personal counseling experience of the editors. We include them here as a point of reference for you as you read through this book; be sure to explore them, and feel free to reference back to them when reading chapters later on, as the authors do not review the full details before discussing the case studies. What results is five different clients, discussed and interpreted in a myriad ways.

Susanna. Susanna is a 15-year-old, cisgender, Mexican American female whose parents identify as part of the Mormon faith. Susanna has been active in her church culture from a young age, and tells you that she finds value in the sense of community, lessons on encouragement, and moral structure that it provides. Recently however, Susanna was referred to you by her guidance counselor for difficulty with grades, social withdrawal, and evidence of self-harm. Her teachers became concerned with the marked change in Susanna's behavior at the start of the school year, as she is normally outgoing, friendly, and high achieving. When Susanna's art teacher noted several fresh score marks on her upper forearm, he became concerned and brought her to the counselor. In meeting with you, Susanna is initially reserved and guarded, describing her behavioral changes as the result of "stress." As the therapy progresses, Susanna reveals that her change in behavior is related to guilt, confusion, fear, and anger that resulted from feelings of same-sex attraction inconsistent with her faith background. She tells you that her same-sex attraction has been present since the start of puberty, but she was able to suppress it by investing her attention in academics. At the start of the school year, Susanna entered into a friendship with a girl in her class that developed into a mutual attraction. When her friend wrote her a note expressing her feelings of attraction, Susanna broke ties and attempted to rededicate herself to her classes and faith; she however describes being "tortured" by romantic thoughts of her former friend and the messages of her family and faith regarding sexual morality.

Marian. Marian is a 62-year-old, cisgender, heterosexual Caucasian woman who currently works as an office manager at a local clinic. Marian comes to treatment after a recent diagnosis of stage three breast cancer, describing ruminative worry, frequent thoughts about death, and panic attacks. She tells you that this is the second incidence of cancer in her life, and that she had gone through a successful chemotherapy/radiation treatment when she was in her early thirties. Although the first incidence of cancer was caught early on, the advanced stage of her current condition and her age have prompted Marian to feel a stronger sense of fear regarding the outcomes. Additionally, she has begun to evaluate her life to this point, and describes feelings of regret and loss regarding missed opportunities and mistakes made. Marian states that she considers the fleeting nature of existence, and worries about what may or may not follow after her passing if the treatment is not successful. She tells you that she identifies as agnostic, and that her open-minded perspectives on faith and spirituality complicate her sense of the future, as well as the value of her life to this point.

Nassir. Nassir is a 40-year-old, heterosexual, cisgender man who is currently in treatment recovering from addiction to prescription pain medication. He identifies as a practitioner of Islam, and states that his addiction is a source of significant moral failure that causes him great pain and distress. Nassir is highly acculturated to the social practices, values, and norms of the dominant culture, having moved to this country from Lebanon at a young age, and currently works as an insurance salesman. He shares that he received soft-tissue and spinal damage when he fell while ice-skating. After taking OxyContin as prescribed for several months while healing from his injury, Nassir developed a dependence on the medication that became apparent when he attempted to follow the doctor's recommendations to gradually wean himself off of use. Nassir began to purchase medication from dealers, spending most of his savings and falling under probation at his work. After an accidental overdose and brief hospitalization, Nassir voluntarily checked himself into a local detox facility, and is in an intensive outpatient program. He shares that he cannot reconcile how he lost so much of himself to his drug abuse, and struggles with how he will reconnect with his faith and faith community after completing treatment. "I feel like I can get the physical things back in order," he says, "but I feel like no one will ever see me like myself again. In my community, I'll always be 'less than' and maybe that's how it should be. I don't know how I'll ever feel like my old self, or feel connected to my faith again."

Lin, Paul, Adam, and John. Lin, a 34-year-old, Asian American cisgender woman, brings her two children (Adam, 14 and John, 11) and husband (Paul, 37) to treatment for family therapy seeking help with behavioral problems her children are currently displaying. Lin and Paul identify as Jehovah's Witnesses, and as such abstain from partaking in the celebration of major holidays and birthdays, as well as certain civic activities, such as serving in the military or saying the pledge of allegiance. The family recently moved for Paul's work, and left their extended family and a strong social support network to come to an area with a smaller faith community and no family support. Lin shares that they have been careful to raise their sons in accordance with the religious teachings of their faith, and that the boys understand what behavioral expectations exist for their conduct in the school and at home. Recently, however, Adam and John have begun to protest not being able to participate in the school's Halloween celebration, where students dress up and trick-or-treat throughout the school. They state that they don't like being the "oddballs," in the school and that they were bullied for not participating in the daily pledge of allegiance. More recently, Adam was invited to a new friend's birthday party, and he insists on going, despite the parent's attempts to reinforce the family's values regarding these issues. Lin and Paul share with you that the boys have been withdrawn and angry, have resisted completing household chores, and that Adam has periodically refused to engage in family prayer. The parents state that they are at a loss for how to help their sons adjust to the new environment and how to address the behavioral resistance without using force or escalating the conflict.

Cecily. Cecily is a 45-year-old, African American, heterosexual, cisgender woman. She comes to treatment at the suggestion of her pastor at a local community church because she has been struggling with symptoms of depression for a period of six months. She states that there was no significant event that precipitated her symptoms, and that the sadness and additional symptoms of worry related to sadness "just sort of crept up on me." She would have difficulty accomplishing obligatory tasks, spent much time sleeping, and cried often, particularly during church services. Cecily shares that she attempted to discuss her intense feelings of hopelessness, worthlessness, and lack of motivation with members of her congregation that she saw as mentors, but was dismayed to become the subject of some church gossip. As people became aware of her struggles, she says that many gave her advice to engage in more prayer, time reading the Bible, and faith in God to resolve her symptoms. Others suggested that she may be the subject of demonic oppression, while others still suggested that her depression was an indication of her lack of spirituality. When asked her perception of the symptoms, Cecily says "I don't know what to think. I just want to feel better. I feel like I'm failing God somehow by not trusting Him. But at the same time, He feels so far away in all of this. Is that because of me?"

Our Hope for You

This book represents a passion project, and we hope that you will find it to be useful both clinically and academically. For the practicing clinician, we hope that you will be able to apply the assessment tools and theoretical perspectives to your work with clients. The trans-theoretical perspectives of assessing and understanding spiritual and religious belief systems will provide a unique lens for conceptualizing their work with you. Depending on your theoretical orientation, we hope that you will find new depth and skills for bringing your particular brand of therapy to the benefit of others. We also believe that this book will provide educators and counselors in training with a common language for understanding each other and potential clients, as well as tools for working with them.

Part I

Counselor Preparation and Understanding the Client in Terms of Spirituality and Religious Issues

1 Counselor Self-Awareness and Counselor Communication

Stephanie F. Dailey

"He who knows others is wise. He who knows himself is enlightened."

—Lao Tzu

Introduction

Central to effective, ethical intervention in any client issue is counselor self-awareness and communication. Those who do not explore and acknowledge their own personal development, cultural heritage, intrapersonal strengths, and inherent biases are not only at risk of failing to develop a positive working alliance with clients (Hagedorn and Moorhead, 2011), but lack the ability to engage with clients in a culturally responsive, ethical manner (Arredondo and Toporek, 2004; Collins and Arthur, 2007; Rosin, 2015). Self-knowledge avails counselors the capacity to be responsive, authentic, and undistortingly centered on the client and counseling process. Thus, facilitating the counselor's ability to recognize, respond to, and utilize client communications regarding spiritual and religious concepts is integral to effective practice.

This chapter will explore the concept of self-awareness and provide counselors with a general understanding of counselor self-awareness as a core value of the counseling profession. The benefits of knowing oneself will be explored and consequences associated with deficiencies in awareness will be presented. Means by which counselors can extend their journey of self-exploration, specifically in relation to the spiritual and religious domain, will be investigated. As conjoint benefits of counselor self-awareness are acknowledged, ways in which the counselor can augment counselor/client communication will be presented. As with other chapters in this book, the reader will explore these concepts to promote a better understanding and utilization of the Association of Spiritual, Ethical and Religious Values in Counseling (ASERVIC) Competencies for Integrating Spirituality and Religion into Counseling (ASERVIC, 2009).

Self-Awareness

Self-reflection and awareness, repeatedly noted as ethical and professional obligations for competent and effective practice, lack clarity within our professional literature (Pompeo and Levitt, 2014; Richards, Campenni, and Muse-Burke, 2010; Rosin, 2015). Western definitions of awareness focus on "consciousness" as a combination of awareness and attention (Brown and Ryan, 2003). Awareness lies in the background as the "detector" of consciousness; a constant monitor of one's intrapersonal and interpersonal landscape. Attention, or *conscious awareness*, is something an individual is cognizant and intentional about. Definitions more specific to counseling highlight counselor self-awareness as an "ongoing process of both reflection and learning from which counselors gain personal understanding as well as insight into how they view clients" (Collins, Arthur, and Wong-Wylie, 2010, p. 340). Levitt and Moorhead (2013) assert that counselors who demonstrate self-awareness are able to "objectively identify their own set of values, beliefs, and biases, and recognize the impact of these things upon their actions" (p. 37).

Fundamental to conscious awareness is the ability of a counselor to be self-reflective of their unique value system for the purpose of constant reflection, or the self-monitoring of how these beliefs impact the counseling relationship (Pompeo and Levitt, 2014). Counselor *self-awareness* is the capacity of individuals to be attentive to their feelings, thoughts, and behaviors in the immediate experience of the counseling relationship (Oden, Miner-Holden, and Balkin, 2009; Richards et al., 2010; Williams, 2008). Self-awareness involves recognizing personal individuality, values, cultural backgrounds, and the lenses through which the world can be viewed. This includes understanding how problems are resolved and our understanding of how change takes place – both in regard to self and others. Self-awareness is the foundation of the counselor's chosen theoretical orientation, whether we realize it or not, and underlies *how* and *why* a counselor applies specific techniques and interventions into the counseling process. Self-awareness informs the counselor's ability to recognize and understand issues, such as ethnocentrism, and how these impact practice (Collins and Arthur, 2010). While there are many definitions, philosophies, and theological approaches to self-awareness, at the core of all of this is the timeless Socratic concept of "know thyself."

Counselor Self-Awareness: A Core Value

The importance of consciousness and self-examination lies at the root of ancient philosophy, historically observed by Socrates, Locke, Descartes, and Aristotle, with varying interpretations and aims. Socrates is perhaps most famous for his dictum "the unexamined life is not worth living." Humanistic, psychoanalytic, and postmodernist theorists held similar ideologies, and although differing in their approach and valuation of self-awareness, all deeply upheld the concept of introspection as a necessary function within the helping process (Hansen, 2009).

Counselor self-awareness is recognized as an ethical mandate. The ACA *Code of Ethics*, F.8.c., highlights personal growth as "an expected component of counselor education" (ACA, 2014, p. 14). For practitioners, the *Code* emphasizes the need for constant exploration and understanding of one's cultural identity and how this may shape his or her value system, as it relates to the counseling process (ACA, 2014). Accreditation standards support the imperative nature of counselor introspection, requiring counselor education programs to assess self-awareness as an indicator of "fitness for the profession" during admissions procedures (CACREP, 2015, p. 33). Likewise, entry-level counselor education graduates must be equipped with "strategies for personal and professional self-evaluation and implications for practice" (ACA, 2014, 2.F.1.k: p. 9).

Looking at the ASERVIC Competencies for Integrating Spirituality and Religion into Counseling (2009), specifically Competencies 3 through 5, it is evident that the need for constant self-exploration, both personally and professionally, is warranted. In an effort to identify limits of understanding, barriers to effective practice, and tools that can facilitate more effective practice, these three competencies require an active exploration of the counselor's attitudes, beliefs, and values about spirituality and/or religion. These competencies highlight both the purpose of evaluating the influence of these beliefs on the counseling process and the importance of counselors being able to objectively recognize limits of understanding and seek consultation and/or collaboration as needed.

The Summit Working Group, which developed the ASERVIC Competencies (see Introduction), emphasized the importance of understanding spiritual concepts in Competencies 1 and 2, and experiential understanding (i.e., self-awareness) of the spiritual domain in Competencies 3, 4, and 5. The subsequent competencies focus on human growth and development and professional practice issues, such as client communication, assessment, and diagnosis and treatment planning. This order was intentional as counselor self-awareness, particularly within the context of understanding counselor/client differences, must supersede practice. Beyond this rationale, counselor self-awareness brings clear gains to the therapeutic process.

Gains of Self-Awareness

The root of the word *psychotherapy* is from the Greek, referring to *soul/spirit/mind*. Thus, by its very nature, psychotherapy involves looking inward. Historically influential psychologists, Gordon Allport (1960), William James (1902/1985), Carl Jung (1958), and Abraham Maslow (1968), all assert that true emotional health involves a connection to spiritual and/or religious practices. Many, including Maslow (1968) and Carl Rogers (1973), posit this connection results in greater client attainment of self-awareness, insight, personal growth, and self-actualization. This growth is not limited to the client. If counseling is likely to include client exploration of spiritual and/or religious concepts, then the counselor must be willing and able to understand the religious and spiritual needs of his or her clients. A critical component of this process is for the counselor to first understand his or her own spiritual and religious beliefs. Notwithstanding the aforementioned ethical mandates, accreditation guidelines, and professional competencies, if counselors are to assist clients in increasing self-awareness of the spiritual domain, is it not imperative that they are able to do the same? In this section, the authors explore both *why* counselor self-awareness is essential and *what* this awareness brings to the counseling relationship.

The Therapeutic Alliance. Decades of research (e.g., Duncan, 2015; Lambert and Barley, 2001; Norcross and Wampold, 2011; Messer and Wampold, 2002) support the notion that the therapeutic alliance is central to positive counseling outcomes. A strong working alliance is the cornerstone of the counseling profession; distinguishing it from psychology, social work, and psychiatry (Kottler and Balkin, 2016). Rogers (1980) believed that empathy, fundamental to the therapeutic alliance, can occur only if the counselor is able to enter the private, perceptual world of the client. This entry, according to Rogers, is gained by building a strong counseling relationship. Kottler and Balkin (2016) write "the relationship is a key component of any helping effort, perhaps even the most significant feature" (p. 8). Therefore, if counselor self-awareness is a requirement for effective client engagement, then it is also a requirement for establishing a positive working relationship with the client. This is particularly relevant to client work which integrates sacred beliefs and spiritual/religious practices.

Counselors who seek to be competent in addressing the spiritual and religious domain with clients must focus on key tenets of the counseling relationship. Such tenets are built upon an active exploration and evaluation of the counselor's attitudes, beliefs, and values about spirituality and/or religion. In addition, the counselor must recognize and reconcile his or her own personal limits of understanding. When a counselor is more spiritually self-aware, his or her ability to recognize client spiritual concerns is greater (Asselt and Senstock, 2009). Understanding the client's spiritual and religious beliefs not only infuses the counselor–client relationship, but also enhances the counselor's non-judgmental openness toward the client. One of the many benefits of this process is an enriched, more objective understanding of the client's culture and worldview.

Multicultural Competence. Counselors are encountering increasingly multifaceted cultural milieu in their work. Given that spiritual and religious beliefs are closely tied cultural systems, it is unlikely that counselors can provide competent care without self-knowledge and self-awareness. Not surprisingly, there is a considerable amount of attention within the multicultural literature pointing to the absolute necessity of counselor awareness regarding personal values, assumptions, beliefs, and biases. Sue and Sue (2012) highlight the need for counselors to continuously and actively investigate their own assumptions and biases, in order to reach even a minimum level of multicultural competence. Collins, Arthur, and Wong-Wylie (2010) assert that "reflective practice is a central component of professional competence and necessarily involves attention to culture" (p. 340). Rationale supporting this notion includes the potential of the influence of *ethnocentricism*. *Ethnocentricism* is described as defaulting primarily to one's cultural lens – inherently laden with certain values and assumptions – in this case, for the purposes of clinical and ethical decision-making (Collins and Arthur, 2010; Levitt and Moorhead, 2013). Enhancing multicultural competence has great value for both understanding the client's spiritual domain and engaging in a better understanding of the impact of the counselor's own spiritual and/or religious belief system within the counseling process. Ho (1995) makes the wise assertion that "those who do not know the culture of others do not really know their own" (p. 11).

Navigating Inner Experiences in Practice. Counselor self-awareness is also required for navigating through the vicissitudes of *transference* and *countertransference* in the counseling relationship (Rosin, 2015). *Transference* involves the projection of feelings, often unconsciously, to another individual. Counselors with minimal self-awareness are prone to unintentional engagement in the transference relationship, thereby potentially harming the client or engaging in practices which are ineffective (Dryden and Reeves, 2008; Rosin, 2015). An example is the use of prayer in counseling. Albeit controversial within the literature, prayer can be an effective therapeutic technique when the client and counselor's religious beliefs are fully understood, and the use of such a technique is part of the informed consent process (Weld and Eriksen, 2007). However, counselors must be aware of the potential for such practices to blur boundaries and heighten transference issues (Cashwell and Young, 2011).

Countertransference refers to the way that a counselor reflexively relates and responds to a client (Dryden and Reeves, 2008); this phenomenon may occur when interacting with someone who is in great opposition to one's own beliefs or when beliefs are seemingly analogous (Udipi, Veach, Kao, and LeRoy, 2008). Continuing with the use of prayer as an example, a counselor who is unaware may unconsciously assume that a client who wishes to utilize prayer as a counseling technique for one presenting problem will want to utilize this strategy for other presenting issues. These unfounded assumptions not only lead to inaccurate postulations about the client's personal values, but directly influence and frustrate clinical decision-making, potentially resulting in decreased counseling outcomes and counselor well-being.

Counselor Well-being. Client work often involves intense, emotional subject matter, which can take an emotional toll on counselors. Furthermore, the work on the part of the counselor to remain aware of both *content* (what the client is saying) and *process* (the meaning behind content) issues during the counseling process can be laborious, particularly to novice or fatigued counselors. The very hallmark of professional burnout is a counselor's inability to recognize and tend to his or her own needs (Levitt and Moorhead, 2013). Not only do counselors experiencing burnout lose their effectiveness in helping others, but they also have little opportunity for continued growth, both as a person and a professional. A lack of self-care is one of the most prominent factors associated with burnout and poor ethical decision-making (Skovholt, Grier, and Hanson, 2001).

In emphasizing self-awareness, it is important to note that counselor self-care is often a by-product of increased awareness (Pompeo and Levitt, 2014). Richards et al. (2010) determined that while there is not a significant relationship between self-care and self-awareness, self-awareness is a likely result of increased counselor well-being. Given the benefits of spiritual investigation and the plethora of literature, which points to the need for counselors to acknowledge and be comfortable with their own spiritual beliefs, the gains of counselor self-awareness are certainly clear with regard to promoting counselor well-being (Capuzzi and Gross, 2003; Fukuyama and Sevig, 1997; Sacks, 1985; Tuck et al., 2001). The following section explores how counselors, both novice and seasoned, can better cultivate levels of self-awareness in the spiritual domain.

Cultivating Counselor Self-Awareness

At the very heart of this chapter is the idea that counselors must engage in ongoing personal self-reflection to effectively understand and address spiritual and/or religious issues in counseling. The reasons are summed up as three basic tenets: (1) counselor self-awareness is an ethical mandate, (2) counselor self-awareness is required for competent practice, and (3) counselor self-awareness is critical to client welfare. Pompeo and Levitt (2014) describe the process of increasing one's self-awareness as "a conscious choice in which one considers and analyzes one's own actions, including being honest about personal intentions and motives" (p. 80). Remley and Herlihy (2010) highlight counselor self-awareness as a core characteristic of virtuous counselors, describing it as one in which the counselor is familiar with his or her own assumptions, convictions, and biases – particularly in terms of how these may impact the counseling relationship. While scholarly discourse has consistently pointed to the need for increased awareness, what is missing is *how* counselors can effectively approach, continuously explore, and recognize limitations in their awareness.

Cottone, Tarvydas and Claus (2007) state that one must *experience values* to uncover them fully. Hansen (2009) defined conditions for establishing the construct of self-awareness, claiming that certain higher-order capacities, most notably the availability of self, must exist to facilitate self-reflection. Thus, counselors must be present and willing to engage in the reflective process. There is also countless evidence pointing to increased levels of counselor self-efficacy, improved client outcomes, strengthening of the therapeutic alliance, increased insight and multicultural understanding, and greater clinical insight resulting from increased counselor awareness. Given these stated benefits, every counselor is encouraged to reflect on their own belief system, culture and worldview, assumptions they make about the world, and how they may operate from an ethnocentric position, particularly in their professional work. The following section provides tools that counselors can use to foster increased awareness and self-knowledge. Outlined are two different processes, self-reflective exercises, which can be used to begin one's journey into counselor self-awareness and those that can be used to maintain or enrich counselor self-awareness. The counselor is encouraged not to think of this as an exclusive list, but rather as tools to be carried along on the journey toward counselor self-awareness.

Beginning the Journey

Like all human beings, mental health professionals possess a unique set of assumptions about human nature. This worldview, largely based on one's personal cultural and ethnic identity, influences all aspects of the counseling process. Thus, the way in which a counselor approaches case conceptualization, problem solving, and ethical decision-making – even his or her day-to-day interactions with clients – is largely influenced by his or her worldview. Essentially, all interactions, not just those related to clinical practice, are related to one's worldview. While the following is not an exhaustive list, these include helpful strategies to deeply explore one's identity as both an individual and a counselor. It is not by chance that these practices relate to exploring one's culture and worldview, as increased awareness of the spiritual domain is irrevocably tied to his or her cultural, racial, and ethnic background.

Narrative Identity. During the last decade, psychologists explored the idea of helping individuals define their narrative identity in an effort to help the storyteller, or narrator, derive emancipation from suffering or adversity (McAdams and McLean, 2013). Curiously, the idea of helping professionals better understand their own life stories by means of a narrative, has surfaced. This reality results from the need for counselors to better understand their values and beliefs, while also confronting biases and convictions.

Counselors can begin to understand their life narrative by reconstructing their past; looking at their life story and identifying what people, places, events, and experiences had the greatest impact in shaping who they are today. Defining one's narrative identity includes identifying life challenges and exploring how these were confronted. The key to greater understanding is accessing interpersonal or external tools and significant figures or organizations that were of assistance during these life challenges. This exercise facilitates the identification of themes in the counselor's narrative. This narrative becomes an "identity" when the counselors can envision meaning and purpose in their story. Emphasis is placed on sources of strength and resilience, using the narrative to understand current actions and future goals. McAdams (1993) explains:

> if you want to know me, you must know my story, for my story defines who I am. And if I want to know myself, to gain insight into

the meaning of my own life, then, I too, must come to know my own story.

(p. 11)

Counselors are encouraged to focus on their narrative in such a way that their values, beliefs, decision-making processes, convictions, and assumptions about the world remain at the forefront of conscious awareness.

Spiritual Autobiography. Akin to the idea of understanding one's narrative identity, is exploring the development of one's spiritual and religious beliefs through a spiritual autobiography. White (1997) suggested that examining events chronologically promotes the development of awareness, while Curry (2009) emphasized that it may be unrealistic to remember all salient events that have shaped one's history. Regardless of the approach, chronological or thematic, spiritual autobiographies serve as a remarkable tool for promoting insight and awareness.

Not intended as a full narrative, a spiritual autobiography is typically written as a reflection of momentous events related to the writer's development as a spiritual and/or religious being. Always related to the development of one's spiritual and/or religious growth, a spiritual autobiography tasks the writer with questions or prompts. Regardless of the format, writers come up with an outline of significant experiences that occurred during these periods. With this outline, the writer explores how the selected items shaped or directed their spiritual and/or religious life. The final piece of the spiritual autobiography is to envision the future in terms of spiritual and/or religious beliefs, reflecting on questions such as, what will be held dear, what will be shed, what will be enriched, etc. The final product promotes a deeper understanding of oneself as a spiritual and/or religious being and informs how this belief system manifests in one's life both in the present and future. Counselors, who are not inclined to write out events, are encouraged to investigate other means, such as, a spiritual timeline or graphing techniques which might include spiritual genograms (see Chapter 10) or spiritual ecomaps (see Chapter 2) (Curry, 2009; Gill et al., 2011).

Three-phased Approach. For those who are more structural or prefer to approach self-awareness from a developmental lens, Pompeo and Levitt (2014) provide a three-phased approach to counselor self-awareness in practice. Their model includes: 1) *Counselor Self-Reflection and Stagnation*, 2) *Self-Awareness Process*, and 3) *Client Growth and Counseling Relationship* phases. The first phase, *Counselor Self-Reflection and Stagnation*, involves the identification of a reflective task. Similar to what counselors focus on during clinical supervision, this phase requires the counselor to identify a clinical issue, which is personal to the counselor. Examples may include feelings of professional insecurity (e.g. imposter syndrome); strong desires to please the client; or reluctance to work with a specific client population. Teasing out these deeply personal issues and working on them individually is necessary to gain perspective into deeper underlying issues which impede efficacious practice.

The second phase, *Self-Awareness Process*, consists of identifying one's moral and ethical reasoning processes (Pompeo and Levitt, 2014). Put into practice, the counselor must identify his or her philosophical approach to decision-making. Based on personal and professional experience, counselors can identify the ethical decision-making philosophy to which they are most inclined. Revisiting the philosophy behind ethical decision-making, specifically the concepts of absolutism, utilitarianism, and feminism, can assist counselors in better understanding how they view the world and make decisions. Tangible experiences, particularly those in everyday life, allow the counselor to investigate the ways in which they judge what the "right action" is. Understanding how and why decisions are made, particularly in terms of moral reasoning, is a vital pathway to understanding one's worldview (Tennyson and Strom, 1986).

The third and final phase of Pompeo and Levitt's (2014) model of counselor self-awareness is *Client growth and counseling relationship*. Although considered a phase, at this stage, the counselor is more self-aware and more heavily focused on client communications and interactions. As the counselor's process to achieve self-awareness occurs, a parallel process of client growth also occurs. Primarily, the counselors' growth experience has facilitated their understanding of client struggles and potential stagnation. This concept is indicative of empathy, a position foundational to counseling practice (Corey et al., 2014; Meier and Davis, 2010). It is during this stage that the client is able to reap the benefits of increased counselor self-awareness.

Experiential Exercises. Counselors who work within the spiritual domain are encouraged to engage in experiential exercises to increase their understanding of spiritual and/or religious issues, which may fall outside their own personal experience. This includes attending spiritual and/or religious activities unfamiliar to the counselor and visiting local faith-based organizations. Not only do these experiences increase the counselor's knowledge of different faiths, practices, and belief systems but also engaging with local resources builds bridges between communities of faith and local counseling resources. Counselors are also encouraged to collaborate with religious and spiritual leaders as part of an interdisciplinary approach. Just as a counselor would consult with a medical doctor, spiritually and religiously orientated clients can benefit from an integrated approach.

Reflective Exercises. Counselors interested in increasing their understanding of the Sacred can also benefit from tools found within the multicultural literature. Aside from being useful in one's journey toward self-awareness, reflective exercises are also favorable to the classroom or as part of clinical supervision. Examples include the *Who Am I?* exercise (see Aparna, 2011; Hagedorn and Gutierrez, 2009); *The Cultural Grid* (see Hines and Pederson, 1980; Pedersen and Pedersen, 1989); *My Culture/ Drawing* (see Pellicier, 2011); and *Identities in Interaction* (see Delgado-Romero and Schwartz, 2011). For a comprehensive examination of cultural reflections see Pope, Pangelinan, and Coker (2011).

Continuing the Journey

The benefits of continued counselor self-awareness cannot be understated. Seasoned counselors understand that the journey toward self-awareness does not have an endpoint; awareness is not a course from which one graduates. Therein lies the requirement of all professional counselors to continue the voyage toward self-knowledge. Those who seek to advance their knowledge of different spiritual and religious traditions in an attempt to gain greater knowledge of the client's belief system, are more likely to engage in some form of personal introspection. For example, a client who talks about the benefits of walking a labyrinth may spark the interest of a counselor who has never engaged in such practices. A devout Catholic client who talks about the cathartic nature of confession, may encourage a counselor to personally investigate the practice of admission and atonement. Regardless of specific practice, engaging in continuous self-awareness allows for greater insight into a client's belief system, while also serving as a resource for future clients (Richards and Potts, 1995). Examples include increased counselor competence in identifying bias and harmful assumptions and enhanced expertise in clarifying one's values, particularly as they shift throughout one's lifespan. Counselors are also able to recognize spiritual or religious "blind spots," particularly those which may cause a counselor to unintentionally disrespect or respond insensitively to a client's spiritual and/or religious values (Bishop, 1992). Below are two ways in which counselors can facilitate continuing the journey.

Reflective Practice. Schön (1991) proposed that self-aware counselors can gain increased awareness when they take a reflective turn and begin a process of observing, describing, and illuminating their practice actions, particularly those which are spontaneous. Schön (1991) outlined two different modes of reflection: *reflection-in-action* and *reflection-on-action*. *Reflection-in-action* can instantaneously alter a counselor's actions by using immediacy (Taylor, 1998). Counselors operating in this mode think about what they are doing in the moment, critically evaluating, shifting, reframing, and questioning implicit and explicit thoughts and behaviors. This allows the counselor to immediately shift, as appropriate, based on the counselor's evaluation of self. *Reflection-on-action*, conversely, is carried out after the fact and usually away from the clinical realm (Schön, 1983). This second mode of reflection is intended to improve future practice and aid the counselor in gaining a better understanding of their motives and intentions with a client. While reflection-in-action emphasizes improvement in the moment, reflection-on-action is focused on future work with clients. Wong-Wylie (2010) added a third component to Schön's reflective practice, termed *reflection-on-self-in/on action*, which involves personal observations of values, biases, and feelings. Based on Connelly and Clandinin's (1988) work on *personal practical knowledge*, Wong-Wylie (2010) proposed this reflective practice as a transformational learning experience aimed at evoking change to one's frame of reference.

One of the most common means by which individuals can promote personal reflection is through *mindfulness* techniques. *Mindfulness* involves "paying attention in a particular way: on purpose, non-judgmentally, in the present moment" (Kabat-Zinn, 1994, p. 4). Elements typical of mindfulness include: (1) stopping in the moment, (2) observing the moment, and (3) returning to the present (Germer et al., 2016). Since counselors must offer true presence and deep understanding of and listening to clients, utilizing mindfulness as a gateway to self-awareness has numerous benefits. At the very basic level, mindful practices allow counselors to tap into both awareness and compassion. Not surprisingly, these attributes serve as the foundation for a positive therapeutic alliance. There are numerous ways in which counselors can cultivate mindfulness, far too many to cover in this section. Thus, counselors are encouraged to investigate mindfulness practices and find one which helps bring them an increased sense of awareness and connectivity to the present moment.

Personal Counseling and Self-Care. Any discussion on self-awareness would be remiss if the recommendation for personal counseling and the identification of individualized self-care strategies was not included. Introductory texts, ethical guidelines, and best practices on clinical supervision all recommend personal counseling as an ongoing outlet to better understand oneself (e.g., Borders et al., 2014; Corey et al., 2014; Gladding, 2012; Meier and Davis, 2010; Remley and Herlihy, 2010). This recommendation infers that counselors remain open to navigating their own difficulties and personal biases, not just early on, but throughout their career. Moreover, because the journey of self-awareness is often fraught with interpersonal challenges, personal counseling and self-care strategies are necessary for the counselor to be present and effective within the counseling relationship (Richards et al., 2010). It is strongly recommended that both novice and seasoned counselors identify personalized self-care strategies and utilize them on their path to self-awareness (Corey et al., 2014; Remley and Herlihy, 2010).

Self-Awareness: The Gateway to Effective Client Communication

Spiritually competent counselors recognize that client disclosures often provide higher levels of meaning and insight into the client's spiritual world (Cashwell and Young, 2011). Thus, counselors must be adept at identifying ways in which they can effectively communicate, utilize, and address spiritual and religion concepts and themes in practice. First, the authors present a discussion on acceptance and sensitivity. The objective is to enhance spiritual and multicultural competence, fostering a better understanding of how assumptions and bias can adversely impact the counseling relationship. Next, a review of how to identify therapeutically relevant practices/beliefs, focusing on spirituality and religion as an area of strength or understanding for the client, will take place. Additionally, strategies that counselors can use to respond to client communications, particularly when the counselor and client have different belief systems are explained. Finally, a discussion on how counselors can help clients deepen their own understanding of their spiritual and religious beliefs will take place.

Acceptance and Sensitivity

Counselors skilled in the spiritual domain recognize the personal nature of client spiritualty, likely because they have higher levels of understanding of their own spirituality. Spiritually competent counselors, as outlined in the ASERVIC spiritual competencies, approach "client communications about spirituality and/or religion with acceptance and sensitivity" (ASERVIC, 2009, p. 1). Thus, counselors must adopt a non-judgmental stance in all communications and be mindful of areas about which they are unfamiliar, lack competence, or are prone to bias. These behaviors adversely impact clinical decision-making and impede the development of a positive therapeutic alliance. Perhaps the most commonly referenced example is related to non-verbal communication. A counselor who considers maintaining eye contact as a sign of openness and interest, may be failing a client who considers prolonged eye contact a sign of disrespect. Counselors who work with clients whose religious, spiritual, or ethnic backgrounds are different or unfamiliar, have a responsibility to learn about these major differences and explore with clients how they express their beliefs in their religious context.

Effective communication about spiritual and/or religious issues in counseling involves a stance of intellectual curiosity (Rollins, 2009) and creating a safe space for clients. Counselors are encouraged to take a "not knowing" posture, allowing the client to be the expert in their own spiritual and/or religious beliefs (Curry and Simpson, 2011). Clients traditionally do not assume that spiritual and religious issues are a part of counseling. Therefore, the responsibility is on the counselor to make the client aware that counseling is a welcome space to discuss their beliefs, matters of faith, and their spiritual and/or religious identity (Rollins, 2009). When warranted (see Chapter 2), questions such as, "How does faith (or spirituality) guide your life?" are unimposing and empower clients to discuss spiritual matters. When professionals appropriately invite clients to talk about spiritual and religious issues, they create a safe environment for clients to discuss their beliefs. Not extending this invitation will likely mean that part of the client's lived experience will remain unknown and, therefore, untapped (Cashwell and Young, 2011). Moreover, clients who may not participate in mainstream religious or spiritual practices often feel their beliefs are disregarded or, in some circumstances, considered pathological (Gill et al., 2011). Therefore, it is the responsibility of the counselor to ethically and appropriately inquire about the client's belief system in a way that is safe and comfortable for the client.

Counselors who work with clients of faith should become comfortable with using basic religious language about the belief system relevant to the client (Curry and Simpson, 2011; Hagedorn and Moorhead, 2011). When discussing spiritual and/or religious matters, counselors should investigate both the content of what a client is saying, as well as underlying themes about the way in which they approach their life (Gill et al., 2011). Counselors should also look for strengths that spiritual and/or religious beliefs provide the client, and examine spiritual and religious behaviors which may be sources of healing. Essentially, counselors need to find out what is important to the client, and areas in which the client has found meaning, happiness, and peace. Do not be rigid or prejudge beliefs, as this sabotages the counseling relationship. For example, a counselor working with a Hindu client may help the client explore his or her life choices through the law of *dharma*; thus, the client is able to explore how they are responsible for their life and the subsequent choices that they make. While this example could be challenging for a counselor unfamiliar with the unique religious and spiritual practices of the client, integration of a general working knowledge of these critical cultural components into the helping process is essential (Hagedorn and Moorhead, 2011).

While counselors simply cannot be responsible for being well-versed in all faith systems, they can maintain a stance of "spiritual curiosity" (Rollins, 2009). An integral part of spiritual and multicultural competence, counselors must ask themselves "how can I use the client's spiritual and/or religious beliefs to help them with their presenting problem?" By utilizing the strengths that the client already possesses, clients can often reframe their struggles or approach them from a different, more desired, perspective.

Strategies for Effective Client Communication

The ASERVIC Competencies for Integrating Spirituality and Religion into Counseling, maintain that spiritually competent counselors employ "spiritual and/or religious concepts that are consistent with the client's spiritual and/or religious perspectives and are acceptable to the client" (ASERVIC, 2009, p. 1). An important distinction is made here. In order to effectively utilize spiritual and/or religious content, the counselor must do so in a manner that is not only appropriate, but endorsed by the client. The counselor must do more than simply understand the client's spiritual and/or religious belief system. This means the counselor utilizes appropriate language, terms, and has the correct frame of reference (Cashwell and Young, 2011). The client should find the spiritual and religious content used by the counselor meaningful and relevant (Corey et al., 2015; Cashwell and Young, 2011; Frame, 2002). In this instance, a very important component of appropriate spiritual integration must not be lost. While the use of spiritual and religious content in counseling is an effective means of client strength and healing, integration must be done in a way that holds appropriate meaning for the client (Cashwell and Young, 2011). Some strategies counselors can use to respond to client communications are suggested below.

Continuously Monitor Assumptions. Previously, the need for acceptance and sensitivity when client beliefs differ from those of the counselor has been highlighted (see ACA, 2014; ASERVIC, 2009; Collins and Arthur, 2010; Day-Vines et al., 2007; Levitt and Moorhead, 2013). However, counselors who believe they are from similar faith systems, such as a Christian counselor working with a Christian client, should never assume that all Christian perspectives are similar. There are hundreds of Christian denominations, many that are vastly different from one another. Looking at the aforementioned example, a foundational belief within Christianity is that God offers forgiveness to everyone and anyone who accepts the gift of forgiveness and believes in Jesus Christ will receive salvation. However, not all Christian denominations approach forgiveness in a similar fashion. Pentecostal Christians deeply believe in the physical experience of God through tongues. A Pentecostal client speaking of their distinct experience of being empowered by *the Spirit* may be grossly misunderstood by a counselor trying to understand this experience through their own Christian paradigm. Thus, counselors are cautioned to carefully investigate assumptions, not only about religious faith, but all matters, in which inherent assumptions are made about the client's worldview.

Implicit Assumptions. Attending to appropriate client communication regarding spiritual and religious issues becomes particularly challenging when counselors are unaware of preconceptions or biases. Managing assumptions, and broaching and navigating values conflicts, all infer that the counselor is aware of spiritual and/or religious matters which may adversely impact the counseling process (see Day-Vines et al., 2007). However, what happens when the counselor is not aware? How can the counselor appropriately and ethically approach client communications about the Sacred? The answer is continued self-awareness and, as mentioned previously, continuing the journey of self-reflection. Having an increased awareness of personal assumptions, values and biases, subsequently increases the counselor's ability to navigate implicit assumptions (Auger, 2004; Dryden and Reeves, 2008). By definition, implicit assumptions fall largely outside of our conscious awareness (Auger, 2004). Broader than explicit biases, implicit assumptions are deeply tied to the cultural context in which we identify. By recognizing the impact that our cultural and racial identity has on our worldview, a topic more thoroughly discussed in the next chapter, counselors can become more adept at identifying their implicit assumptions. This is particularly relevant when working with culturally different clients or clients in which we *assume* we understand their cultural background (Sodowsky, Kuo-Jackson, and Loya, 1997).

Broaching. Borrowed from the multicultural literature, broaching can be used when discussing the sacred in counseling (Day-Vines et al., 2007), particularly when the counselor feels spiritual and religious issues may influence the client's counseling concerns. Broaching allows the counselor to initiate conversations of faith and respond to these issues during the course of counseling. It includes openness, sensitivity, immediacy, and a genuine commitment to continual exploration of relevant spiritual/religious issues as they are relevant to treatment.

Values Conflicts. Counselors, particularly when working with spiritual and religious issues, need to be aware of and attend to values conflicts that arise in practice. Consistent with the ACA *Code of Ethics* (A.4.b; 2014), counselors need to avoid imposing their own values, beliefs, and behaviors onto clients. Perhaps the most commonly cited example of differing belief systems is instances in which the counselor and client are members of different religious or spiritual communities – a Jewish counselor working with a Buddhist client or a Pagan counselor working with a Christian client. In these instances, the counselor must attend to counselor/client differences with a sense of openness and curiosity (Rollins, 2009; Asselt and Senstock, 2009). While it is not the client's job to educate the counselor on the client's faith system, the counselor can initiate a conversation about how the client expresses their religious and spiritual beliefs within their ethnic context. Using the example above, the Jewish counselor might ask "Tell me how Buddhism influences your daily life experience?" The Pagan counselor might ask a Christian client "What role has your religion played in your life?" Both clients could be asked about ways in which their religion has served as a source of strength or whether their religion has currently or historically served as a stressor. These questions are best positioned from an open, unassuming stance.

Self-disclosure. Do not be afraid, only prudent, regarding self-disclosure of the counselor's beliefs (Levitt and Moorhead, 2013; Corey et al., 2015). One must ask "Am I bringing this into the room for me or for the client?" Clearly, if the disclosure is to alleviate any discomfort or anxiety on the part of the counselor, it should remain undisclosed. However, there are some instances in which counselors reveal their own beliefs to increase the client's comfort level in discussing these issues or illustrating that differing views are acceptable, and that the counselor is not trying to change or influence the client in any way. The purpose is to alleviate any anxiety on the part of the client, such as the fear that the counselor will judge them. Simply stated, all clients typically want to know is "are you okay with me?"

Having cultivated the journey of counselor self-awareness and maintained an open and non-judgmental stance, counselors who are looking to appropriately utilize the client's belief system must seek to understand how the client's presenting problem and treatment can be conceptualized within their own frame of reference (Collins and Arthur, 2010; Frame, 2002). For example, if a client uses the term *Higher Power*, then the counselor should use that reference. If a client speaks of things such as prayer, connecting with nature, *dharma*, or meditation, counselors need to seek to understand how the client conceptualizes these practices and how they play a role in the client's life. Curry and Simpson (2011) call for counselors to listen "between the lines" for spiritual and/or religious references. While formal and informal assessment of the client's spiritual domain is necessary, oftentimes, meaningful content generates as a part of the counseling process (Gill et al., 2011). Thus, counselors should integrate this content and these themes, accordingly. A client who routinely refers to prayer as a source of strength, should be encouraged to talk about this and integrate practice into the healing process. In the next section, how to effectively identify spiritual themes which are relevant to counseling practice will be discussed.

Effectively Identifying Therapeutically Relevant Practices and Beliefs

When listening for themes in client communications, counselors must attend to how the client's spiritual and religious beliefs shape his or her perception of the world (Cashwell and Young, 2011). As the counselor becomes more capable of responding, recognizing, and utilizing spiritual and/or religious concepts, the more skilled they are at identifying therapeutically relevant themes (Collins and Arthur, 2010; Curry, 2009). This includes ways in which clients find meaning and purpose in life, their belief (or disbelief) in a fair and just universe/world, and client's beliefs about death and loss. Spiritual themes can be communicated in a number of contexts, but most often surround existential issues of meaning, purpose, responsibility, forgiveness, community, and other values held dear to the client.

Sources of strength are often related to the client's spiritual and/or religious nature, and practices related to these can serve as an invaluable tool for coping with therapeutic issues (Bergin and Richards, 1997). A client's concept of truth and reality, oftentimes reflected in their spiritual belief system, can lead to greater insight into the client's worldview (Cashwell and Young, 2011; Frame, 2002). Asking a client, "What brings you joy?" often yields an answer entrenched with spiritual meaning. Depending on the client's spiritual and/or religious practices and presenting problem, these answers often yield vital internal resources for the client (Gill et al., 2011). Similar to how a counselor would listen for practices and/or beliefs, which serve as a source of strength, counselors must also listen for themes which indicate conflicts or problems of a spiritual nature.

As helping professionals, counselors know that, sometimes, clients are suffering because of the way they look at things, or, their conceptual understanding of the world (Rollins, 2009). Oftentimes, this understanding is related to how the client views the Sacred (Bergin, 1991; Frame, 2002). Counselors can open the door by using open ended questions (Gill et al., 2011) such as, "Are your spiritual and/or religious beliefs important to you and do you want to include these as part of the counseling process?" This question serves a dual purpose. First, it identifies whether the client wants to talk about spiritual and religious issues. Second, it grants permission for the client to discuss spiritual matters.

Considering that most Western approaches to health overly focus on symptom identification, aligning with the medical model, the approach to assessing for spiritual variables must be initiated by the counselor, as further described in Chapter 2. As stated previously, many clients do not know that counseling involves *all* parts of the individual – including the spirit (Bergin and Richards, 1997; Rogers, 1980). Using the tool of broaching (Day-Vines et al., 2007), counselors can re-open the door of spirituality and faith, frequently, and investigate matters of faith as a vital resource or, in some circumstances, as a contributor to the client's presenting concerns.

As a Contributor to Emotional Difficulty. Counselors must address whether spiritual issues are part of the client's presenting problem or if there are spiritual issues (e.g. 'unhealthy' religion) which are or may adversely impact client functioning (Bergin, 1991; Frame, 2000). At face value, the idea of spiritual beliefs contributing to the client's presenting problem may seem counterintuitive to what has been presented in this chapter. However, counselors often help clients work through their problems by examining conflict between a client's beliefs and behaviors (Curry and Simpson, 2011). Clients often come to counseling with problems based largely on an internal conflict between what a client is doing (i.e. getting a divorce) and their beliefs and values (i.e. marriage is sacred). It is important that counselors do not limit themselves to the idea that only devout clients experience impasses of faith. Clients who hold the earth as a sacred space, who pronounce themselves as "spiritual but not religious," can experience struggles of the very same nature.

It is important to note that a counselor faces considerable challenges when trying to decipher the "health" of a client's spirituality. Unhealthy practices might include: preoccupation with sinfulness, cult membership, religious paranoia, spiritual delusions or hallucinations, demonic possession, masochism, and/or frequent denominational shifting (Bergin and Richards, 1997; Frame, 2002; Meadow and Kahoe, 1984). This is also relevant when the client's application or interpretation of a religious belief induces maladaptive behavior. For example, a client who is vegetarian because she believes in reincarnation is not exhibiting pathology. However, a client who believes that anyone who eats meat is "going to hell" and who presents with severe preoccupation regarding the certain damnation of her family who eat meat, is experiencing symptoms that impact her ability to function. Therefore, it is more important that counselors investigate client functioning when considering whether a belief system has detrimental effects. In the following chapter, belief systems are described in detail.

Counselors should not impose their values upon clients regarding spiritual and/or religious problems that clients may be having (ACA, 2014; Levitt and Moorhead, 2013). If a client believes that he or she will attain enlightenment because of duties to their church, and this is not "unhealthy" in nature, counselors work with the client to help them integrate these beliefs into their lives. It is the role of the counselor to help integrate these belief systems into the client's thoughts, feelings, and actions, and help relieve any distress that these issues may be causing them.

If psychological distress can originate from religious or spiritual concerns, what about clients who profess they are not religious or spiritual? While the counselor must be careful not to push issues that the client does not feel are relevant, Frame (2002) posits that sometimes a lack of interest or refusal to discuss spiritual and/or religious issues can be indicative of problems or conflicts within the client's belief system. This is common in individuals who experience significant trauma, are haunted by the death of a loved one, or who may have experienced severe life circumstances, such as disaster victims, abuse survivors and/or rape victims. Conversely, other clients may feel marginalized by their identity as atheist, agnostic, or a "non-believer" and avoid discussions in counseling related to spiritual and/or religious identity (D'Andrea and Sprenger, 2007). These illustrations are just a few examples of the ways in which clients present with spiritual concerns. Counselors are encouraged to seek continued supervision, consultation, and training, particularly when working outside one's areas of competence or when faced with challenging client concerns.

Tips for Client Communications

- Guard against the tendency to assume an extreme position (e.g. black and white thinking) when talking with clients about spiritual and/or religious belief systems.
- Create a safe climate in which clients can examine their thoughts, feelings, and actions.
- When working in the spiritual domain, pause and consider the client's position, including biases and/or other interpersonal issues they might face.
- Careful reflection on one's own worldviews and experiences with religion and spiritual practices is essential. Not addressing these situations appropriately can lead the client to feel a sense of shame or marginalization.
- Counselors may need to give referrals – particularly when a faith leader could augment counseling, and should keep a current referral list of faith leaders and community resources at their disposal.
- Be open to seeking continuing education to further develop knowledge and skills related to working with clients from diverse spiritual/faith traditions.
- Counselors should seek supervision/consultation when experiencing values conflicts and/or to periodically assess how their own experiences and worldviews may be impacting competence.

References

Allport, G. W. (1960). *Personality and social encounter: Selected essays*. Boston, MA: Beacon Press.

American Counseling Association. (2014). *Code of ethics.* Alexandria, VA: Author.

Anandarajah, G., and Hight, E. (2001). Spirituality and medical practice. *American Family Physician,* 63(1), 81–88.

Aparna, I. G. (2011). Who am I? In M. Pope, J. S., Pangelinan, and A. D. Coker (Eds.). *Experiential activities for teaching multicultural competence in counseling.* Alexandria, VA, US: American Counseling Association.

Arredondo, P., and Toporek, R. (2004). Multicultural counseling competencies and ethical practice. *Journal of Mental Health Counseling,* 26(1), 44–55.

Asselt, K. W., and Senstock, T. D. B. (2009). Influence of counselor spirituality and training on treatment focus and self-perceived competence. *Journal of Counseling & Development,* 87(4), 412–419.

Association for Spiritual, Ethical and Religious Values in Counseling. (2009). *Spiritual competencies: Competencies for addressing spiritual and religious issues in counseling.* Retrieved from http://www.aservic.org/resources/spiritual-competencies/.

Auger, R. W. (2004). What we don't know can hurt us: Mental health counselors' implicit assumptions about human nature. *Journal of Mental Health Counseling,* 26(1), 13–24.

Bergin, A. E. (1991). Values and religious issues in psychotherapy and mental health. *American Psychologist,* 46(4), 394–403.

Bergin, A. E., and Richards, P. S. (1997). *A spiritual strategy for counseling and psychotherapy.* Washington, DC: American Psychological Association.

Bishop, D. R. (1992). Religious Values as Cross-Cultural Issues in Counseling. *Counseling and Values,* 36(3), 179–191.

Borders, L. D., Glosoff, H. L., Welfare, L. E., Hays, D. G., DeKruyf, L., Fernando, D. M., and Page, B. (2014). Best practices in clinical supervision: Evolution of a counseling specialty. *The Clinical Supervisor,* 33(1), 26–44.

Briggs, M. K., and Rayle, A. D. (2005). Incorporating spirituality into core counseling courses: Ideas for classroom application. *Counseling and Values,* 50(1), 63–75.

Brown, K. W., and Ryan, R. M. (2003). The benefits of being present: mindfulness and its role in psychological well-being. *Journal of Personality and Social Psychology,* 84(4), 822.

Capuzzi, D., and Gross, D. R. (2003). *Theories of psychotherapy.* Upper Saddle River, NJ: Prentice.

Cashwell, C. S., and Young, J. S. (2004). Spirituality in counselor training: A content analysis of syllabi from introductory spirituality courses. *Counseling and Values,* 48(2), 96–109.

Cashwell, C. S., and Young, J. S. (2011). *Integrating spirituality and religion into counseling. A guide to competent practice.* Alexandria, VA: American Counseling Association..

Collins, S., and Arthur, N. (2007). A framework for enhancing multicultural counselling competence. *Canadian Journal of Counselling,* 41(1), 31–49.

Collins, S., and Arthur, N. (2010). Culture-infused counselling: A fresh look at a classic framework of multicultural counselling competencies. *Counselling Psychology Quarterly,* 23(2), 203–216.

Collins, S., Arthur, N., and Wong-Wylie, G. (2010). Enhancing reflective practice in multicultural counseling through cultural auditing. *Journal of Counseling & Development,* 88(3), 340–347.

Connelly, F. M., and Clandinin, D. J. (1988). *Teachers as curriculum planners. Narratives of experience.* New York: Teachers College Press.

Corey, G., Corey, M. S., Corey, C., and Callanan, P. (2014). *Issues and ethics in the helping professions with 2014 ACA codes.* Nelson Education.

Corey, G., and Corey, M., Corey, C., Callanan, P. (2015). *Issues and ethics in the helping professions* (9th edition). Stamford, CT: Cengage.

Cottone, R. R., Tarvydas, V. M., and Claus, R. E. (2007). Ethical decision-making processes (pp. 85–113). In R. R. Cottone and V. M. Tarvydas (Eds). *Counseling ethics and decision making*. New York: Pearson.

Council for Accreditation of Counseling and Related Educational Programs. (2015). *2016 CACREP Standards*. Alexandria, VA: Author. Retrieved from http://www. cacrep.org/for-programs/2016-cacrep-standards/.

Curry, J. R. (2009). Examining client spiritual history and the construction of meaning: The use of spiritual timelines in counseling. *Journal of Creativity in Mental Health*, 4(2), 113–123.

Curry, J. R., and Simpson, L. R. (2011). Communicating about spirituality in counseling (pp. 119–140). In C. S., Cashwell and Young, J. S. (Eds). *Integrating spirituality and religion into counseling: A guide to competent practice*. Hoboken, NJ: John Wiley & Sons.

D'Andrea, L. and J. Sprenger (2007). Atheism and nonspirituality as diversity issues in counseling. *Counseling and Values*, 51: 149–158.

Day-Vines, N.L., et al. (2007). Broaching the subjects of race, ethnicity, and culture during the counseling process. *Journal of Counseling & Development*, 85, 401–409.

Delgado-Romero, E. A., and Schwartz, E. A. (2011). Identities in interaction: A role-play. In M. Pope, J. S., Pangelinan, and A. D. Coker (Eds.). *Experiential activities for teaching multicultural competence in counselling* (p. 99). Alexandria, VA: American Counseling Association.

Dryden, W., and Reeves, A. (Eds.). (2008). *Key issues for counselling in action*. Thousand Oaks, CA: Sage.

Duncan, B. L. (2015). The person of the therapist: One therapist's journey to relationship. In K. J. Schneider, J. F. Pierson, and J. F. Bugental (Eds.), *The handbook of humanistic psychology: Theory, research, and practice* (2nd ed., pp. 457–472). Thousand Oaks, CA: Sage Publications.

Favier, C. M., O'Brien, E. M., and Ingersoll, R. E. (2000). Religion, guilt & mental health. *Journal of Counseling and Development*, 78, 155–161.

Frame, M. W. (2000). Spiritual and religious issues in counseling: Ethical considerations. *The Family Journal*, 8(1), 72–74.

Frame, M. W. (2002). *Integrating religion and spirituality into counseling: A comprehensive approach*. Belmont, CA: Wadsworth.

Fukuyama, M. A., and Sevig, T. D. (1997). Spiritual issues in counseling: A new course. *Counselor Education and Supervision*, 36(3), 233–244.

Germer, C. K., Siegel, R. D., and Fulton, P. R. (Eds.). (2016). *Mindfulness and psychotherapy*. New York: Guilford Publications.

Gill, C., Harper, M. C., and Dailey, S. (2011). Assessing the spiritual and religious domain. pp. 141–162. In C. Cashwell and Young, J. S. (2011). *Integrating spirituality and religion into counseling: A guide to competent practice*. Alexandria, VA: American Counseling Association.

Gladding, S. T. (2012). *Counseling: A comprehensive profession*. New York: Pearson.

Hagedorn, W. B., and Gutierrez, D. (2009). Integration versus segregation: Applications of the spiritual competencies in counselor education programs. *Counseling and Values*, 54(1), 32–47.

Hagedorn, W. B., and Moorhead, H. J. H. (2011). Counselor self-awareness: Exploring attitudes, beliefs, and values (p. 71–96). In C. Cashwell and Young,

J. S. *Integrating spirituality and religion into counseling: A guide to competent practice.* Alexandria, VA: American Counseling Association.

Hansen, J. T. (2009). Self-Awareness Revisited: Reconsidering a Core Value of the Counseling Profession. *Journal of Counseling & Development* , 87(2), 186–193.

Hines, A., and Pedersen, P. (1980). The cultural grid: Matching social system variables and cultural perspectives. *Asian Pacific Training and Development Journal*, 1(1).

Ho, D. Y. (1995). Internalized culture, culturocentrism, and transcendence. *The Counseling Psychologist*, 23(1), 4–24.

James, W. (1902). The varieties of religious experience. New York: Collier. Reprinted in Smith, J.E. (Ed.). (1985). *The works of William James* (Vol. 15). Cambridge.

Jung, C. G. (1958). *A psychological view of conscience. Collected works*, 10, 437.

Kabat-Zinn, J. (1994). *Wherever you go. There you are: Mindfulness meditation in everyday life.* New York: Hyperion.

Kottler, J. A., and Balkin, R. S. (2016). *Relationships in Counseling and the Counselor's Life.* Hoboken, NJ: John Wiley & Sons.

Lambert, M. J., and Barley, D. E. (2001). Research summary on the therapeutic relationship and psychotherapy outcome. *Psychotherapy: Theory, Research, Practice, Training*, 38(4), 357.

Lao-tzu (1988). *Tao te ching: A new English bersion* (S. Mitchell, Trans.). New York: Harper & Row.

Levitt, D. H., and Moorhead, H. J. H. (Eds.). (2013). *Values and ethics in counseling: Real-life ethical decision making.* New York: Routledge.

Maslow, A. H. (1968). *Toward a psychology of being (2nd ed.).* New York: Van Nostrand.

McAdams, D. P. (1993). *The stories we live by: Personal myths and the making of the self.* New York: Guilford Press.

McAdams, D. P., and McLean, K. C. (2013). Narrative identity. *Current Directions in Psychological Science*, 22(3), 233–238.

Meadow, M. J., and Kahoe, R. (1984). *Psychology of religion: Religion in individual lives.* New York: Harper & Row.

Meier, S., and Davis, S. (2010). *The elements of counseling.* Scarborough, ON: Nelson Education.

Meissner, W.W. (1996). The pathology of beliefs and the beliefs of pathology (pp. 241–267). In Shafranske, E.P. (Ed.), *Religion and the clinical practice of psychology*. Washington D.C.: American Psychological Association.

Messer, S. B., and Wampold, B. E. (2002). Let's face facts: Common factors are more potent than specific therapy ingredients. *Clinical Psychology: Science and Practice*, 9(1), 21–25.

Ni, H. C. (1995). *The complete works of Lao Tzu: Tao teh ching & hau hu ching.* Los Angeles, CA: Sevenstar Communications.

Norcross, J. C., and Wampold, B. E. (2011). What works for whom: Tailoring psychotherapy to the person. *Journal of Clinical Psychology*, 67(2), 127–132.

Oden, K. A., Miner-Holden, J., and Balkin, R. S. (2009). Required counseling for mental health professional trainees: Its perceived effect on self-awareness and other potential benefits. *Journal of Mental Health*, 18(5), 441–448.

Pedersen, A., and Pedersen, P. (1989). The Cultural Grid: A framework for multicultural counseling. *International Journal for the Advancement of Counselling*, 12(4), 299–307.

Pedersen, A., and Pedersen, P. B. (1985). The Cultural Grid: A personal cultural orientation. In L. Samovar and R. Porter (Eds.), *Intercultural Communication: A Reader* (pp. 50–62). Belmont, CA: Wadsworth.

Pellicier, A. S. (2011). My culture/drawing. In M. Pope, J. S., Pangelinan, and A. D. Coker (Eds.). *Experiential activities for teaching multicultural competence in counselling* (p. 43). Alexandria, VA: American Counseling Association.

Pompeo, A. M., and Levitt, D. H. (2014). A path of counselor self-awareness. *Counseling and Values*, 59(1), 80–94.

Pope, M., Pangelinan, J. S., and Coker, A. D. (Eds.). (2011). *Experiential activities for teaching multicultural competence in counseling*. Alexandria, VA: American Counseling Association.

Remley Jr, T. P., and Herlihy, B. (2010). *Ethical, legal, and professional issues in counseling* (3rd ed.). Upper Saddle River, NJ: Prentice Hall.

Richards, K., Campenni, C., and Muse-Burke, J. (2010). Self-care and well-being in mental health professionals: The mediating effects of self-awareness and mindfulness. *Journal of Mental Health Counseling*, 32(3), 247–264.

Richards, P. S., and Potts, R. W. (1995). Spiritual interventions in psychotherapy: A survey of the practices and beliefs of AMCAP members. *Issues in Religion and Psychotherapy*, 21(1), 4.

Rogers, C. R. (1973). My philosophy of interpersonal relationships and how it grew. *Journal of Humanistic Psychology*, 13(2), 3–15.

Rogers, C. R. (1980). *A way of being*. Boston: Houghton Mifflin.

Rollins, J. (2009). Crossing the great divide. *Counseling Today*, 52(1), 28–32. Retrieved from http://ct.counseling.org/2009/07/crossing-the-great-divide.

Rosin, J. (2015). The necessity of counselor individuation for fostering reflective practice. *Journal of Counseling & Development*, 93(1), 88–95. doi:10.1002/j.1556-6676.2015.00184.x.

Sacks, J. M. (1985). Religious issues in psychotherapy. *Journal of Religion and Health*, 24(1), 26–30.

Schön, D. (1983) *The Reflective Practitioner: How Professionals Think in Action*. Guildford, UK: Arena.

Schön, D. A. (1991) *The Reflective Turn: Case Studies In and On Educational Practice*. New York: Teachers Press.

Skovholt, T. M., Grier, T. L., and Hanson, M. R. (2001). Career counseling for longevity: Self-care and burnout prevention strategies for counselor resilience. *Journal of Career Development*, 27(3), 167. doi:10.1023/A:1007830908587

Sodowsky, G. R., Kuo-Jackson, P. Y., and Loya, G. J. (1997). Outcome of training in the philosophy of assessment: Multicultural counseling competencies. In D. B. Pope-Davis and H. L. K. Coleman (Eds.), *Multicultural aspects of counseling series, Vol. 7. Multicultural counseling competencies: Assessment, education and training, and supervision* (pp. 3–42). Thousand Oaks, CA: Sage Publications.

Souza, K. Z. (2002). Spirituality in counseling: What do counseling students think about it? *Counseling and Values*, 46(3), 213–217.

Sue, D. W., and Sue, D. (2012). *Counseling the culturally diverse: Theory and practice*. Hoboken, NJ: John Wiley & Sons.

Taylor, E. W. (1998). *The Theory and Practice of Transformative Learning: A Critical Review*. Washington, DC: ERIC Clearinghouse on Adult, Career, and Vocational Education, Center on Education and Training for Employment.

Tennyson, W., and Strom, S. M. (1986). Beyond professional standards: Developing responsibleness. *Journal of Counseling & Development*, 64(5), 298–302.

Tuck, I., Wallace, D., and Pullen, L. (2001). Spirituality and spiritual care provided by parish nurses. *Western Journal of Nursing Research*, 23(5), 441–453.

Udipi, S., Veach, P. M., Kao, J., and LeRoy, B. S. (2008). The psychic costs of empathic engagement: personal and demographic predictors of genetic counselor compassion fatigue. *Journal of Genetic Counseling*, 17(5), 459–471.

Weld, C., and Eriksen, K. (2007). The ethics of prayer in counseling. *Counseling and Values*, 51(2), 125.

White, R. 1997. Time for history: Some ideas for teaching chronology in Year 2. *Teaching History*, 89: 22–25.

Williams, E. N. (2008). A psychotherapy researcher's perspective on therapist self-awareness and self-focused attention after a decade of research. *Psychotherapy research*, 18(2), 139–146.

Wong-Wylie, G. (2010). *Counsellor "Know Thyself": Growing Ourselves, Shaping Our Professional Practice, and Enhancing Education Through Reflective Practice*. VDM Publishing.

Young, J. S., Wiggins-Frame, M., and Cashwell, C. S. (2007). Spirituality and counselor competence: A national survey of American Counseling Association members. *Journal of Counseling & Development*, 85(1), 47–52.

2 Understanding Worldview and the Impact of Spiritual Systems through Assessment

Open and Closed Faith Systems

Carman S. Gill and Robert R. Freund

> "True wisdom comes to each of us when we realize how little we understand about life, ourselves, and the world around us."
>
> —Socrates

Introduction

As described in Chapter 1, the journey of self-awareness emphasizes an examination of the counselor's personal worldview and culture as an essential step toward becoming competent to work in the spiritual and religious domain. ASERVIC's spiritual competencies (2009) build upon this through highlighting the crucial importance of understanding the client's culture and worldview, particularly in the areas of spirituality and religion. ASERVIC states that "[t]he professional counselor recognizes that the client's beliefs (or absence thereof) about spirituality and/or religion are central to his or her worldview and can influence psychosocial functioning" (2009, p. 1.). In this chapter, we describe culture and worldview, discuss definitions of spirituality and religion, as well as, how such these factors impact client functioning. Religiosity will be analyzed in terms of characteristics of open and closed belief systems, rather than specific denominations. We describe a practical conceptualization of belief systems, based on a dimensional assessment of characteristics that are common to most belief systems, rather than the traditional categorical system of religions. Assessment strategies aimed at understanding these systems are described and we apply a qualitative assessment to a case example.

Client Culture

The term *culture* is often used and defined in a variety of ways. For instance, Haviland (1975) defines culture as "a set of shared assumptions where people can predict each other's actions in a given circumstance and react accordingly" (p. 6). The Oxford English Dictionary Online (Simpson and Weiner, 1989) states that culture refers to "ideas, customs and social behavior of a particular group of people or society" (n.p.). Whereas a debate occurs about when human beings are first exposed to culture, at or prior to birth, we know that culture is not innate (unlike other factors, such as some personality influences, sexuality, and gender). Culture (ideas, customs and social behaviors) is created for a purpose and passed down or amended through groups and systems. For instance, infants are not born as "clean slates"; however, neither do they come into the world with clothing. Clothing is an example of the social behavior aspect of culture that has changed dramatically over time, and often varies significantly from group to group. As with other aspects of culture, we can typically tell something about a person based on what they wear. For example, a yarmulke tells us something about an individual's culture, as well as their religion.

Clearly, culture permeates every part of our lives, often below conscious awareness. Every aspect of what we know and do, the very ideas upon which our lives are built, stem from our current and past experiences within our cultures. These cultural experiences are inherently tied to race, gender, socioeconomic status, and ethnicity. Further, they influence the way we attend to spiritual and religious practice. At birth, culturally based expectations, rules and behavioral training begins in earnest, based on factors such as race and assigned sex. As we seek to belong to the group, we increasingly adapt to its cultural practices, and begin to notice differences in those of whom are not members. Robertson and Young (2011) note that spirituality and religion are a part of this cultural process and we argue that, for many clients, they are at the core of their cultural process.

Adler theorized that all human behavior serves an overarching goal of establishing connection to and security within the larger social group (Sweeney, 2009). Consistent with this perspective, a group's *social behavior* orients individuals toward important goals for belonging and serves as an identifier for group membership. In a religious or spiritual context, this may involve specific practices that serve as rituals for connection and vehicles for communicating shared meaning between members (Basham, 2011). Communication, in general, serves an important role of separating, identifying, and sustaining those within the group, even within the sub-cultures of specific religious groups. Further, language is an important part of communication. Beyond the basics of different languages working to identify or separate cultures within subgroups, language and key words work to create a culture. For instance, the term "born again" will have a different meaning and be used in a different context for Evangelical Christians than it would be for someone who is unfamiliar with that religious tradition. Whereas, though "Ave Maria" is readily recognizable for most of the Christian world, those with limited experience in that religious culture will not fully understand the depth of meaning behind those words.

Communication, as a part of social behavior, includes more than the speech patterns alone; it incorporates both verbal and nonverbal content. The concept of verbal communication includes both the verbal content, as well as, vocal cues (pitch, speed, and rhythm of delivery). Nonverbal communication, however, is both physical and physiological, incorporating body posturing, facial expression, and motor movements. Ekman (2003) pioneered research that supported Darwin's theory of emotion universality, in which he tested and verified that six core emotions (happiness, sadness, anger, disgust, surprise, and fear) are present across all cultures. Nuanced versions of these basic emotions (such as remorse or wistfulness) may be more culturally defined. Additionally, the social norms and cultural expectations (known display rules) govern the way in which emotions are expressed during interpersonal communication (Ekman, 2007). The expression of emotion and nonverbal behavior is therefore both universal but culturally bound, and may impact the way in which individuals engage with religious practices. Specific faith cultures may have prescribed means of verbal communication (e.g. the Quaker tradition formerly prescribed "plain speech", as a means by which to be set apart from the dominant society), as well as nonverbal communication (e.g. the Anabaptist tradition of greeting one another with a "holy kiss", as a way of signifying group inclusion). The processing of grief in religious ceremonies, for example, may be vastly different in an Anglo-Saxon religious culture versus a Judaic culture (e.g. "sitting shiva").

Multiculturalism is a frequently used term in the counseling setting. CACREP (2015) defines multicultural as "denoting the diversity of racial, ethnic, and cultural heritage; socioeconomic status; age; gender; sexual orientation; and religious and spiritual beliefs, as well as physical, emotional, and mental abilities" (p. 42). At its most basic level, the influence of culture is experienced through implicit, explicit, personal, and group ideas that are reinforced through customs and norms. It is a fitting simile to liken culture to the air that we breathe, as it so saturates our daily experience of the world that we fail to take notice. Each person sees the world through their own lens of cultural experiences, creating a unique challenge for us as counselors. At a micro level, we all experience our culture uniquely and, at a macro level, we live in a diverse, multicultural society. This results in the challenge of understanding not only basic religious beliefs associated with the numerous religions represented in our country, but also each client's personal experience of the Sacred. Adding to the challenge of understanding culture on a macro and micro level, as counselors we must know our own unique culture and how it impacts our understanding of the client and the client's system. Muddying the waters even further is the role of worldview.

Worldview

Derived from the German word "Weltanschauung" (Wiggins, 2011), *worldview* is often discussed in terms of the individual's unique outlook and internalized messages about self, others, life, and the world (Sperry and Sperry, 2012). Worldview differs from culture in that it is a uniquely and personally created set of beliefs or roadmap for processing and responding to one's environment. Adler referred to worldview as "lifestyle" or a road map one uses for understanding life's events (Sweeney, 2009). For example, someone who views the world as unyieldingly cruel or unfair may decide to avoid taking risks or be predisposed to interpreting life events negatively. One's culture, particularly in terms of spirituality and religion, has a significant impact on worldview development. For instance, the childhood religious belief that humans are unredeemable sinners could result in a worldview that others cannot be trusted. For a counselor to begin understanding the client in terms of culture and worldview, the counselor must understand their own cultural beliefs and worldview, as described in Chapter 1. Further, the counselor should be able to accurately assess client culture and worldview. An understanding of spirituality and religion, in terms of similarities and differences, is crucial to assessing culture and worldview and to the integrity of the counseling process.

Defining Spirituality

Spirituality has been defined in multiple ways across numerous cultures, theologians, researchers, and counselors. The definition is as unique as each individual; perhaps, because perceptions and practices of spirituality are unique to each person. The term itself originates from the Latin word *spiritus*, referring to "the breath of life" (Kelly, 1995). The spiritual is often seen as the source of life, the Divine from which meaning in life, love and humanity is derived, and that of which lends to humanity. Myers, Sweeney and Witmer define it as "an awareness of a being or force that transcends the material aspects of life and gives a deep sense of wholeness or connectedness to the universe" (2000, p. 252). Young and Cashwell state that spirituality is "the universal human capacity to experience self-transcendence and awareness of sacred immanence, with resulting increases in greater self-other compassion and love" (2011, p. 7). They conceptualize this within a developmental perspective, believing that a person's definitions of spirituality will evolve as she or he progresses through various life events. Piedmont, Ciarrochi, Dy-Liacco, and Williams (2009), on the other hand, describe spirituality as an individual attribute, and in terms of a personal relationship with transcendent realities. Whereas the definitions may vary, most theorists agree that spirituality is a deeply personal, multifaceted concept, making it difficult (though not impossible) to quantifiably assess.

The available models of spirituality, formed around the varied perspectives of many theorists, are plentiful. Noteworthy models in the counseling profession include Ellison's Model of Spiritual Well-being (1983), which has been heavily applied in research, and was one of the first to be operationalized and measured through a quantitative assessment. Spiritual Well-being is seen to have two dimensions: "a sense of well-being in relation to God and a sense of well-being in relation to life and its purpose" (Richards et al., 2009, pp. 73–74). These domains reveal clients' beliefs about whether God loves them, is concerned about them, and provides a source of support. For example, a client who believes God has abandoned him may present as particularly despondent after losing a job. Spiritual well-being can be assessed through interview and utilization of the Spiritual Well-Being Scale (Ellison, 1983).

The Humanistic Model of Spirituality was posited in the late 1980s by Elkins et al. (1988), and is based on the works of Maslow, Frankl, Jung, and Dewey. They believed that spirituality is multidimensional and has nine components. These components include: transcendent dimension, meaning and purpose in life, mission in life, sacredness of life, material values, altruism, idealism, awareness of the tragic, and fruits of the spirit (Elkins et al., 1988). Westgate approached the complex issues of multidimensional spirituality with her Spiritual Wellness Model, proposed in 1996. Based on a thorough review of the literature, she described four components of spirituality, which include: transcendence, meaning and purpose in life, innerness or intrinsic values, and community of shared values. These themes are consistent with those measured by the Spiritual Assessment Scale (SAS) created by Howden (1992), and are discussed toward the end of this chapter.

The models above are a sample of the many posited regarding spirituality, and describe themes that are found throughout spirituality literature. Ideas of meaning and purpose in life, one's internal approach to connections and values, transcendence, spiritual journey, and in relating to others, are consistently reflected in literature and research. Understanding spirituality in terms of these components gives the counselor insight into the extent to which clients are connected to their own healthy spirituality. Further, in their 2009 study, Piedmont et al. determined that, for the individual, spirituality "may operate as a source of motivation that impacts growth and development" (2009, p. 170). Their research also concluded that spirituality and religion are highly correlated, but distinct constructs that are not interchangeable as variables. To this effect, ASERVIC (2002) reports, "[s]pirituality is not the same thing as religion. While religion may be one way in which persons express or experience their spirituality, it is not the same as spirituality, itself" (p. 2).

Defining Religion

Derived from the Latin word *religio*, signifying a bond between humans and a power greater than themselves (Hill et al., 2000), *religion* is often defined in terms of how it differs from spirituality or as an outcome of spirituality. ASERVIC, in their division "white paper," described religion "as the organization of belief which is common to a culture or subculture" (2002, p. 2). Myers, Sweeney and Witmer (2000) argued that a distinction should be made between spirituality and religion. They believed that religion is narrower in focus, referring to the external expression of the internal spiritual being, often within institutional belief and behaviors. Acknowledging the roots of the word, Pargament (1997) defined religion as "a search for significance in ways related to the sacred [sic]" (p. 240). He stated that religion is a uniquely human phenomenon, and that it includes qualities related to the Divine, such as holiness, blessedness, transcendence and other associated concepts.

As with spirituality, theorists acknowledge that religion is multifaceted, and the models of religion and religiousness reflect this idea. For instance, one of the first models of religion, Glock and Stark's Five Dimensional (5D) model (1965) includes the experiential, the ritualistic, the ideological, the intellectual, and the consequential components. In his well-known model of Religious Coping (1997), Pargament proposed a theory that involves two basic assumptions: first, stressful life events occur for every individual; second, individuals choose from multiple methods of coping, including religion (Harrison et al., 2001). He defined religious coping as "a specific mode of coping that is inherently derived from religious beliefs, practices, experiences, emotions, or relationships" (Abu-Raiya and Pargament, 2015, p. 25). Whereas multiple models of spirituality and religion have been posited over the years, most, if not all of these, report that a system of "belief" is at the heart of religion.

Understanding Belief Systems

Most of the world's religions and belief systems have a core set of fundamental principles, tenets if you will, despite their differences. Prior efforts in exploring multicultural considerations in counseling have often assumed a categorical approach to describing belief systems. While this may be convenient for identifying broad religious identities, it bears a limited and questionable utility. Clients' dynamics are only partially based on religious affiliation, and the expression of that affiliation is impacted by a plethora of cultural, developmental and emotional factors. To attempt to discuss the widely varied presentations of a diverse set of belief systems would be a disservice to the counselor and dismissive of the client; therefore, we attempt to discuss the universal dynamics of religion and belief systems in a way which is practical for individual assessment and treatment. We believe that discussing these groups along a continuum of open and closed systems allows clinicians to tailor their assessments, rather than attempting to compartmentalize the myriad religions and denominations in our society with specific facts. This is not intended to diminish the significance of the client's broader religious orientation; but rather, to supplement the clinician's conceptualization, diagnosis, and treatment planning process. Such an approach will allow counselors to honor the specific constructs of spirituality in clients' lives while also accurately representing the interconnected influences of culture and development.

In order to accomplish this task effectively, it is important to first have a clear definition of 'belief systems.' The terms 'faith' and 'belief' are often colloquially used synonymously. While belief is frequently associated with both spirituality and religion, faith and belief are not interchangeable terms.

'Belief' is defined by Oxford English Dictionary Online (Simpson and Weiner, 1989) as "something one accepts as true or real" (n.p.). Hagedorn and Hartwig Moorhead (2011) assert that spiritual beliefs are part of a larger cultural system. Foster and Holden described the purpose of faith as "a common belief system through which a person forms an identity" (2011, p. 99). The authors (2011) conceptualize *belief systems* in terms of the cognitive framework or schemas upon which faith is built. If faith is then built upon a set of beliefs, faith can be described as the activation of that belief system. In certain traditions faith is described as "the evidence of things not seen" (Hebrews 11:1, King James Version), implying that faith is the external action associated with a belief or belief systems. From a certain standpoint, faith and belief are therefore overlapping, where faith is a more active term (i.e. "to have faith in something"). Within this section, we will discuss the implications of religious belief systems. In the next chapter, we will discuss faith development. Further, the authors do not wish to ascertain that one system is better than another. Rather, we wish to present the ways in which belief systems differ, depending on the degree to which they are open or closed.

In the 1960s, Milton Rokeach conceptualized beliefs systems on a continuum, based on characteristics ranging between what he referred to as 'open' and 'closed' dynamics (1960). Whereas he applied these concepts broadly to belief systems in general, we will attempt to describe this continuum specifically in terms of religious belief systems. There are many facets to open–closed systems (to be further discussed), but Rokeach distills the concepts to a hallmark feature that differentiates the concepts, stating "the fundamental basis is the extent to which there is a reliance on absolute authority" (1960, p. 60). Following this model, we believe that closed religious belief systems are defined specifically by the degree to which a "top-down" relationship with authority exists. In more closed systems, authority figures will apply rewards and punishment, as needed, to reinforce their role in communicating axioms and rules. Individuals are accepted based on conformity with this authority. Consider the difference within Christian denominations. While some denominations promote a constructivist, internalized authority (e.g. Universalist Unitarian churches) others rely more heavily, and to varying degrees, upon the role and authority of church leadership to guide practice and belief (e.g. Catholic churches).

Closed systems are characterized in varying degrees by reactions to other systems with differing beliefs. A belief system that trends toward being closed, may perceive an unfamiliar system as inferior or even immoral. Whereas rejecting a system that varies dramatically from one's own beliefs is not uncommon, extremely closed systems tend to have a high degree of denunciation for other belief systems, even when the other system is similar in nature (Rokeach, 1960). For example, a fundamentalist Baptist belief system may react negatively to individuals who participate in another Baptist system that accepts women as religious leaders. This rejection is often associated with fear of the "other" system and penalties, such as, the perception of not following "God's will." The rejection of differing systems can be so extreme that individuals do not discriminate amongst different religious systems, seeing all others as "wrong" and applying penalties as a result. Communication limited to the authority figure alone, and fear of interaction with others, may result in a reinforced cycle that prevents these systems from engaging in cognitive processes or questioning, which could result in change. A lack of individual evaluation or independent action is, in varying degrees, typically associated with highly closed belief systems. As the system becomes more closed in nature, fear of questioning authority results in feelings of isolation; and potentially, a fearful worldview. Distant future orientation becomes more and more the focus for closed systems, contrasting the balance of past, present, and future orientations found in more open systems (Rokeach, 1960).

In keeping with the idea of conceptualizing belief systems on a continuum, the extent to which a system is open is characterized by the degree to which authority is shared, rather than absolute. Authority is shared to varying degrees and acceptance into the belief system is not based on the extent to which individuals agree with authority figures. Individuals in open systems are able to differentiate between the truth of information and the source of information (authority figure). As a result, communication from authority figures is processed within the group, as well as by individuals, and accepted based on its merits or perceived veracity. In addition, communication with people engaging in different belief systems becomes more acceptable, resulting in less rejection of others and decreased fear of the world. Individuals engaging in more open belief systems can independently evaluate information on its merits and value open communication regarding differing belief systems, creating a cycle that resists hard and fast ideals. Conversely, more closed systems perpetuate static beliefs in that they resist new ideas, which may challenge the closed system. While this description paints a picture of dichotomy with belief systems, we wish to emphasize that most faith systems can be conceptualized along a continuum. Not doing so is the very definition of a closed system approach. For counselors, open versus closed faith systems have specific implications for practice.

Counselors often struggle with determining healthy, versus unhealthy, religious or spiritual perspectives and behavior. In keeping with Rokeach's ideas, Gold (2010) posits that choice is a key element of healthy religious belief systems. Within healthy systems, emotional sanctioning or repercussion does not occur in association with questioning, self-exploration or leaving the belief system. Thus, the element of choice is a determining factor in whether a belief system is healthy or unhealthy for an individual. At the extreme, closed-off belief systems may encourage an unhealthy, negative view of the world. Researchers demonstrate that extremely closed belief systems, including fundamentalism, can be highly related to fear of others. This may associate with prejudice, which often leaves individuals

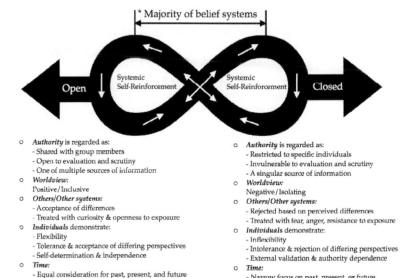

Figure 2.1 Continuum of Open and Closed Belief System Characteristics

experiencing issues with different cultures or groups that foster interpersonal difficulties in a variety of environments (Doehring, 2013). Those systems that fall on the most extreme closed end of the spectrum are often referred to as "cults" or "radicals". Gold (2010) lists seven characteristics of cults that are consistent with the idea of extremely closed-off systems. The impact of these systems on individuals may include anxiety, excessive guilt, anger, fear of the outside world or of leaving the system, or, in extreme cases, violence toward outsiders. Further, the quality of individual coping can be adversely affected when clients are engaged with an unhealthy belief system. Revisiting the idea of choice, whether an open or closed belief system is healthy, is dependent upon the individual's level of autonomy in participation.

Counselors need to be aware of the impact of religious practices on client coping. In terms of positive and negative religious coping, Pargament, Tarakeshwar, Ellison and Wulff (2001) state that "positive religious coping methods reflect a secure relationship with God, a belief that there is a greater meaning to be found in life, and a sense of spiritual connectedness with others. In contrast, the negative religious coping pattern involves expressions of a less secure relationship with God, a tenuous and ominous view of the world, and a religious struggle to find and conserve significance in life" (p. 498). Pargament, Smith, Koenig, and Perez (1998) found that positive religious coping, such as seeking spiritual support, expressing spiritual contentedness, benevolent reframing of stressful events, and congregational support, were associated with low rates of depression. Conversely, they found that negative religious coping, such as negative reframing, spiritual discontent, and religious conflict, were related to negative mental health outcomes. When working with spiritually impacted client concerns, counselors should look for these themes, building upon strengths and addressing unhealthy patterns from within a theoretical framework.

In terms of counseling theory, Rokeach (1960) suggests that clients will benefit from a theoretical framework that acknowledges the degree of openness of their belief system. For example, he suggests that clients who present with a more open belief system may benefit more from Gestalt; on the contrary, classic psychoanalysis or behaviorism may be more effective for clients whose belief systems tend to be closed. Depending upon the degree of openness, we also recommend Transpersonal, Existential and Narrative therapy. In terms of beliefs systems that lean more toward a closed nature, we recommend Third Wave Cognitive-Behavioral therapies, as well as 12-Step spirituality. Additional approaches that work well with many of these clients include creative arts, Adlerian and Family Systems.

Whereas we have discussed and defined spirituality and religion in this chapter, most clients will not necessarily make a distinction between these two concepts or discuss them in these terms. Understanding the extent to which a client operates in the spiritual domain and religious domain in separate or overlapping ways, is key to addressing the associated strengths and challenges. Young and Cashwell (2011) describe five patterns clients tend to follow, including those who are both spiritual and religious; spiritual and not religious; religious but not spiritual; religiously tolerant and indifferent; and religiously antagonistic. The extent to which religion is embedded within the client's culture or worldview also plays an influential role. For example, a client's moderately closed system can also be culturally bound, such as the faith of Hasidic Jews, which may completely overlap with cultural identification. In such situations, one may be culturally religious but not spiritually inclined (though this of course is dependent upon each individual). The key to understanding a client's culture, worldview, belief system, and coping is engaging in thorough and accurate assessment.

Assessment

Assessment is one of the most vital components of successful mental health treatment. Successful treatment of mental health and wellness issues is often predicated upon an appropriate and accurate assessment process. ASERVIC's spiritual competencies (2009) mandate that professional counselors strive to understand spiritual and religious functioning, by means of acquiring related information from the client and others within the client's system. As a result, it is imperative for counselors to understand the assessment process, the purpose for using assessments, and how assessment relates to other spirituality competencies. Hodge (2013) argues that this process is focused on determining the impact of spiritual and religious systems on the client's overall functioning. Further, Hodge (2013) defines assessment within this context as "the process of gathering, analyzing, and synthesizing information about these two interrelated constructs into a framework that provides the basis for practice decisions" (p. 93).

Oxford English Dictionary Online (Simpson and Weiner, 1989) defines assessment as both the action of measuring and type of measurement, i.e. "to determine the importance, size, or value of." Locke, Myers, and Herr (2001) defined assessment as the means by which the counselor facilitates awareness of the client's belief systems that are "relevant to the resolution of issues that the clients bring to counseling" (p. 608). For the purpose of this chapter, *assessment* is defined as the act of determining the amount of value or importance an individual assigns to a specific construct, such as spiritual functioning. Counselors must be aware, not only of the actions they are taking when assessing a client; but also, the extent to which they are determining the portion of value or amount of importance that the client assigns to spirituality. Because of this responsibility, counselors should understand the utility of assessing client spirituality.

Rationale for Assessing. The rationale for assessing, or choosing to utilize a particular type of assessment, usually drives assessment process. Gill, Harper, and Dailey (2011) state that the assessment process gives the counselor an opportunity to gather information about the client, the client's world, and issues he or she may face. A solid assessment lays the ground work for diagnosis and case conceptualization (which we discuss in Chapter 4), and determining resources, treatment planning, and selecting interventions (which we cover in Part II of this book). Further, assessment offers an avenue for building the working alliance and increasing the level of safety for the client, ultimately leading to more disclosure. Exploration into the Sacred can give a counselor a much deeper insight into the client's culture and worldview, as well as the impact of spirituality, religion, and belief systems on the client's overall wellness. We also note that, as the counselor gains insight into the client's world, often the client's self-awareness increases, as well. The overlap between assessment and intervention is well documented, and measures such as spiritual timelines are also regarded as interventions. Further, the benefits gained from assessing the spiritual domain generally fall into increased understanding of the client in one of the following five categories: context and worldview, spiritual and religious issues and impact on functioning, strengths and resources, interventions, and client self-exploration (Gill et al., 2011).

Assessment Process. Pargament and Krumrei (2009) discuss spiritual assessments as a three-stage process, inclusive of initial assessment, extensive assessment and implicit assessment. Also, clients are generally assessed at Level I, the initial encounter, and Level II, which is a more in-depth follow-up. Similar to the initial assessment, Level 1 assessment is conducted at the first meeting for basic data gathering and determinations pertaining to the necessity of follow-up (Hodge, 2013). This type of assessment is generally conducted using forms, observations, and direct interviews (Gill et al., 2011).

Level II is considered the extensive assessment and is used to gain more in-depth information (i.e. formal quantitative instruments or qualitative measure such as spiritual genograms), following a Level I assessment. Implicit assessment requires the counselor to listen for spiritual themes and references in the client's presentation or language and ask further probing questions about these experiences (Pargament, 2007). A subtle approach to assessment is recommended when working with clients who are resistant to religious or spiritual discourse, but present with problems in those domains. We will cover this issue as part of the presentation on Level II assessments.

The assessment process begins as soon as the client walks into the room. The counselor and the client begin forming hypotheses about each other that lay the groundwork for future interactions. Observations are generally the first form of assessment, and can be the key to beginning initial discourse about spiritual and religious themes. Formal assessment typically begins with Level I, on an intake form. Questions regarding spirituality and religion are much more commonplace, and most agencies include some basic questions. However, the counselor often leads the way in terms of initial topics introduced, and it is imperative that ideas of spirituality and religion are addressed and introduced using open, non-judgmental or leading language. Counselors should focus on determining whether the client sees themselves as a spiritual or religious person, the impact of spirituality and religion on the presenting issue, and the role of spirituality and religion in coping with issues (Pargament and Krumrei, 2009). The counselor should keep in mind the five patterns clients tend to follow and where the client's religion falls in terms of open and closed systems, as well as the level of spiritual development of the client. Spiritual development will be discussed in the following chapter.

Guided by information gained from Level I assessments, the counselor needs to decide what type of follow-up is needed. In general, counselors may want to follow-up with a more in-depth, Level II extensive assessment, and there are plenty from which to choose. However, if the client is religiously antagonistic or indifferent, implicit assessment may be most appropriate. Counselors should keep in mind the culture and worldview of the client when deciding on Level II assessments. Further, Pargament and Krumrei (2009) emphasize that this should be a "rich, multidimensional process used to capture a phenomenon as multifaceted as spirituality" (p. 101). In keeping with this statement, we review various qualitative and quantitative assessments, though we encourage counselors to remember that results of assessments are only as helpful as the processes by which they are presented and processed with the client.

Types of Assessments. Assessments in generally fall into three categories: qualitative, quantitative, or a combination of both. *Qualitative assessments* focus on questions and conversations, while quantitative methods rely on objective instruments and inventories. Qualitative methods may include verbal histories, observations, intake forms, structured interviews, and open-ended questions (Gill et al., 2011). Other qualitative methods of assessment include the creation of a spiritual map (Hodge, 2001), spiritual ecomaps, spiritual histories, and sentence stems (Gill et al., 2011). We have briefly touched upon observations and intake forms in this chapter; sentence stems will be covered as part of implicit assessments. Further, spiritual histories, genograms and maps will be discussed as interventions in Section II of this book. In accordance, we choose to discuss spiritual ecomaps here, in the qualitative assessment chapter, remembering that this tool can also be used as an intervention.

Spiritual Ecomaps. These are used to portray the spiritual domain of the client's immediate family system, and often results in a document that is useful throughout the counseling process (Gill et al., 2011). Hodge states that "eco-maps focus on clients' present, existential relationships with spiritual and religious systems" (2013, p. 109). Counselors and clients can co-create spiritual ecomaps to gain a deeper understanding of the interaction between the spiritual domain and the client's most salient systems, in a way that is respectful to the spiritual tradition. These graphic depictions of inter-related client systems will help the counselor uncover specifics regarding client issues, as well as, encourage client self-awareness. Using this process, a baseline can be established and changes to pertinent systems can be tracked.

Much akin to a genogram-style representation of the client's immediate family system, an ecomap is created by placing the names of the client and client's immediate family in the middle of the page and drawing a circle around that family system (Hodge, 2013). Additional circles can be added outside of the main circle representing other systems or components that impact the client and/or family's spiritual domain. The counselor and client can use various types of lines to depict different types of relationships. Heavy solid lines indicate close relationships, lighter lines indicate weaker relation-ships, broken lines indicate disconnected relationships, and jagged lines indicate strained or conflicted relationships (McGoldrick and Gerson, 1985). The counselor can explore these spiritual systems with the client, using basic counseling skills and open-ended questioning. The client can add additional lines between the family and each spiritual system, and between pertinent family members and each spiritual system. Some of the suggested systems for discussion include: transcendence, rituals and practices, faith community, spiritual leaders, parent's traditions and transpersonal beings (Gill et al., 2011). As the process unfolds, the counselor and client can adapt or change the ecomap to facilitate a better understanding of the systems. Descriptive notes can be added, as well. An example of an ecomap is given at the end of this chapter, which demonstrates the volume of qualitative data that can be gathered using these assessments, as compared to quantitative, numbers-driven assessments.

Quantitative Assessment. This type of assessment consists of the use of standardized instruments and inventories. Standardized instruments should have undergone tests of reliability and validity, as well as, the inclusion of normative data. They should be relevant to counseling and include clear instructions for administering and scoring (Richards et al., 2009). In some instances, quantitative instruments can be more beneficial than qualitative methods. They are efficient, can be completed outside of the counseling session, used to establish a baseline and track progress, provoke the client's thought process about spirituality, and provide information about specific domains of spirituality to the counselor (Richards et al., 2009). Still, many instruments fail to meet Richards et al.'s (2009) aforementioned criteria and often have issues with generalizability and unclear definitions (Oakes and Raphel, 2008). Despite the challenges of assessing spirituality through qualitative methods and the efficiency of quantitative methods, many researchers stress the value and usefulness of qualitative assessment versus quantitative (Oakes and Raphel, 2008; Steen et al., 2006; Richards et al., 2009). Steen et al. (2006) stress the "value of subjective human experience above objective empiricism" (p. 110).

In terms of quantitative assessments, we can make recommendations for clinicians who wish to assess specific aspects of spirituality and religion. For those seeking to more fully understand the client's spiritual coping and/or struggles, Pargament's positive and negative Brief RCOPE may prove helpful. Based on the Model of Religious Coping described previously in this chapter, the RCOPE includes questions focused on quantitatively assessing positive and negative religious coping cognitively, emotionally, and behaviorally (Pargament et al., 2011). This 14-item assessment allows for responses to be given on a four-point Likert-type scale, ranging from "not at all" to "a great deal" (Pargament et al., 2011). Total possible scores range from 7 to 28 for each of the seven-item positive and negative coping subscales. Internal consistencies are reported as .90 for the positive coping scale and .81 for the negative coping scale. The instrument includes questions such as "[f]elt punished by God for my lack of devotion," "[s]ought God's love and care" and "[w]ondered whether my church had abandoned me" (Pargament et al., 2011, p 57). Results could provide counselors with important information related to the impact of religious coping on the client's approach to his or her worldview and presenting problem. Research on religious coping using religiously diverse versions of this assessment is available, as are the various versions addressing multiple varied religious traditions (Abu-Raiya and Pargament, 2015).

Howden's Spiritual Assessment Scale (SAS, 1992), which includes themes that are consistent with Westgate's Spiritual Wellness model (1996), provides insight into the client's spiritual domain, in terms of overall spirituality and spiritual components including transcendence, purpose and meaning in life, connections, and unifying interconnectedness. This is a brief, 28-item assessment that uses general language in terms of spiritual concepts, and has been used in research because of the high levels of reliability and validity associated with the scale and subscales (Gill et al., 2011). When working from a 12-Step model, Veach and Chappel's

Spiritual Health Inventory (SHI, 1992), an 18-question, Likert-type assessment with strong reliability, is a helpful instrument. The four themes underlying the instrument are consistent with 12-Step spirituality and include personal experience, spiritual well-being, sense of harmony, and personal helplessness. The instrument is easy to score and includes items such as "[i]t is my experience that developing and maintaining spiritual health requires effort and work" and "God, the Creator, or Higher Power is so powerful that nothing I do makes any difference" (Veach and Chappel, 1992).

From time-to-time in counseling, we encounter clients who, for various reasons, do not want to discuss spirituality or religion. These individuals may be religiously intolerant or indifferent. They may be in a developmental stage of faith that includes anger, may not be able to identify spiritual or religious concerns, or they may simply distrust a mental health professional with such information. When this occurs, and it is apparent to the counselor that spirituality and religion contribute to the issue, implicit assessment may be necessary. Implicit assessment follows or focuses on themes that may be spiritual and religious in nature (Pargament and Krumrei, 2009). These themes can include meaning in life, hope, forgiveness, guilt and shame, inspiration, love, death, and beyond. Recognizing these themes as spiritual in nature and following up appropriately, will give the clinician insight into a client's spiritual perspective. Further, cueing in on the metaphors associated with these themes can be a very powerful tool (2009). For instance, a client may relegate a circumstance to "God's hands," identifying themselves as "helpless," or refer to another individual as "irredeemable" and "damned." We also recommend a qualitative assessment, the Oshodi Sentence Completion Index (OSCI; Oshodi, 1999). Employing Afrocentric perspective mastery, the Oshodi scale offers sentence completion stems related to spiritual themes, such as, "[w]ith my human spirit..." and "[w]hen good or bad things happen to me, I attribute them to..." (1999).

Case Study

The present case study applies a spiritual systems assessment to Susanna, a 15-year-old, cisgender, Mexican-American female whose family identifies as part of the Mormon faith. For more information on Susanna's presenting issues, please reference her full profile in the Introduction of this book.

In the initial session, Susanna is guarded but responsive to Level 1 assessment questions. The counselor is able to ascertain that she identifies herself as a religious and spiritual person, but doesn't seem to differentiate between these concepts. She has a strong sense of community and regard for the Divine. She is heavily committed to Mormonism, the family's religion. It is clear from her description that her belief system is moderately closed, as she states that she "received many uncompromising messages about purity,

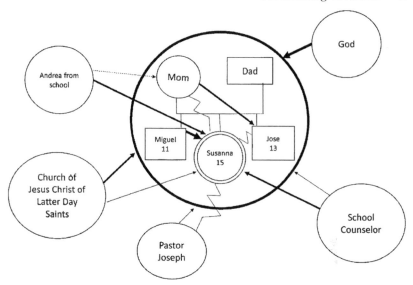

Figure 2.2 Susanna's Ecomap

morality, and sin from her parents" and she is "expected to follow these rules without question." She also assures you that her beliefs prohibit her from killing herself and she is not actively suicidal.

Based on this initial information, the counselor believes that co-creating an ecomap, a Level II assessment, will provide the best opportunity to understand the interplay of the systems impacting Susanna's presenting problem, as well as, their functions. Also, a graphic display of these systems will provide the counselor insight into Susanna's baseline, inform future areas to explore, and encourage her involvement and insight. After a brief discussion of the process, Susanna agrees and is guided through the steps. As expected, Susanna is eager to follow the rules and get the ecomaps "right."

Susanna's ecomap gives the counselor valuable insight into Susanna's world. The bold lines connecting her church and God to her family system indicate Susanna's perception of their heavy influence over her family. She has not connected these as strongly to herself. This is in contrast to the bold lines she has drawn connecting herself to her school counselor and to her friend, Andrea. Further, the jagged lines that she uses to connect herself with her mother, youngest brother and pastor provides some insight into her negative perception of those relationships. Follow up questions are necessary for clarification and a full assessment. However, this information not only provides a vehicle for deeper communication and insight, it informs case conceptualization and treatment planning, which will also benefit from understanding Susanna's spiritual development.

References

Abu-Raiya, H., and Pargament, K. I. (2015). Religious coping among diverse religions: Commonalities and divergences. *Psychology of Religion and Spirituality*, 7(1), 24–33. http://dx.doi.org/10.1037/a0037652.

ASERVIC. (2002). *A Position Paper of the Association for Spiritual, Ethical, and Religious Values in Counseling*. Retrieved October 27, 2002, from http://www.counseling.org/aservic/Spirituality.html.

Association for Spiritual, Ethical, and Religious Values in Counseling. (2009). *Spiritual Competencies: Competencies for integrating spirituality into counseling*. Retrieved from http://www.aservic.org/competencies.html.

Basham, A. (2011). Ritual in counseling. In C. S. Cashwell and J. S. Young (Eds.), *Integrating spirituality and religion into counseling: A guide to competent practice* (2nd ed.) (pp. 209–224). Alexandria, VA: American Counseling Association.

Council for Accreditation of Counseling and Related Educational Programs. (2015). *Accreditation manual*. Alexandria, VA: Author. Retrieved from http://www.cacrep.org/wp-content/uploads/2016/06/2016-Standards-with-Glossary-rev-2.2016.pdf.

Doehring, C. (2013). An applied integrative approach to exploring how religion and spirituality contribute to or counteract prejudice and discrimination. In K. I. Pargament, A. Mahoney, and E. P. Shafranske (Eds.), *APA handbook of psychology, religion, and spirituality (vol 2): An applied psychology of religion and spirituality* (pp. 389–403). Washington, DC: American Psychological Association. doi:10.1037/14046–020.

Ekman, P. E. (2003). *Unmasking the face: A guide to recognizing emotions from facial expressions*. Los Altos, CA: Malor Books.

Ekman, P. E. (2007). *Emotions revealed: Recognizing faces and feelings to improve communication and emotional life* (2nd ed.). New York, NY: Owl Books.

Elkins, D. N., Hedstrom, L. J., Hughes, L. L., and Leaf, J. A. (1988). Toward a humanistic phenomenological spirituality: Definition, description, and measurement. *Journal of Humanistic Psychology*, 28, 5–18.

Ellison, C.W. (1983). Spiritual well-being: Conceptualization and measurement. *Journal of Psychology and Theology*, 11, 330–340.

Foster, R. D., and Holden, J. M. (2011). Human and spiritual development and transformation. In C. S. Cashwell and J. S. Young (Eds.), *Integrating spirituality and religion into counseling. A guide to competent practice* (pp. 97–118). Alexandria, VA: American Counseling Association.

Gill, C. S., Harper, M. E., and Dailey, S. F. (2011). Assessing the client's spiritual domain. In C. S. Cashwell and J. S. Young (Eds.), *Integrating religion and spirituality in counseling: A guide to competent practice* (2nd ed.) (pp. 141–162). Alexandria, VA: American Counseling Association.

Glock, C. Y., and Stark, R. (1965). *Religion and society in tension*. Chicago, IL: Rand McNally Co.

Gold, J. M. (2010). *Counseling and Spirituality: Integrating spiritual and clinical orientations*. Upper Saddle River, NJ: Pearson Education Inc.

Hagedorn, W. B., and Hartwig Moorhead, H. J. (2011). Counselor Self-Awareness: Exploring attitudes, beliefs, and values. In C. S. Cashwell and J. S. Young (Eds.), *Integrating religion and spirituality in counseling: A guide to competent practice* (2nd ed.). (pp. 71–96). Alexandria, VA: American Counseling Association.

Harrison, M. O., Koenig, H. G., Hays, J. C., Eme-Akwari, A. G., and Pargament, K. I. (2001). The epidemiology of religious coping: A review of recent literature. *International Review of Psychiatry*, 13, 86–93.

Haviland, W. A. (1975). *Cultural Anthropology*. New York, NY: Holt, Rinehart & Winston.

Hill, P. C., Pargament, K. I., Hood, R. W., McCullough, M. E., Swyers, J. P., Larson, D. B., and ZinnbauerB. J. (2000). Conceptualizing religion and spirituality: Points of commonality, points of departure. *Journal for the Theory of Social Behavior*, 30, 51–77.

Hodge, D. R. (2001). Spiritual genograms: A generational approach to assessing spirituality. *Families in Society: The Journal of Contemporary Human Services*, 82, 35–48.

Hodge, D. R. (2013). Assessing spirituality and religion in the context of counseling and psychotherapy. In K. I. Pargament (Ed.), *APA handbook of psychology, religion, and spirituality: Vol. 2. An applied psychology of religion and spirituality* (pp. 93–123). Washington, DC: American Psychological Association.

Howden, J. W. (1992). Development and psychometric characteristics of the Spirituality Assessment Scale. Dissertation Services. Ann Arbor, MI: Bell & Howell Company.

Jalāl, D. R. (1995). *The essential Rumi* (C. Barks, Trans.). New York, NY: Harper Collins.

Kelly, E. K. (1995). *Spirituality and religion in counseling and psychotherapy: Diversity in theory and practice*. Alexandra, VA: American Counseling Association.

Locke, D. C., Myers, J. E., and Herr, E. L. (2001). *The Handbook of Counseling*. Thousand Oaks, CA: Sage.

McGoldrick, M., and Gerson, R. (1985). *Genograms in family assessment*. New York: W. W. Norton.

Myers, J. E., Sweeney, T. J., and Witmer, J. M. (2000). Counseling for wellness: A holistic model for treatment planning. *Journal for Counseling & Development*, 78, 251–266.

Oakes, E. K., and Raphel, M. M. (2008). Spiritual assessment in counseling: Methods and practice. *Counseling and Values*, 52(3), 240–252. doi:10.1002/j.2161–2007X.2008.tb00107.x.

Oshodi, R. E. (1999). The construction of an Africentric sentence completion test to assess the need for achievement. *Journal of Black Studies*, 30, 216–231.

Pargament, K. I. (1997). *The Psychology of religion and coping: Theory, research, practice*. New York, NY: The Guilford Press.

Pargament, K. I. (2007). *Spiritually integrated psychotherapy: Understanding and addressing the sacred*. New York: Guilford Press.

Pargament, K. I., and Krumrei, E. J. (2009). Clinical assessment of clients' spirituality. In J. Aten and M. Leach (Eds.), *Spirituality and the therapeutic process: A guide for mental health professionals* (pp. 93–120). Washington DC: American Psychological Association Press.

Pargament, K., Feuille, M., and Burdzy, D. (2011). The brief RCOPE: Current psychometric status of a short measure of religious coping. *Religions*, 2, 51–76. doi:10.3390/rel2010051.

Pargament, K. I., Smith, B. W., Koenig, H. G., and Perez, L. (1998). Patterns of positive and negative religious coping with major life stressors. *Journal for the Scientific Study of Religion*, 37, 710–724.

Pargament, K. I., Tarakeshwar, N., Ellison, C. G., and Wulff, K. M. (2001). Religious coping among the religious: The relationships between religious coping and well-being in a national sample of Presbyterian clergy, elders, and members. *Journal for the Scientific Study of Religion*, 40(3), 497–513.

Piedmont, R. L., Ciarrochi, J. W., Dy-Liacco, G. S., and Williams, J. E. G. (2009). The empirical and conceptual value of the Spiritual Transcendence and Religious Involvement scales for personality research. *Psychology of Religion and Spirituality*, 1, 162–179. doi:10.1037/a0015883.

Richards, P. S., Bartz, J. D., and O'Grady, K. A. (2009). Assessing religion and spirituality in counseling: Some reflections and recommendations. *Counseling and Values*, 54, 65–79.

Robertson, L. A., and Young, M. E. (2011). The Revised ASERVIC Spiritual Competencies. In C. S. Cashwell and J. S. Young (Eds.), *Integrating religion and spirituality in counseling: A guide to competent practice* (2nd ed.) (pp. 25–42). Alexandria, VA: American Counseling Association.

Rokeach, M. (1960). *The Open and Closed Mind: Investigations in to the nature of belief systems and personality systems*. New York, NY: Basic Books.

Simpson, E. S. C., and Weiner, J. A. (Eds.) (1989). *The Oxford Encyclopaedic English Dictionary*. Oxford: Clarendon Press.

Sperry, L., and Sperry, J. (2012). *Case conceptualization: Mastering this competency with ease and confidence*. New York, NY: Routledge.

Steen, R. L., Engels, D., and Thweatt, W. T. (2006). Ethical aspects of spirituality in counseling. *Counseling and Values*, 50, 108–118.

Sweeney, T. J. (2009). *Adlerian Counseling and Psychotherapy: A practitioner's approach* (5th ed.). New York, NY: Routledge.

Veach, T. L., and Chappel, J. N. (1992). Measuring spiritual health: A preliminary study. *Substance Abuse*, 13, 139–147.

Westgate, C. E. (1996). Spiritual wellness and depression. *Journal of Counseling and Development*, 75, 26–35.

Wiggins, M. I. (2011). Culture and worldview. In C. S. Cashwell and J. S. Young (Eds.), *Integrating religion and spirituality in counseling: A guide to competent practice* (2nd ed.) (pp. 43–70). Alexandria, VA: American Counseling Association.

Young, J. S., and Cashwell, C. S. (2011). Integrating spirituality and religion into counseling: An introduction. In C. S. Cashwell and J. S. Young (Eds.), *Integrating spirituality and religion into counseling: A guide to competent practice* (2nd ed.) (pp. 1–24). Alexandria, VA: American Counseling Association.

3 Understanding the Development of Spirituality, Religion, and Faith in the Client's Life

Robert R. Freund and Carman S. Gill

"It does not matter how slowly you go so long as you do not stop."
—Confucius

Introduction

In order for a clinician to competently work with clients' spiritual and religious issues, it is necessary that he or she be able to place the client's beliefs into an appropriate developmental context. This developmental perspective is essential for treatment planning and the selection of effective interventions. In this chapter, Fowler's faith stages (1981), Genia's psychospiritual development (1995), and integral psychology (Wilber, 2000) will be described in terms of predicted growth trajectories and hallmarks for identifying each stage of development. Additionally, Fowler and Genia's theories are applied to the case of Cecily (see Introduction) as an example of how these may be used in clinical situations.

In reviewing the available content, we decided to follow the pragmatic mission of the text. Rather than presenting a brief overview of all the available theories of spiritual development, three of the predominant perspectives were selected. This serves multiple purposes. First, the authors can communicate a detailed explanation of the developmental theories rather than only enough information to communicate each theory's essence. This expanded presentation will allow the reader to more readily take this information and apply it to clinical practice. Additionally, the distinctly different foundations (cognitive, psychodynamic, and holistic/wellness) of the three theories will mesh well with a variety of theoretical orientations. If readers wish to learn about additional theories of spiritual development, we recommend referencing Sperry's (2012) *Spirituality in Clinical Practice* and Cashwell and Young's (2011) *Integrating Spirituality and Religion into Counseling,* as well as Oser and Gmünder's (1991) *Religious Judgement: A Developmental Approach.*

Fowler's Stages of Faith

Fowler's Stages of Faith are based on integrations of pre-existing structural theories of human development, including those of Piaget and

Kohlberg (Fowler, 1981). Fowler proposed that faith development occurs in discrete stages that are consistent with the cognitive abilities and limitations of a given developmental stage. Different aspects of faith perspective and understanding emerge at specific points in an individual's life, building upon prior developments and serving as a foundation for the next. Additionally, the development of someone's faith and the way that it is expressed depends on the psychosocial experiences he or she makes. Developmental events in a given stage therefore also have a resonant effect on someone's faith perspectives later in life.

Fowler describes spiritual development as occurring in six stages, which can be useful for determining the capabilities and limitations of a client's spiritual functioning (Fowler, 1981). Because psychosocial experiences will impact spiritual development, it is important to be able to pair the events of a client's history with the timeline for spiritual development (e.g. a significant family illness prompting the client and family to begin observing spiritual or religious practices, etc.) The family culture and religious dynamics of early childhood can significantly impact a client's stage of developmental functioning. For example, the degree of religiosity in a family will impact the degree of religious practice observed throughout his or her development. It is also important to note that the ages indicated here are estimates, and not concrete indications; individual variations in experience (as with all development) are always expected.

Stage 0: Infancy and Undifferentiated Faith

The initial stage of faith development occurs in infancy. Because infants are wholly dependent on parent figures for nourishment and safety, interaction with their caregivers fosters the capacity for basic trust and an understanding of the mutuality of interaction (e.g. that I can both influence and be influenced by others.) Fowler (1981) suggested that as children connect with parent figures, making eye contact, smiling, and having immediate needs met serve as a pre-linguistic foundation for an understanding or concept of the Divine. If basic emotional and physical needs aren't met in a health way (either by too little or too much) a child's capacity for trust and mutuality can become skewed, resulting in egocentric, isolating, or disconnecting interaction styles with others. This can also translate to difficulties connecting with a concept of the Divine; individuals may struggle with narcissistic or disconnected spiritual relationships with his or her god-figure (Fowler, 1981).

Stage 1: Intuitive-Projective Faith (Ages 2–7)

Between the ages of two and six or seven, children enter into the "Intuitive-Projective" stage of faith and develop a fluid, imaginative theory of deity and spirituality (Fowler, 1981). The religious symbols and imagery to which children are introduced become the building blocks of a magical and egocentric understanding of who the Divine is, and how one interacts with the Divine. Because children at this age lack the cognitive ability to empathize and adopt the perspectives of others, they tend to believe that their perspective is universal – even extending to the Divine. This spiritual perspective is fluid, and easily adjusted to suit the needs of a particular situation as children borrow from the most salient aspects of familial or cultural messages regarding the Divine. In this stage of development, spirituality is based off of the feelings triggered by a particular experience, rather than logical evaluation. While this process obviously changes as a child ages, the emotional context of the faith narrative has long lasting developmental impact; the emotional valence (punitive, versus positive and hopeful messages) can influence the flexibility and adaptive qualities of personality in adulthood (Fowler, 1981).

Stage 2: Mythic-Literal Faith (Ages 8–12)

The spirituality of children in the "Mythic-Literal" stage of faith is hallmarked by their newly developed, logic driven, creative problem solving skills (Fowler, 1981). Faith perspectives and spiritual narratives are no longer governed by fantastic projections of the internal experience. Instead, a child's internal motivation to develop a sense of clarity regarding "what is real, and what is not" becomes the focus for orienting to a construct of spirituality (p. 135). As such, concrete demonstrations of faith (rituals, practices, etc.) and religious stories take on significant roles in organizing their faith perspectives. The religious stories a child is told serve as concrete guides for moral interpretation, and are unquestioningly incorporated into his or her definition of spirituality. Children can also understand others' motivations or perspectives beyond their own. In this framework, the Divine can have his/her own reasons for a course of action that is beyond one's personal awareness. Fairness and reciprocity are also important concepts for children in this stage of faith; how well one adheres to the 'rules' of engagement determines his or her standing in the religious community, as well as their relationship with the Divine. These beliefs can linger into adulthood, as some individuals structure their expectations and attitudes toward the Divine based on obedience and reciprocity (e.g. "I faithfully pray and attend church, therefore I expect that God will bless me") (Fowler, 1981). If this occurs, it can often result in inflexible and maladaptive responses to religious, environmental, or interpersonal challenges in which spiritual considerations are operative.

Stage 3: Synthetic-Conventional Faith (Adolescence)

Individuals entering puberty develop the cognitive capacity for abstract thought and meta-cognition; creativity is no longer bound by concrete logic. While children in the Mythic-Literal stage of development literally interpret religious stories, those in the Synthetic-Conventional stage instead assess for patterns of meaning in those stories (aligning with the formal operational stage of cognitive development) (Fowler, 1981). Individuals operate out of a capacity for abstract, non-egocentric perspective-taking that nuances spiritual perspectives. Relationships with the Divine also shift from an expectation of concrete reciprocity to one of relational intimacy (e.g. "God loves me, is always with me, and guides me daily"). Affirmation of the faith experience therefore comes from a subjective, unexamined internal sense of "knowing." Interpersonal relationships in general take on special significance; while Mythic-Literal faith discerns "right" and "wrong" in the context of the concrete faith narratives, Synthetic-Conventional faith discerns these concepts in light of group expectations and a relationship-based understanding of the Divine figure(s). In this way, authority feels personal while being external, and the expectations of others help to focus an individual's commitment to her/his values. Despite the personal nature of one's faith experience, it is still largely unexamined, and many individuals enter a kind developmental equilibrium that is maintained across the lifespan. So long as the interpersonal contracts of the faith community remain unbroken, and the implicit relationship with the Divine remains unthreatened, many people will continue to operate from an externalized, socially constructed concept of authority and spiritual truth that still feels very personal (Fowler, 1981).

Stage 4: Individuative-Reflective Faith (Young Adulthood – Early-Forties)

A disruption of the relational and spiritual equilibrium must occur in order for someone to begin transitioning into Individuative-Reflective Faith. Traumatic events, existential conflicts, social upheaval, or faith crises can prompt individuals to evaluate the systems that dictate their previously unquestioned beliefs and faith identity (Fowler, 1981). When this occurs, a necessary distancing from external authority figures (whether social or spiritual) takes place. The validity of faith symbols, practices, spiritual narratives are no longer assumed, and instead are evaluated in the context of systemic utility. Symbols are broken, evaluated, and the inherent meaning becomes explicitly observed. Individuals may feel that they have lost the sanctity of their faith elements under this scrutiny, and many people risk becoming disenfranchised from the values of their faith system, now that "feeling right" is no longer an acceptable criterion for validity. Personal autonomy and an individualized perspective of spiritual values may prompt individuals to move toward hybridized or alternative faith systems. Alternatively, this period of evaluation may result in the individual renewing ties to their former faith system; many find a new equilibrium between Synthetic-Conventional and Individuative-Reflective faith. However an individual proceeds, the effusive authority of spiritually significant others is lost in exchange for an internalized system of values and authority that is explicitly, personally adopted (Fowler, 1981).

Stage 5: Conjunctive Faith (Midlife – Advanced Age)

As those in Individuative-Reflective faith explore the nuanced elements of a faith system, they may eventually determine that certain aspects of worship and the Divine resist examination (Fowler, 1981). Acknowledging that there is a greater complexity in the consideration of spirituality than can easily be explained, individuals may cultivate an added willingness to be influenced by the faith perspectives of others, including those in one's native faith culture. This marks the entrance into Conjunctive faith; understanding that a concept, like truth, is more nuanced and interdependent with other factors than one specific faith tradition can address, individuals allow themselves to explore additional perspectives of faith or truth. It's important to note that this does not suggest that an individual necessarily abandons her or his original faith system, nor that they uncritically accept any new truth narrative. This faith stage builds on the critical and evaluative nature of Individuative-Reflective faith processes and deliberately incorporates elements of other truth narratives that resonate with one's values orientation. As individuals non-defensively interact with alternate truth perspectives, they will often develop a new appreciation for faith symbols and rituals. These faith elements come to be understood not only for the systemic utility, but also for their value in connecting with larger spiritual truths. While Individuative-Reflective faith breaks down faith elements into their most basic understood parts, Conjunctive faith realizes that the sum of the whole is greater than its parts. This realization will prompt individuals to seek to unify perspectives that appear opposite and renew a deeper experience of the Sacred (Fowler, 1981).

Stage 6: Universalizing Faith

This last stage of faith development is rare, and not easily encapsulated by simple terms. Universalizing faith builds on the multiple truths perspective of Conjunctive faith, but expands that awareness to a cosmic level. Individuals in this faith stage take on a self-sacrificing, socially unifying perspective, to the extent that one's desire for justice exceeds considerations of personal safety or wellbeing (Fowler, 1981). As such, individuals in this stage of faith tend to engage in socially radical, and by many accounts, subversive behaviors, for the sake of a spiritual vision and understanding greater than their own lives. They view themselves and others from a perspective of universal interconnectedness, and do not limit the connection of living beings to social, ethnic, or religious boundaries. Because of this, individuals in this stage of faith work from a spiritual ideology of what mankind is intended to be, rather than what is, and are willing to sacrifice themselves for the sake of furthering that ideology. This is threatening to social and religious authorities, as it undermines the socio-political infrastructure, and it is not infrequent that someone will be martyred for the values they support. Individuals meeting these criteria are rare, and have a profound, often pivotal impact in their culture. They include such spiritual revolutionaries as Gandhi, Rev. Martin Luther King Jr., and Mother Teresa. Spiritual founders, such as Jesus Christ, Moses, Confucious, the Buddha, and others also are considered to have operated from this stage of faith (Fowler, 1981).

Using Stages of Faith Theory in Counseling

We posit that the benefits in working with Fowler's theory come from the logical indications for modifying interpersonal goals and interactions in the therapeutic relationship and larger clinical work. The best therapeutic relationships are based around a dynamic adjustment of interpersonal engagement on the part of the clinician in response to client needs (Duncan et al., 2010). Therefore, awareness of the subjective experiential differences for each client can help counselors to more successfully modify approaches to initiating discussions around spiritual issues in a way that better builds rapport. Being aware of the developmental influences on a client's faith will provide the counselor with a sense of expected perceptions, goals, movement, and challenges that will present in the therapy. Counselors can therefore operate in a way that meets client's developmental capacities, while also facilitating growth toward later developmental stages. In the event that a client is not in a spiritual crisis, or ready to move into a new stage of development, the hallmarks of different stages can help counselors work toward maximizing the client's spiritual functioning in that stage (Fowler, 1981).

Coupled with an assessment of the client's belief system dynamics, as described in Chapter 2, counselors can more precisely identify the individual "sticking points" of one's spiritual development. For example, systems leaning toward the closed end of the spectrum may influence clients to retain characteristics of Mythic-Literal faith in adulthood (Rokeach, 1960; Fowler, 1981). Systems with especially closed dynamics will encourage dichotomous thinking patterns inherent in Mythic-Literal faith, while also reinforcing the significance of external authorities. Individuals in Conjunctive faith may demonstrate more variability in rigidity and flexibility; however more closed belief systems could make it difficult for an individual to begin examining authority narratives and move toward Individuative faith. In this vein, we surmise that the challenges and crises of latter developmental stages, particularly Individuative faith, would be, to varying degrees, exacerbated by closed belief system dynamics. A potential positive side effect of these struggles may also be that individuals who successfully navigate these greater struggles can experience more significant personal and spiritual gains (Rokeach, 1960; Fowler, 1981). It is important to realize that the conclusions one makes in these evaluations is highly dependent on the nuanced interactions of these developmental and systemic factors.

Genia's Psychospiritual Development

Genia (1995) criticized the predominant theories of spiritual development for excluding the contributions of psychoanalytic and object relations theories to the understanding of human development. She considered the theoretical frameworks as relying too heavily on cognitive and psychosocial factors, and posited the theory of Psychospiritual Development as an additional framework for interpreting clients' spiritual functioning. This theory is, in many ways, an expansion of cognitive developmental theories, as it adds psychoanalytic elements to the developmental benchmarks already understood in cognitive and psychosocial theory. For this reason, it serves as an effective alternative to the major cognitive-developmentally based theories like Stages of Faith and Integral Psychology (Fowler, 1981; Cashwell and Young, 2011). This theory may be particularly useful for clinicians who operate out of a psychoanalytic or similar psychodynamic theoretical orientation (Genia, 1995).

Genia's (1995) theory centers around the perspective that children form a sense of the Divine as a direct result of their parent relationships. In fact, there are many commonalities between Genia and Fowler's theories given that they center on the subjective developmental experiences of children, as they mature toward adulthood. Similar again to Fowler, Genia proposes that faith development is lifelong, and occurs in discrete stages. Genia differs from Fowler in that, while Fowler anticipates that traces of each stage may be present in an individual's current functioning, Genia considers indicators of earlier developmental stage to be signs of regression and potential pathology. The offsetting influence of stress-induced regressions contributes to the highly individual nature of spiritual development, and is qualified by crises, resources, and other circumstances; as a result, development may occur intermittently, with gaps and spurts, or be offset by stress-induced regressions (Genia, 1995).

Stage 1: Egocentric Faith

In this stage, individuals who fail to form secure relationships in the preverbal phase of development become unable to form lasting internal constructs of other people and attachment figures (Genia, 1995). As a result, those in Egocentric Faith tend to act narcissistically and in a self-serving manner in spiritual and other processes. The determination of whether one's deity is good or bad is typically entirely dependent on whether their own needs are being met. As a result, perceptions of one's deity may fluctuate depending on how a person perceives their circumstances. Depending on if things are going well versus poorly, their God-figure may be considered unequivocally good, or alternatively comprehensively bad or abandoning. In many ways, because individuals lack a healthily developed ego, the Divine becomes an extension of the self, and there is limited capacity for conceptualizing one's deity as being "other" than one's self. Interactions with the Divine are typically petition based, and any penitence is generally made out of fear of punishment (Genia, 1995).

Stage 2: Dogmatic Faith

Genia posited that if an individual is able to develop a basic sense of trust in others, he or she can be in Dogmatic Faith, and tend to rely heavily on a given set of behavioral expectations for religious conformity (Genia, 1995). Fairness and reciprocity are central to the way individuals function, and these are determined specifically by religious texts and spiritual authority figures. Self-worth, belonging, and spiritual soundness are based very strongly on the approval of others within a spiritual community. Often times, individuals will form authoritarian, rigid, and very controlled spiritual beliefs. The emotional constructs of guilt, a desire for acceptance, and fear of rejection play very heavily into the conduct of these individuals. As such, one protects his or her own faith and security through aggression or judgment toward others, not in alignment with their personal belief system (Genia, 1995).

Stage 3: Transitional Faith

The hallmark behaviors of Transitional Faith are experimentation with and exposure to faith systems that are alternative to one's native faith (Genia, 1995). Moral reciprocity becomes exchanged for interpersonal relationship and perspective taking; as such, individuals become capable and disposed to questioning or examining the rigid and conformist nature of previous faith experiences. Genia suggests that this process is necessary for one's faith to make a transition from extrinsic to intrinsic religiosity. It is a process that can be filled with interpersonal and emotional difficulty, as the individual struggles to identify belief systems that are personally viable. This requires intense support from others, however it yields the benefit of an authentic, deliberate, and clarified faith experience for those that successfully make the transition (Genia, 1995).

Stage 4: Reconstructed Internalized Faith

Once someone successfully progresses through Transitional Faith and develops an intrinsic sense of religious involvement, they enter into Reconstructed Internalized Faith (Genia, 1995). During this stage, the deliberate application and internalization of spiritual or religious values allows an individual to interact with doctrines or practices in a prosocial, rather than psychodynamically defensive way. Faith also becomes more nuanced and context specific. Individuals understand and apply their faith in a way that is sensitive to the systemic, cultural, and interpersonal factors of a given environment. Interaction with the Divine also becomes less petition and punishment oriented, and more focused on praise and devotion. Guilt may remain operative in the spiritual process, but originates out of one's internal processes for living out their values, rather than based on adherence to external standards. There additionally may be an increased acceptance of and appreciation for other faith traditions, however individuals tend to resist being influenced by these alternatives (Genia, 1995).

Stage 5: Transcendent Faith

This stage of faith development is very similar to that of Reconstructed Internalized Faith, but with some significant differences. Whereas individuals in Stage 4 are guided by the internalized doctrines of their chosen faith system, individuals in Transcendent Faith have internalized a universal construct of morality (Genia, 1995). It may be more fitting to say that individuals in this stage of faith have connected their internalized religious values to universalized morality, and begin to operate out of this new perspective. As such, there is an increased openness to the influence of others and their faith perspectives. Individuals in Transcendent Faith remain committed to their own faith perspectives, but demonstrate a vulnerable approach to diversity, uncertainty, and alternative experiences. Socially, these individuals demonstrate a significantly higher commitment to social contribution and justice (Genia, 1995).

Using Psychospiritual Development Theory in Counseling

We posit that some of the greatest utility for Genia's (1995) theory comes from the interchangeable connection between one's relationship with the Divine, and one's relationship with others. Genia stresses that dysfunction in the spiritual domain is likely reflected in dysfunction of interpersonal functioning as well. Spirituality therefore becomes a convenient substitute for addressing broader, potentially more widespread psychological concerns. From a psychodynamic perspective, this allows counselors to interact with developmental and psychological constructs within the vehicle of spirituality (Genia, 1995).

The value of this theory becomes most apparent in the combined informative relationship between one's self, others, and the Divine; while development is continuous, the idea that one can regress or become "stuck" in another developmental stage provides counselors with valuable information regarding wellness and potential pathology. For example, individuals operating out of egocentric faith dynamics may present with self-serving or unstable interpersonal patterns (consistent with Narcissistic, Borderline, and other personality disorders). These patterns may be fostered and stabilized, or disrupted by the belief system dynamics in which an individual operates (Rokeach, 1960). In a closed belief system, egocentric clients may be successful and rise to positions of authority, while more open systems could challenge their perspectives on the Divine. The fluidly developmental perspectives in Genia's theory allow counselors to implement a more dynamic and continuous approach to incorporating spirituality into treatment planning. For example, Genia's concept of faith development may provide useful indications for assessing readiness for change; individuals in egocentric faith may be in a precontemplative change mindset, while those in transitional faith may be in either preparation for change or action mindsets (Prochaska and DiClemente, 1983). This integrative approach to assessing client's functioning can be tailored to the counselor's preferences and personal approach.

Wilber's Integral Psychology

Ken Wilber is possibly best known for the development of his own theory, *integral psychology*, in which he argues for intrinsic connections between all human experience and academic knowledge and posits that these fit together coherently when viewed through a particular lens (Rentschler, 2006). This metatheory includes five main components: developmental levels or waves of consciousness; developmental lines or streams of consciousness; normal and altered states of consciousness; the self or "self-system"; and the *AQAL* (Wilber, 2000). The AQAL matrix, "all-quadrants, all-levels" (which itself is short for "all-quadrants, all-levels, all-lines, all-states, and all-types"), contains four different perspectives from which anything can be viewed at any given period in time and circumstance (Rentschler, 2006). The first two perspectives are located inside the person and exterior to the person, that is "interior individual" and "exterior individual." The final two perspectives are located within and outside as well, but are viewed from a third person, collectivist, or "we" perspective and called *interior collective* and *exterior collective*. In addition to the AQAL matrix, this section focuses specifically on development levels or waves, sub-categories of developmental levels, and pathology; however, *Integral Psychology: Consciousness, Spirit, Psychology, Therapy* (Wilber, 2000) is a great resource for readers interested in more depth.

Based on the assumption that everything in the universe is spiritual and is at some level of self-realization, Wilber's theory of development levels or waves of consciousness integrates ideology from Eastern states of consciousness with Western development theories (Foster and Holden, 2011). He proposes levels of development as follows: prepersonal, personal, and transpersonal. Prepersonal refers to the time of life wherein an individual demonstrates no firm identity but is devoted to the process of developing a sense of self for managing life, lasting from birth to about age seven (Cowley, 2010; Foster and Holden, 2011). Generally proceeding from this point to around age 21, the personal level mirrors individuation in that, the individual continues through a process of forming and elaborating the developing sense of self. Cowley states, "this level includes, at the upper limits, a well-developed value structure of a self-actualized person" (2010, p. 86). The transpersonal level is characterized by going beyond ego toward self-transcendence, including a mature character and a realization that personal identity is inclusive of humanity, nature, and the nonmaterial (Cowley, 2010; Foster and Holden, 2011). Wilber asserted that all aspects of spiritual development unfold in stages that one cannot skip (2000).

Wilber arbitrarily divided the developmental levels into nine sub-categories or stages as follows: (Stage 1) sensorimotor, (Stage 2) phantasmic-emotional, (Stage 3) re-mind, (Stage 4) rule/role mind, (Stage 5) formal-reflexive, (Stage 6) vision-logic, (Stage 7) psychic, (Stage 8) subtle, and (Stage 9) causal (2000). The first three sub-categories are associated with the prepersonal level, sub-categories four through six with the personal level, and the final three are associated with the transpersonal level (Foster and Holden, 2011). As beings journey through the process of fuller realization of the spiritual, pathology is believed to result from difficulty moving through fulcrums, or the developmental milestones associated with progressing to the next sub-categories or stage. He states "thus, the differentiation-and-integration process can go wrong at each and every self-stage (or fulcrum) and the level of the fulcrum helps to determine the level of pathology" (p. 93). He believes different symptomology will emerge based on the developmental levels and stages and recommends specific therapeutic approaches (Wilber, 2000). For instance, at the transpersonal level, existential crises may occur, similar to those discussed by Frankl. In each of the associated sub-categories, including psychic, subtle, and casual, difficulties delineate the nature of the issue. Within the psychic sub-category (Stage 6) of the transpersonal level, spiritual crises may emerge as a dark night of the soul and/or free-floating anxiety (Cowley, 2010). Meditation, exercise, and contemplative practice are a few of the recommended interventions (2010).

Applying Developmental Theories: The Case of Cecily

Stages of Faith

Cecily is coming to treatment in Fowler's third, or Synthetic-Conventional stage of faith. This is indicated by her affiliation with a specific faith group, and the role that her pastor has played in connecting her with the clinician. The vignette is not specific, but it's possible that Cecily views counseling as a last resort for healing, after having explored spiritually based solutions (e.g. prayer, trying to grow closer to God, consulting with the pastor and other congregants). Her external authority figures have thus far largely dictated her mental health practices, and her attempts at healing, even coming to counseling, have been prescribed by others. Her orientation to God is as a spiritual significant other or outsider, and how this dictates her distress; she is concerned with failing God, and that trust is at the center of her struggles. At the same time, the tacit assumptions of her faith system are in crisis. She has been faithful to God, and expects him to be faithful to her (here, we see some vestiges of Mythic-Literal faith). As she fails to receive an answer or felt sense of intimacy with God that soothes her pain, Cecily's relationship with Him feels jeopardized. This situation is one that could prompt Cecily to enter into the early stages of Individuative-Reflective faith. Developmentally, she is later than most would be in entering into this stage, so there is a possibility that she may come to cling more to the Synthetic-Conventional aspects of her faith. A necessary element in moving into the fourth stage includes distancing herself from the religious authority figures of her faith community, so that she can begin to explore and examine her values, as well as the assumptions that lead her to believe that her depression is the result of moral failing. The counseling environment itself may serve as a springboard for, at least, mentally distancing herself and beginning this process of examination, as she works through her depressive symptoms.

Psychospiritual Development

Cecily displays elements of Dogmatic Faith (Stage 2) and Transitional Faith (Stage 3). She is strongly impacted by the judgments of others, and has a strong desire for acceptance within her community, as well as with her God. Again, the elements of externalized authority figures play heavily in determining her behavior. These factors suggest that she has not quite moved beyond the dynamics of Dogmatic Faith. However, despite her expectations for quasi-reciprocity with God, Cecily contextualizes this heavily in relationship terms. The struggles that she faces in feeling that God is distant, and how that factors into her depressive symptoms, suggest that she is struggling toward internalizing her faith. In worrying about the quality of her relationship with God, Cecily may be initiating a process of evaluating which of her beliefs are personally viable and how they should be personally lived out. The counselor can reasonably expect that her questioning will intensify as she continues in this process, and that emotional support, both in counseling and church, will be essential for her to successfully transition through Stage 3 and into Reconstructed Internalized Faith (Stage 4).

Integral Theory

Cecily is in the personal developmental level. Because Cecily is beginning to question the authority and doctrine of the church, her counselor believes she is struggling with the transition or fulcrum from the fourth sub-category of rule/role mind and entering the fifth sub-category, formal-reflexive. Within the fifth, formal-reflexive sub-category, individuals move from learning and following social expectations (rule/role) to questioning them. Cecily begins experiencing symptoms related to existential questioning and finds that her normal religious coping methods are not helping. The danger is that role conflict can occur, wherein Cecily attempts to continue to conform, but still experiences chronic inner turmoil, resulting in pathology (Cowley, 2010). Based on this integral theory integration, the counselor realizes that Cecily is moving toward the upper stages of the personal development level and is searching for deeper realization of the spiritual. As a result, the counselor employs Experiential and Existential therapies, two strategies recommended by Wilber (2000).

References

Cashwell, C. S., and Young, J. S. (2011). *Integrating spirituality and religion into counseling: A guide to competent practice.* Alexandria, VA: American Counseling Association..

Confucius (2016). *A treasury of wisdom: Expounding the Bhagavad Gita, and epitome of all teachings and learnings* (R. Pal Baran, Trans.). East Midnapore, WB, India: Partridge.

Cowley, A. S. (2010). Cosmic consciousness: Path or pathology? *Social Thought*, 20(1–2), 77–94.

Hubble, M. A., Duncan, B. L., Miller, S. D., and Wampold, B. E. (Eds.). (2010). *Heart and soul of change: Delivering what works in therapy* (2nd ed.). York, PA: American Psychological Association.

Foster, R. D., and Holden, J. M. (2011). Human and spiritual development and transformation. In C. S. Cashwell and J. S. Young (Eds.), *Integrating spirituality and religion into counseling: A guide to competent practice* (pp. 97–118). Alexandria, VA: American Counseling Association.

Fowler, J. W. (1981). *Stages of faith: The psychology of human development and the quest for meaning.* New York, NY: Harper One.

Furey, R. J. (1993). *Joy of kindness.* Spring Valley, NY: Crossroad Publishing.

Genia, V. (1995). *Counseling and Psychotherapy of Religious Clients: A developmental approach.* Westport, CT: Praeger Publishers.

Prochaska, J. O., and DiClemente, C. C. (1983). Stages and processes of self-change of smoking: Toward an integrative model of change. *Journal of Consulting and Clinical Psychology*, 51(3), 390–395.

Sperry, L. (2012). *Spirituality in clinical practice: Theory and practice of spiritually oriented psychotherapy* (2nd ed.) New York, NY: Routledge.

Rentschler, M. (2006). AQAL Glossary. *AQAL: Journal of Integral Theory and Practice*, 1(3), 1–39.

Rokeach, M. (1960). *The Open and Closed Mind: Investigations in to the nature of belief systems and personality systems.* New York, NY: Basic Books.

Oser, F. and Gmünder, P. (1991). *Religious Judgement: A developmental approach.* Birmingham, AL: Religious Education Press.

Wilber, K. (2000). *Integral psychology: Consciousness, spirit, psychology, therapy.* Boston, MA: Shambhala.

4 Understanding the Spiritual Domain through Case Conceptualization

George Stoupas, Vassilia Binensztok, and Len Sperry

"Life can only be understood backwards; but it must be lived forwards."
—Søren Kierkegaard

Introduction

How do counselors know what to do? How do they come to decide on the correct causes of clients' problems and the right course of action? Collecting and organizing the various pieces of information a client brings to treatment can be a daunting task, especially when complex issues related to religion and spirituality are included in the clinical picture. Case conceptualization is the clinical competency that addresses this challenge. It is defined as "a method and clinical strategy for obtaining and organizing information about a client, understanding and explaining the client's situation and maladaptive patterns, guiding and focusing treatment, anticipating challenges and roadblocks, and preparing for successful termination" (Sperry, 2010a, p. 110). Case conceptualization provides a bridge between assessment and treatment. In essence, a case conceptualization is a story crafted by the counselor. This story includes important details about the client's past, as they pertain to the presenting problem. It also serves as a guiding light, illuminating the road ahead and revealing potential obstacles. If the story is accurate and thorough, then it will lead to the desired outcomes (i.e. positive change, symptom remission, etc.). If, however, the story is inaccurate or missing important pieces, then the client most likely will not change – and may even get worse.

Case conceptualization is critical for effective treatment. Indeed, theorists refer to case conceptualization as "the heart of evidence-based practice" (Bieling and Kuyken, 2003, p. 53). Counselors' ability to conceptualize client cases is associated with a number of important outcomes, including enhanced clinician empathy, stronger therapeutic alliances, client perceptions of clinician effectiveness, and maintenance of treatment gains following termination (Crits-Christoph et al., 1993; Eells, 2015; Jacobson et al., 1989; Morran et al., 1994). In the world of managed care, counselors are increasingly expected to justify their treatment decisions with specific details about the individual client. Spiritual and religious issues must be assessed and included in the counselor's explanation of the client's problems if treatment is to be appropriate and successful.

There are many different case conceptualization models from which to choose. Many of these are based on specific theories, such as the Cognitive-Behavioral (Wright et al., 2006), Psychodynamic (Levenson and Strupp, 2007), and Adlerian (Dinkmeyer and Sperry, 2000). However, the overwhelming majority of case conceptualization models do not routinely include a thorough assessment of client spirituality. Moreover, only a few who write about spiritually oriented psychotherapy address this competency in detail (Aten and Leach, 2009; Sperry, 2012). This chapter provides a framework for case conceptualization that emphasizes religious and spiritual factors. This framework is based on Len Sperry's (2010a) integrative case conceptualization method, which is expanded in Sperry and Sperry (2012). It includes four components related to diagnostic, clinical, cultural, and treatment formulations, as well as the "5 Ps" – *presentation, precipitant, pattern, predisposition,* and *perpetuant* that serve as hallmarks to the process. Each of these elements will be presented in detail, with specific examples to illustrate how they pertain to spiritually oriented counseling. The chapter will end with an extended case vignette that demonstrates this integrative model.

Diagnosis and Case Conceptualization

Of its many attributes, case conceptualization is, first and foremost, a "bridge" that connects assessment and diagnosis with treatment (Sperry, 2010a; Sperry, 2012). One of the four components of a case conceptualization is diagnostic formulation. This component answers the question: "what happened?" and, in part, is often specified with a Diagnostic and Statistical Manual of Mental Disorders (*DSM*) diagnosis. The current *DSM* (5th ed.; *DSM-5*; American Psychiatric Association [APA], 2013) is relatively sensitive to and respectful of spiritual and religious issues. However, that has not always been the case, and, in fact, earlier editions of the *DSM* discouraged a focus on religion. The reason for this is reflected in the history of the relationship between religion and mental illness and the changing diagnostic formulation of specific psychiatric presentations with religious content.

Since the latter part of the nineteenth century and much of the twentieth century, psychiatrists and other mental health professionals have too often misdiagnosed or over diagnosed religious hallucinations and delusions reflective of the prevailing professional attitudes and practices of those times. The point of this section is to convey that an accurate diagnosis is necessary in developing an effective case conceptualization. Until recently, the history of religion and mental health has demonstrated that too often a misdiagnosis was likely to occur which resulted in an inappropriate case conceptualization and an ineffective treatment outcome.

A brief historical review is useful in understanding how mental health professionals' attitudes and practices influenced the way their patients or clients were diagnosed and treated. From earliest times, mentally ill individuals were understood to be possessed by evil spirits. In eras during which people believed these possessed individuals were also believed to be contagious, it is not surprising that such individuals were confined to mental institutions to "protect" the public. Fortunately, the majority of world religions championed the care of these mentally ill individuals. "Many of the most important breakthroughs in compassionate treatment of the mentally ill were made by persons of faith crusading for those who did not have the power to speak for themselves" (Koenig, 2005, p. 39).

In modern times, people such as Sigmund Freud and Albert Ellis significantly influenced mental health providers' professional attitudes and practices. In six publications Freud insisted that religion was the universal obsessional neurosis of humanity, "a system of wishful illusions together with a disavowal of reality such as we find in an isolated form nowhere else but amentia, in a state of blissful hallucinatory confusion…" (Freud, 1930, p. 43). Freud's position was most influential in forming and reinforcing providers' professional attitude that religious beliefs were harmful. Later, Albert Ellis extended Freud's critique in several books, articles, presentations, and in newspaper interviews. His most devastating portrayal was a very telling contrast between the emotionally healthy individual and the devoutly religious individual. Emotional health was characterized through flexibility, openness, tolerance, and ability to change, while the devoutly religious were characterized by inflexibility, close mindedness, intolerance, and inability to change (Ellis, 1980). The influence of these two men and others on professional practice was even more profound. By 1980, psychiatric units at major academic medical centers, including the Methodist-affiliated Duke University Department of Psychiatry, had removed all religious influence in its treatment of the mentally ill. Of note is that later in life, Ellis, while remaining an atheist, acknowledged that belief in a loving God could be psychologically healthy (Ellis, 2000).

What is also surprising is how these negative attitudes toward religion influenced the personal religious beliefs of most mental health professionals. Surveys conducted in the 1980s and 1990s showed that while only 4 percent of Americans did not believe in God, the greater majority of psychologists and psychiatrist were non-believers. These personal and professional beliefs significantly influenced their treatment of religious patients and clients. Although more than 90 percent of mental health professionals endorsed a link between religion and mental health and believed in addressing this in treatment, 58 percent of surveyed psychiatrists never referred their patients to clergy (Koenig, 2005).

It should not be surprising that the diagnostic manual of the 1980s and 1990s also reflected these negative biases toward religion. A review of *DSM-III* (3rd ed.; *DSM–III*; American Psychiatric Association [APA], 1980) showed a disproportionate number of examples that illustrated serious mental conditions, particularly religious hallucinations and delusions (Richardson, 1993). Furthermore, a review of the religious content in *DSM-III-R* (3rd ed., rev.; *DSM–III–R*; American Psychiatric Association [APA], 1987) showed that more than 22 percent of all illustrations of mental illness included religious descriptions (Larsen et al., 1993).

DSM-5 *and Religious/Spiritual Diagnostic Issues*

As previously noted, *DSM-5* is more sensitive to religious and spiritual issues than previous editions. This reality is evident in two ways. First, with regard to an updated definition of delusion, and second, with the V-code designation.

Updated Definition of Delusion. *DSM-5* defines delusion as follows:

> a false belief based on incorrect inference about external reality that is firmly held despite what almost everyone else believes and despite what constitutes incontrovertible and obvious proof or evidence to the contrary. The belief is not ordinarily accepted by other members of the person's culture or subculture (i.e., it is not an article of religious faith).
> (American Psychiatric Association [APA], 2013, p. 819)

In short, there are three elements to this definition: a false belief that is fixed or firmly held, and is not accepted in the person's culture or subculture. While *DSM-IV* (4th ed.; *DSM–IV*; American Psychiatric Association [APA], 1994) and *DSM-IV-TR* (4th ed., text rev.; *DSM–IV–TR*; American Psychiatric Association [APA], 2000) also identify these three elements, *DSM-III* (APA, 1980) and *DSM-III-R* (APA, 1987) did not include the cultural element.

It was this omission of culture that "allowed" individuals with certain beliefs (e.g., that God talks to them, or that spirits of dead relatives influence their lives, as religious hallucinations) to be diagnosed with religious delusions, even though other members of their culture held such beliefs. A review of hospital medical records from the 1960s through the early 1990s are likely to show that African-Americans who revealed that God talks to them were more likely to be misdiagnosed with schizophrenia. Change began when the *DSM-IV* (APA, 1994) became the standard for diagnoses in 1994 and the cultural element became key to a correct diagnosis and diagnostic formulation.

V-code for Religious or Spiritual Problem. *DSM-5* (APA, 2013) provides a V-code for Religious or Spiritual Problem (V 62.89) as follows:

> This category can be used when the focus of clinical attention is a religious or spiritual problem. Examples include distressing experiences that involve loss or questioning of faith, problems associated with

conversion to a new faith, or questioning of spiritual values that may not necessarily be related to an organized church or religious institution.

(American Psychiatric Association, 2013, p. 725).

Although V-codes are considered non-clinical codes, that the *DSM-5* includes them suggest that this code is important and clinically useful for planning treatment.

Diagnostic Formulation

The first component of an integrative case conceptualization is the diagnostic formulation. As previously stated, it answers the "what happened" question in counseling (Sperry and Sperry, 2012). Diagnostic formulations are descriptive in nature, and include information related to the presenting problem, its precipitants, and the client's pattern. Accordingly, the three components of a diagnostic formulation are presentation, precipitant, and pattern. These are described in detail in the sections below.

Presentation

A client's presentation includes the presenting problem and the client's typical response to precipitating factors (Sperry and Sperry, 2012). A client's presentation is largely tied into his patterns and personality dynamics, which will be discussed further in this chapter. For example, Joe, a client with narcissistic personality dynamics, will often react negatively to being challenged. He presents with anger and depression after an argument with his wife, in which he did not feel valued enough.

Religious and spiritual issues can tie into client presentation in a number of ways. The client may be experiencing a spiritual emergency, struggle or a clash between spiritual/religious values and personal values. Clients may be faced with strife between themselves and religious communities. For example, a client, active in a moderately closed Mormon belief system, may be struggling to come to terms with his homosexuality. This client may present with anxiety and isolation as he tries to resolve his feelings about his sexual orientation, questions about his faith, and the reaction from his religious community. Conducting a spiritual assessment, as described in Chapter 2, is key to understanding how religious and spiritual issues affect presentation.

Religious and spiritual factors that should be assessed for their role in the client presentation include spiritual history, spiritual wellbeing, values-lifestyle congruence, and religious problem-solving. Spiritual history is an assessment of an individual's spiritual and religious influences, life, and wellbeing. A semi-structured interview is a good method for conducting spiritual history assessments (Sperry, 2011). Spiritual wellbeing is seen to have two dimensions: "a sense of well-being in relation to God and a sense of well-being in relation to life and its purpose" (Richards et al., 2009, pp. 73–74). These domains reveal clients' beliefs about whether God loves them, is concerned about them, and provides a source of support. For example, a client who believes God has abandoned him may present as particularly despondent after losing a job.

Spiritual practices refer to a client's use of prayer, meditation, and other rituals (Sperry, 2011), and value-lifestyle congruence refers to "the degree to which a person's lifestyle choices and behaviors are congruent with his or her professed moral, religious, and spiritual values" (Richards and Bergin, 2005, p. 229). Incongruence between values and lifestyle can lead to guilt, anxiety, and difficulty in interpersonal relationships (Richards et al., 2009). As in the aforementioned example of the Mormon client coming to terms with his homosexuality, this client's experience of values-lifestyle incongruence contributes significantly to his presentation. Although instruments measuring this dimension are lacking, counselors can use the Theistic Spiritual Outcome survey to assess moral congruence (Richards and Bergin, 2005).

Religious problem solving refers to the way in which individuals use spiritual beliefs to solve problems. This dimension can help counselors understand their client's relationship with religion and its effect on problem solving and coping (Richards et al., 2009). Richards and colleagues identified three religious problem-solving styles: *self-directing, deferring,* and *collaborative* (Pargament et al., 1988). Individuals using the *self-directing style* see themselves as solely responsible for decisions without the influence of God. Individuals using the *deferring style* take little to no responsibility for problem solving, relying on God to provide answers and directions. Individuals using the *collaborative style* see themselves as working in conjunction with God to generate solutions. The deferring style is associated with a decrease in sense of control, self-esteem, and tolerance of ambiguous situations while the self-directing and collaborative styles are associated with an increase in sense of control and self-esteem. Two clients may be suffering from marital discord but may present differently depending on religious problem-solving styles. A client with a self-directing style may appear confident but isolating and resistant to help, believing he alone is responsible for solving his problem. On the other hand, a client with a deferring style may present as helpless and dependent, waiting for solutions from God. Counselors can assess this dimension through interviewing and the use of the Religious Problem-Solving Scale (Pargament et al., 1988).

Precipitant

A precipitant is a trigger that activates the client's pattern (as described in the following section) and results in the presenting problem (Sperry and Sperry, 2012). People react to experiences in different ways, largely dependent on patterns, schemas, and personality dynamics. Identifying the precipitant helps the clinician understand why the client is presenting in a particular way at a specific time. For example, if a client maintained sobriety for 15 years and relapses after divorce, the clinician may wonder why previous stressors in the client's history, such as job loss and the death of a friend, did not precipitate relapse. Of all stressors, why is divorce the precipitant to the client's presenting problem of substance use? This information gives the clinician insight into the client's pattern; subsequently, helping to treat the presenting problem and prevent further relapse.

When evaluating precipitants in terms of the spiritual and religious domain, the clinician should be mindful of spiritual factors that may have caused or contributed to the presenting problem. A client facing job loss, for example, may interpret the situation differently depending on his spiritual beliefs, leading to different possible presentations. The client may be unmotivated if he or she has a deferring religious problem-solving style and/or is moving through Fowler's Individuative-Reflective faith stage (Fowler, 1981). The client may express symptoms of depression if he or she feels angry at or abandoned by God during this time. Similarly, a client who committed an act that is incongruent with his or her religious values may experience anxiety about divine consequences, whereas a client who lacks these beliefs would not have a similar experience.

Additionally, spiritual crises and emergencies may themselves be precipitants. Clients may face crises of faith and meaning resulting from any number of stressors (Sperry, 2011). Pargament (2007) defines these as spiritual struggles: "Spiritual struggles are signs of spiritual disorientation, tension, and strains. Old roads to the sacred and old understandings of the sacred itself are no longer compelling" (p. 112). Three kinds of spiritual struggles are identified: *interpersonal*, *intrapersonal*, and *divine*. *Interpersonal struggles* involve friends and loved ones and are concerned with matters of hypocrisy, disagreement with doctrine, gossiping, and other social constructs. *Intrapersonal struggles* involve doubts and confusion about one's personal spiritual traditions. *Divine struggles* involve an individual's struggle with the Divine, often including questioning of faith or the perception of God during difficult life events. Struggles with the Divine are also referred to as "crises of faith." These difficulties may simply be temporary or may result in anxiety, depression, and a decrease in functioning (Exline and Rose, 2005).

Pattern

A client's pattern refers to his typical way of thinking, perceiving, and behaving, or personality traits. Identifying client patterns helps link precipitants to the presentation and explain the client's problems. Patterns are viewed as *adaptive or maladaptive* and may occur through the lifespan or only in certain contexts. *Maladaptive patterns* tend to cause distress and may be severe enough to warrant a personality disorder diagnosis, while *adaptive patterns* are effective, flexible, and appropriate to the situation (Sperry and Sperry, 2012).

Originating in the work of Alfred Adler and Karen Horney, pattern is frequently defined in terms of movement in relation to others, the purpose or intended goal of the movement, and the person's activity level (Sperry and Sperry, 2012). Counselors can categorize each personality style or disorder according to these variables. For example, people who move toward others can be active in their movement, as in the case with those who have a histrionic personality style/disorder and want attention. Alternatively, this movement toward others can be passive, as in the case of dependent personality style/disorder wherein the person seeks to please others. Other movement types include: against (narcissistic and antisocial); away (avoidant and schizoid); and ambivalent (passive-aggressive and obsessive-compulsive). Clients presenting to counseling may exhibit one or more of these types of patterns for various purposes. These range from self-protection and perfectionism to retaliation and the desire for special treatment.

The goal in a spiritual case conceptualization is to identify the client's maladaptive patterns, as well as those that are more adaptive ones and could serve the client more effectively. Spiritual and religious issues can manifest differently depending on the client's pattern and may serve as helpful clues when conceptualizing pattern. A client with a deferring religious problem-solving style may manifest a dependent pattern, whereas one with a self-directing style may have more of an obsessive-compulsive pattern. Areas to assess and include in this portion of the case conceptualization are values-lifestyle congruence, religious problem-solving, God representation, spiritual identity, and orthodoxy.

God representation, or "God image," is the way in which an individual represents God, and the characteristics an individual attributes to God (Sperry, 2011; Richards et al., 2009). As described in Chapter 3, the impact of the open or closed belief system, as an individual progresses through development stages, will influence his or her God image. A client may view God as loving, frightening, or even vengeful; these representations help reveal the client's patterns. The client with an avoidant pattern might view God as frightening, for example, while a client with a more narcissistic pattern could view God as impotent, with the client as the more God-like figure. God image can be assessed through an informal interview (Sperry, 2011) and using The God Image Inventory (Lawrence, 1991).

A client's level of *orthodoxy* can also provide useful clues to his pattern. Involvement in a spiritual and religious community involves a client's level of engagement in a faith community, the history of the client's relationship to that community, and the faith community's influence over the individual (Sperry, 2011). The latter area is encompassed by religious orthodoxy (Richards and Bergin, 2005). Comparable to the open and closed belief systems model described in Chapter 2, religious orthodoxy refers to the degree of faith an individual has and his adherence to religious traditions. Belief orthodoxy refers to an individual's level of belief in religious doctrine while behavioral orthodoxy refers to the individual's practice of religious traditions (Richards and Bergin, 2005). Clients who identify as highly orthodox are more likely to desire counselors who share their beliefs and are more likely to view their beliefs as related to their presenting problems (Richards et al., 2009). One may completely devote himself to a life of solitude, ascetic worship, and prayer not only because of faith but also because of personality dynamics. Additionally, orthodoxy can affect the development of a pattern as early as childhood, as explained in the socio-cultural portion of the case conceptualization. Orthodoxy can be assessed through informal interview and using instruments such as the Christian Orthodoxy Scale (Fullerton and Hunsberger, 1982).

Clinical Formulation

Moving on from the "what happened?" question in the diagnostic formulation, the clinical formulation provides answers to the question "why did it happen?" The purpose of the clinical formulation is to explain the client's presenting problem and symptoms (Sperry, 2010b). The clinical formulation is the central component of integrative case conceptualizations, connecting diagnosis to treatment (Sperry, 2011). It is also in this section that spiritual and religious considerations are explored in greatest detail. The clinical formulation includes *predisposition* and *perpetuants*, described in detail below.

Predisposition

Predisposition, or predisposing factors, include all possible explanations for why the client is experiencing his or her current problems (Sperry, 2011; Sperry and Sperry, 2012). Another term for this is "etiological factors." Essentially, these help explain how clients came to be the way they are. In order to identify a client's predisposing factors, counselors typically look to the client's history. Predisposing factors may come from a variety of sources, including biological, psychological, and sociocultural. Biological predisposing factors may include illnesses (e.g. cancer, HIV/AIDS), injury, disabilities and impairments (e.g. amputation, substance abuse, trauma), or a family history of issues related to the presenting problem (e.g. depression, suicide). During the assessment process, counselors can obtain information related to biological predisposing factors with detailed medical and developmental histories.

Psychological predisposing factors include intelligence, personality style and dynamics, belief system (including schemas, intermediate beliefs, and automatic thoughts), self-concept, and related intrapsychic factors. Vulnerabilities here can manifest in emotional and behavioral problems. While psychological factors can be a source of strength and resilience for some individuals, those that contribute to the client's presenting problem can be seen as liabilities. Examples include low self-esteem, mistrust of others, poor self-regulation, and negative emotions, such as depression and anxiety. Information about psychological predisposing factors can come from a variety of sources, such as standardized assessments (e.g. MMPI) or semi-structured clinical interviews. Finally, *sociocultural predisposing factors* refer to a variety of possible contributing factors in the client's current and past social contexts. These include family history, such as family-of-origin dynamics, members' roles, boundaries, and interaction styles. For some clients, this may also include histories of physical, emotional, sexual, or other forms of abuse and/or neglect. Counselors can conduct a thorough assessment of the client's family history, paying particular attention to family functioning and style. For example, how did this client's family respond to unexpected challenges (e.g. illness)? Were there family secrets? What was the quality of affection among family members? Additionally, sociocultural predisposing factors include information about the client's current social world. Here, counselors should gather information about current peer relationships, romantic involvement, school or work status, support system or lack thereof, and other current environmental factors. Of particular importance throughout these three sections is information related to the client's spiritual and religious experiences – both past and present. Clients' engagement in spiritual practices, involvement in a spiritual or religious belief system, faith development stage, and sense of spiritual or religious identity from childhood onward provides valuable insights when crafting a spiritually integrative case conceptualization.

Taken alone, none of the factors outlined above, in and of themselves, may entirely explain the client's presenting problem; as a group, however, these predisposing factors provide the conditions, or "ingredients," necessary to explain why the problem occurred. When developing case conceptualizations from a spiritually integrative framework, it is important to consider how biological, psychological, and sociocultural factors specifically relate to the client's religious and/or spiritual experiences. This is illustrated in the following example: A 28-year-old male presents for treatment of symptoms related to Generalized Anxiety Disorder. He has a history of childhood leukemia, resulting in multiple hospitalizations during adolescence. Throughout this time, the client was very fearful of dying. This fear was exacerbated by the death of his only friend, a young man being treated in the same hospital. The client came to see himself as fragile, and life as harsh and unpredictable. While the client did, secretly, have questions about God and the afterlife, his agnostic parents, engaged in a very open belief system, did not initiate a discussion about these concepts, as they did not see them as important. This left the client feeling fearful and alone. The client's cancer eventually remitted, however he remained constantly on edge about whether or not it would return. This fear generalized to other areas of the client's life, resulting in an overall sense of worry. In this case, the presenting problem (anxiety) is rooted in the client's history of biological, psychological, and social predisposing factors. Understanding how these relate to the problem is crucial for developing an effective treatment plan that includes appropriate religious and/or spiritual interventions.

Perpetuant

Perpetuants are factors that maintain or exacerbate the client's presenting problems (Sperry and Sperry, 2012). They serve to keep the client stuck in his or her present state by reinforcing maladaptive functioning and insulating against change. In other words, perpetuants keep the problem going. Perpetuants can come from a variety of sources, including skills deficits, interpersonal interactions, and living or work environments. In the example outlined in the preceding section, lack of social support, isolation, self-medication with alcohol or other substances, and continued reluctance to fully explore spiritual and/or religious explanations for his childhood illness and friend's death are potentially perpetuating factors. Predisposing factors may also act as perpetuants for the client's problem if these are ongoing. For instance, a client who has an obsessive-compulsive personality style might focus on being perfect in his or her adherence to religious rituals, criticizing others who he does not see as meeting the same standards of devotion. This client is likely to fall into Genia's stage 2, dogmatic faith (Genia, 1995), and is comfortable with more closed off religious systems. This predisposing personality style results in ongoing interpersonal conflicts with others and alienation, which reinforces the client's anxiety and drive to control. Counselors may find the task of separating perpetuants and predisposing factors challenging, because of this overlap.

Cultural Formulation

The *cultural formulation* adds depth to the clinical formulation by answering the question "what role does culture play?" (Sperry and Sperry, 2012). As with the clinical formulation, this component of an integrative case conceptualization provides an opportunity to explore the client's spiritual and religious experiences, values, and practices. The cultural formulation is based on four elements, described below: *cultural identity, acculturation and acculturative stress, cultural explanation, and culture versus personality.*

Cultural Identity

The relationship between spirituality and culture is complex. Spirituality may appear in all of the various dimensions of culture (e.g. ethnicity, race, national origin, gender, sexual orientation, etc.) because culture is the context in which spirituality often exists (Sperry, 2012). However, it is important to note that one's sense of spirituality is not necessarily directly related to culture. Martsolf (1997) notes that culture, and personal experiences unrelated to culture, or some combination of both that might deviate from cultural norms could entirely define spirituality. In determining the client's cultural identity, counselors should rely on the person's own self-appraisal and not base this on appearance or demographics. For example, a first-generation American of Syrian descent may not identify with Arab culture or the Muslim religion, even though his parents may find both very important. In this case, to make assumptions and attempt spiritual interventions that are based on Islam would be inappropriate and could be perceived by the client as disrespectful. Cultural identity is about perceived membership in a particular group, as chosen by the individual. The client described above may identify as a Buddhist due to his experiences with meditation, or may define himself in strictly non-religious or non-spiritual terms. Spiritual identity and cultural identity are not considered one and the same.

Acculturation and Acculturative Stress

Acculturation is the process by which individuals adapt to a culture different from their culture of origin (Sperry and Sperry, 2012). This typically refers to the experience of immigrants, though it may also describe the transition between minority and majority cultures within the same country or society. *Acculturative stress* can be the result of the acculturation process. It involves varying degrees of psychological harm brought about by experiences such as racism and discrimination, language barriers, and conflicts between one's values or practices and those of the dominant culture, just to name a few. In the case of acculturative stress related to religious and spiritual identity, individuals may feel particularly threatened because of the significant role these play in their self-concept. For example, an Orthodox Jewish man may experience this stress when expected to sit next to a female passenger on a plane, in violation of the religious laws to which he adheres. Another point to consider is how clients use spirituality in response to acculturative stress that may be unrelated directly to spirituality or religion. Sanchez, Dillon, Concha, and De La Rosa (2015) examined religious coping practices among recent Latino immigrants. They found that positive religious coping behaviors, such as forgiveness and seeking spiritual support, protected against acculturative stress. When completing a spiritually integrative case conceptualization, using formal assessments, such as the Brief Acculturation Scale, may be useful to determine the client's level of acculturation (Panigua, 2005).

Cultural Explanation

It is crucial that counselors assess and understand clients' own explanations for why they are experiencing problems or symptoms. While the counselor may have a hypothesis about the causes of the presenting problem, the client's view might be completely different. This may lead to inappropriate treatment recommendations, client resistance, or early termination, among other undesirable outcomes. The *cultural explanation* section of the cultural formulation outlines the client's explanatory model. It includes the client's beliefs about the causes of distress as well as the client's expectations and preferences for treatment (Sperry and Sperry, 2012). In the case of religious or spiritual issues, this case conceptualization component takes on added significance. For example, a client may believe that negative events in his life, from losing a job to flat tires, are punishments from God for his previous sins. His response to this might include feelings of sadness, anger, and behavioral withdrawal. Without understanding the client's explanation, the counselor could attribute the client's symptoms to irrational thinking and recommend some form of cognitive therapy. Because treatment did not take into account the client's perspective of the problem, it is likely to be ineffective in producing positive change. In this example, integrating the client's cultural explanation means addressing his beliefs about the Divine, sin, and divine punishment. This may lead to treatment interventions specifically designed to address the client's beliefs, such as confession or some form of atonement ritual. Formal assessments, such as the Views of Suffering Scale (VOSS; Hale-Smith et al., 2012), may assist in identifying the client's explanation. In this section, counselors should also note the client's previous experiences with treatment and whether or not specific religious and/or spiritual healing practices have been helpful.

Culture versus Personality

The final part of the cultural formulation involves weighing the relative influence of culture and personality dynamics, as they pertain to the client's presenting problems. The counselor's task here is to determine whether or not, and to what extent, the individual client's problems are attributable to his or her personality as opposed to cultural identity or context. In other words, how different is this individual from other members of his culture, and which one better explains his or her problems? As noted in Sperry and Sperry (2012), cultural dynamics have relatively little impact on presenting problems for individuals with high levels of acculturation. In this case, personality style is likely to be the main source of problems. For clients with low levels of acculturation, however, culture may play a significant – or primary – role in the development and maintenance of the presenting problems, as in the case of acculturative stress. Following the initial assessment, counselors may confirm one of three possibilities: that personality dynamics are primarily operative, that cultural dynamics are primarily operative, or that the client's problems are attributable to some combination of the two. At first glance, it would appear that the Orthodox Jewish man from the previous example would fall into the second category, in that his symptoms are due to cultural factors. However, upon further assessment the counselor may conclude that this *specific* individual's response to the precipitating event deviates from most other member of the male Orthodox community; he is exceptionally upset or angry. The counselor may find that this personality style is evident in the client's life in many other areas, and has little to do with his religious identity. In this case, the counselor can understand the client's presenting problem as a combination of both personality and cultural dynamics. As with cultural issues in general, it is important that counselors become educated about the beliefs, practices, values, and other cultural variables of their clients. Failure to do so may result in mistaking cultural dynamics for personality or vice versa.

Treatment Formulation

The final component of the integrative case conceptualization model is the treatment formulation. It answers the question: "How can it change?" (Sperry and Sperry, 2012, p. 11). So long as counselors have an accurate diagnosis and developed a comprehensive picture of the preceding case conceptualization components, treatment planning should flow logically. The treatment formulation contains a number of elements, including goals, strategies, anticipated obstacles, and interventions.

The remaining chapters of this book contain information on specific treatment interventions counselors can use when working in the spiritual and religious domains. This chapter will conclude with a detailed case vignette that illustrates the integrative case conceptualization model when working with a client who presents with spiritual concerns.

Case Study

Susanna is a 15-year-old, cisgender, Mexican-American female whose family identifies as part of the Mormon faith. For a full description of Susanna's profile and presenting issues, please reference the Introduction to this book.

In meeting with you, Susanna is initially reserved and guarded, describing her behavioral changes as the result of "stress." After conducting an ecopmap assessment and related questioning, Susanna reveals that her change in behavior is related to guilt, confusion, fear, and anger that resulted from feelings of same-sex attraction inconsistent with her faith background. She tells you that her same-sex attraction has been present since the start of puberty, but she was able to suppress it by investing her attention in academics. At the start of the school year, Susanna entered into a friendship with a girl in her class that developed into a mutual attraction. When her friend unexpectedly kissed her, Susanna broke ties and attempted to rededicate herself to her classes and faith; however, she describes being "tortured" by romantic thoughts of her former friend and the messages of her family and faith regarding sexual morality.

The following is the counselor's written case conceptualization of Susanna:

DSM-5 Diagnoses: 309.0 (F43.21) Adjustment Disorder with depressed mood; (V62.89) Religious or Spiritual Problem, Non-suicidal self-injury; Obsessive-compulsive personality style

Susanna presents with feelings of guilt, anger, confusion, and fear. She is also experiencing academic problems and social withdrawal. The client recently started cutting her upper arm. She denied wanting to kill or seriously harm herself, explaining that cutting was a means to relieve her negative thoughts regarding a recent event *(presentation)*. Susanna reported that a mutual sexual attraction between her and a female friend had been ongoing for the past few months. The client's symptoms, however, did not appear until her friend kissed her a few weeks ago *(precipitant)*. She states that she now feels "tortured" by her feelings and thoughts about the situation. The client punishes herself when she fails to be perfect *(pattern)*. The counselor can understand her reaction to the precipitating event in light of her history. According to Susanna, this pattern began in early childhood. She stated that she used to recite prayers until she "got them perfect," and was an exceptional student until recently. The client shared that she received many uncompromising messages about purity, morality, and sin from her parents throughout childhood, particularly from her father. She remembers one occasion in which her father, upon seeing a news segment about same-sex marriage on television, commented, "those people are disgusting." The client reported that she was expected to follow rules without question, and developed an overly conscientious and perfectionistic way of dealing with life. Susanna's family was deeply involved with the Mormon Church, endorsing a more closed belief system, throughout her childhood, and their current social network consists entirely of other Mexican-American Mormon families. Susanna denied any family history of mental illness, though she stated that her mother is "an anxious person." Susanna reported that she herself had a tic (blinking) in elementary school, but this resolved spontaneously after one year *(predisposition)*. Susanna reported that she continues to see her friend at school, which causes ongoing feelings of guilt. Her social withdrawal at school and with her family, as well as ongoing messages about acceptable behavior during weekly church services, serve to maintain the presenting problems *(perpetuants)*.

Susanna self-identifies as a Mexican-American. She speaks Spanish fluently, and participates in Mexican traditions with her family – most recently her *quinceañera*. She reported that her involvement in the Mormon Church is extremely important to her. Susanna shared that she and her family spend each Sunday together with members of the religious community, and frequently communicate with them throughout the week. She described her view of God as a demanding judge who rewards compliance and punishes rule breaking *(cultural identity)*. Despite being born in the United States, Susanna's level of acculturation is in the moderate range. Her upbringing in the small Mexican Mormon community within her town is markedly different from the experiences of most of her peers at school. Susanna's parents immigrated to the United States shortly before her birth; their acculturation level is lower than hers. This client appears to be experiencing considerable culture-related stress, as evidenced by her cultural explanation of the presenting problems *(acculturation and stress)*. While Susanna initially attributed her behavior to "stress," she later acknowledged the influence that her Mormon faith, Mexican heritage, and strong paternal injunctions against "deviant" sexual behavior had on her response to the precipitating event. She believes that she has failed her family and the Church, and therefore deserves punishment *(cultural explanation)*. In Susanna's case, it appears that both personality and culture are operative. As previously indicated, both her Mexican heritage and the teachings of the Mormon faith influenced her interpretation of events; however, Susanna's obsessive-compulsive personality style complicated this crisis and resulted in increased distress and her particular maladaptive coping behaviors *(culture v. personality)*.

This client's treatment should aim to first reduce her presenting symptoms and achieve stability in daily life. This includes interventions aimed at decreasing negative emotions and self-injury, while increasing social support. Second order treatment goals will involve shifting her maladaptive pattern, from punishing herself in response to not feeling perfect to being flexible and kind with herself as she processes her conflicting feelings. Specific treatment interventions are designed to identify, challenge, and gradually replace Susanna's rigid and perfectionistic way of thinking.

Because of the significant role that Susanna's faith plays in her presenting problems, a religious/spiritual intervention is indicated. A marker of effective therapy will be a softening of her image of God to a less demanding and more loving image. The counselor will administer the God Image Inventory (Lawrence, 1991) periodically through the course of therapy to track changes in Susanna's image of God. As Susanna's symptoms improve, her image of God is expected to become less rigid, critical, and punitive (Cheston et al., 2003).

References

American Psychiatric Association. (1980). *Diagnostic and Statistical Manual of Mental Disorders* (3rd ed.). Alexandria, VA: Author.

American Psychiatric Association. (1987). *Diagnostic and Statistical Manual of Mental Disorders* (3rd ed., rev.). Alexandria, VA: Author.

American Psychiatric Association. (1994). *Diagnostic and Statistical Manual of Mental Disorders* (4th ed.). Alexandria, VA: Author.

American Psychiatric Association. (2000). *Diagnostic and statistical manual of mental disorders* (4th ed., text rev.). Alexandria, VA: Author. doi:10.1176/appi.books. 9780890423349.

American Psychiatric Association. (2013). *Diagnostic and Statistical Manual of Mental Disorders* (5th ed.). Alexandria, VA: Author.

Aten, J. D., and Leach, M. M. (2009). *Spirituality and the therapeutic process: A comprehensive resource from intake to termination.* Washington, DC: American Psychological Association.

Bieling, P. J., and Kuyken, W. (2003). Is cognitive case formulation science or science fiction? *Clinical Psychology: Science and Practice*, 10(1), 52–69.

Cheston, S. E., Piedmont, R. L., Eanes, B., and Lavin, L. P. (2003). Changes in clients' images of God over the course of outpatient therapy. *Counseling and Values*, 47(2), 96–108.

Crits-Christoph, P., Barber, J., and Kurcias, J. (1993). The accuracy of therapists' interpretations and the development of the therapeutic alliance. *Psychotherapy Research*, 3(1), 25–35.

Dinkmeyer, D., and Sperry, L. (2000). *Counseling and psychotherapy: An integrated, individual psychology approach.* Upper Saddle River, NJ: Prentice Hall.

Eells, T. D. (2015). *Psychotherapy Case Formulation.* Washington, DC: American Psychological Association.

Ellis, A. (1980). Psychotherapy and atheistic values: A response to A.E. Bergin's "psychotherapy and religious values". *Journal of Consulting and Clinical Psychology*, 48, 635–639.

Ellis, A. (2000). Can rational emotive behavior therapy (REBT) be effectively used with people who have devout beliefs in God and religion? *Professional Psychology: Research and Practice*, 31(1), 29–33.

Ellison, C. W. (1983). Spiritual well-being: Conceptualization and measurement. *Journal of Psychology and Theology*, 11, 330–340.

Exline, J., and Rose, E. (2005). Religious and spiritual struggles. In R. Paloutzian and C. Park, *Handbook of the psychology of religion and spirituality* (pp. 315–330). New York, NY: Guilford Press.

Fowler, J. W. (1981). *Stages of faith: The psychology of human development and the quest for meaning.* San Francisco, CA: Harper & Row.

Freud, S. (1930). *Future of an illusion.* New York, NY: Norton.

Fullerton, J. T., and Hunsberger, B. (1982). A unidimensional measure of Christian orthodoxy. *Journal for the Scientific Study of Religion*, 21, 317–326.

Genia, V. (1995). *Counseling and Psychotherapy of Religious Clients.* Westport, CT: Praeger.

Hale-Smith, A., Park, C. L., and Edmonson, D. (2012). Measuring beliefs about suffering: Development of the views of suffering scale. *Psychological Assessment*, 24, 855–866.

Jacobson, N. S., Schmaling, K. B., Holtzworth-Munroe, A., Katt, J. L., Wood, L. F., and Follette, V. M. (1989). Research-structured vs. clinically flexible versions of social learning-based marital therapy. *Behavior Research and Therapy*, 27(2), 173–180.

Kierkegaard, S. (1843/1975). *Søren Kierkegaard's journals and papers: Volume 4, S-Z* (H. V. Hong and E. H. Hong, Trans.). Bloomington, IN: Indiana University Press.

Koenig, H. (2005). *Faith and mental health: Religion resources for healing.* West Conschocken, PA: Templeton Foundation Press.

Larsen, D., Thielman, S., Greenwold, M., Lyons, J., Post, S., and Sherrill, K. (1993). Religious content in the DSM-III-R glossary of technical terms. *American Journal of Psychiatry*, 150, 1884–1885.

Lawrence, R. T. (1991). *The God Image Inventory: The development, validation and standardization of a psychometric instrument for research, pastoral and clinical use in measuring the image of God* (Doctoral dissertation). Available from Dissertation Abstracts International. (52 (3-A), 952).

Levenson, H., and Strupp, H. (2007). Cyclical maladaptive patterns: Case formulation in time-limited dynamic psychotherapy. In T. D. Eells (Ed.), *Handbook of psychotherapy case formulation* (2nd ed.) (pp. 164–197). New York, NY: Guilford Press.

Martsolf, D. (1997). Cultural aspects of spirituality in cancer care. *Seminars in Oncology Nursing*, 13, 231–236.

Matthews, D. (1998). *The faith factor: Proof of the healing power of prayer*. New York, NY: Viking.

Morran, D. K., Kurpius, D. J., Brack, G., and Rozecki, T. G. (1994). Relationship between counselors' clinical hypothesis and clinical ratings of counselor effectiveness. *Journal of Counseling and Psychology*, 72, 655–660.

Panigua, F. (2005). *Assessing and treating culturally diverse clients: A practical guide* (3rd ed.). Thousand Oaks, CA: Sage.

Pargament, K. I. (2007). *Spiritually integrated psychotherapy: Understanding and addressing the sacred*. New York, NY: Guilford Press.

Pargament, K. I., Kennell, J., Hathaway, W., Grenvengoed, N., Newman, J., and Jones, W. (1988). Religion and the problem solving process: Three styles of coping. *Journal for the Scientific Study of Religion*, 27, 90–104.

Richards, P. S., and Bergin, A. E. (2005). *A spiritual strategy for counseling and psychotherapy* (2nd ed.). Washington, DC: American Psychological Association.

Richards, P. S., Bartz, J. D., and O'Grady, K. A. (2009, October). Assessing religion and spirituality in counseling: Some reflections and recommendations. *Counseling and Values*, 54, 65–79.

Richardson, J. (1993). Religiosity as deviance: Negative religious bias in and misuse of the DSM-III. *Deviant behavior*, 14(1), 1–21.

Sanchez, M., Dillon, F., Concha, M., and De La Rosa, M. (2015). The impact of religious coping on the acculturative stress and alcohol use of recent Latino immigrants. *Journal of Religious Health*, 54, 1986–2004.

Sperry, L. (2010a). *Highly effective therapy: Developing essential clinical competencies in counseling and psychotherapy*. New York, NY: Routledge.

Sperry, L. (2010b). *Core competencies in counseling and psychotherapy: Becoming a highly competent and effective therapist*. New York, NY: Routledge.

Sperry, L. (2011). *Spirituality in clinical practice: Theory and practice of spiritually oriented psychotherapy*, 2nd edition. New York, NY: Routledge.

Sperry, L., and Sperry, J. (2012). *Case conceptualization: Mastering this competency with ease and confidence*. New York, NY: Routledge.

Wright, J., Basco, M., and Thase, M. (2006). *Learning cognitive-behavior therapy: An illustrated guide*. Washington, DC: American Psychiatric Press.

Part II
Theories and Interventions

5 Spirituality and Existentialism

Jodi L. Tangen and Andy D. Felton

"Death and life are important. Don't suffer them in vain."

—Bodhidarma

Introduction

Existentialism and spirituality are alike, in that they are both difficult to define, because they are inherently intangible and elusive. To use a common English idiom, defining these concepts is "sort of like trying to nail Jell-O to the wall." Because of this, we endeavor to concretize the concepts, connections, and interventions associated with existentialism and spirituality as much as possible, all the while knowing that the foundational roots of these constructs lie deep within… in a place that is inherently ineffable. Throughout this chapter, we will briefly highlight tenets of existentialism, discuss spirituality in the context of existential theory, describe a few interventions, and provide a case study illustrating a blend of existential and spiritual counseling.

Existentialism

Existential theory poses universal questions and explores an individual's experience being in the world (Corey, 2013; Eliason et al., 2010; Murdock, 2013). Although there are many existential theorists and components of existentialism (based on theorists), two common concepts include the four givens of existence (Yalom, 1980) and Logotherapy (Frankl, 1959).

Givens of Existence

At the root of universal questions of being are inescapable *givens* that encompass our existence (Yalom, 1980). These givens, consisting of death, freedom, isolation, and meaninglessness, are what motivate and inspire us while also creating significant barriers, concerns, struggles, and anxiety in our lives (Corey, 2013; Murdock, 2013; Yalom, 1980).

Death. This given acknowledges that one day we will no longer exist. People tend to evade thoughts about our own deaths in an effort to avoid great angst (Murdock, 2013). Learning to embrace our non-existence can provide a platform in which people live life to the fullest (Corey, 2013, Yalom, 2008). Openly talking with individuals about death allows them to confront their fears around death, which in turn can help them assess how well they are living the life they want and can begin to make choices and act to enhance their quality of life (Yalom, 2008).

Freedom. Existentialism emphasizes the role and responsibility in which people play in their own destiny. This means that individuals have the capacity to make choices, reflect on their choices, and take action in an effort to make changes in our lives (Schneider and Krug, 2010). Ultimately, we are to hold ourselves accountable for the quality of life we live. This translates to us being the authors of our lives; we are the creators of our problems, and we are responsible for then changing them (Corey, 2013; Yalom, 1980).

Isolation. Longing for connection with ourselves and with others is a natural part of our existence. We experience levels of isolation from ourselves when we struggle to take responsibility in our lives and live inauthentically (Corey, 2013). To help fill our intra-personal void, we often seek solace in relationships. Though we can share experiences with others, our uniqueness in the world makes it difficult to fully connect with others, further reinforcing our feelings of isolation (Eliason et al., 2010; Yalom 1980). When isolation is properly explored, much can be gained. Through the acceptance of our aloneness and uniqueness, deeper connections with ourselves can evolve. As people recognize their responsibilities and abilities and live authentically, they can then rely on themselves to decide how to live (Corey, 2013).

Meaninglessness. The meaning making process is an ongoing struggle which can change based on a person's engagement with the world and the individual's values (van Deurzen, 2002; Vontress, 2008). Viktor Frankl (1959) made use of Logotherapy, emphasizing the significance of having purpose in our lives. Through the construction of meaning, people can increase levels of motivation and inspiration while gaining a sense of accomplishment in their lives (Yalom, 1980).

Though each of these givens has a separate entity, they are simultaneously engaging one another and impacting our lives. Through reflection, awareness, and decision-making, we can embrace the different possibilities and opportunities of human life (Eliason et al., 2010; Yalom, 1980). In practice, counselors support individuals to explore, integrate, and embrace these essential givens in effort to live authentically (Corey, 2013; Murdock, 2013).

Logotherapy

A Holocaust survivor, Frankl (1959) posited that individuals could withstand any amount of suffering provided that they find meaning in that suffering. Furthermore, he stated that meaning is found in three different ways:

"(1) by creating a work or doing a deed; (2) by experiencing something or encountering someone; and (3) by the attitude we take toward unavoidable suffering" (Frankl, 1959, p. 111). Applied to counseling, Frankl's Logotherapy is characterized by recognizing the trials and tribulations in life, and searching for possible underlying reasons behind these challenges. This approach lends itself to spirituality and religion, as individuals often look toward their conceptions of a Higher Power to understand life's sorrows. We explore the connections between spirituality and both types of existentialism further in the next section.

Spirituality and Existentialism

There are a variety of ways to conceptualize spirituality, many of which have already been explored in this text. To distinguish our theory a little more, we chose three definitions that illuminate the *bridge* between spirituality and existentialism, rather than focusing on spirituality alone. Based on the theory of existentialism, Kaut (2002) defined spirituality as "... a dimension of personhood defining the essence of humanity" (p. 226). With this definition, we see an emphasis on the common *humanity* aspect of spirituality, which relates to existentialism's focus on the givens of the human condition (e.g., freedom, isolation, meaning, death; Yalom, 1980). Moving even closer to the theory of existentialism, Webb, Toussaint, and Dula (2014) defined spirituality as "the salient, searching pursuit of the transcendently sacred ritualistic, theistic, and/or existential aspects of the human condition" (p. 974). Here, existentialism is literally named as a component of spirituality. Finally, Hodge (2005) stated, "... *spirituality* is defined as an existential relationship with God (or perceived Transcendence) that fosters a sense of meaning, purpose, and mission in life" (p. 77). Moving even closer together, the concepts of spirituality and existentialism here are essentially intertwined. To understand their similarities and differences a little more closely, we examine the role of spirituality within the context of existentialism.

Role of Spirituality within Existentialism

Many scholars have postulated that the connection between spirituality and existentialism lies in the process of making meaning of one's life and struggles (Eliason et al., 2010; Faller, 2001; Kaut, 2002; Snodgrass and Sorajjakool, 2011; Young et al., 1998). In other words, when a person encounters the "groundlessness of existence" (Schneider, 2015, p. 21) – which could include inescapable losses, traumatic experiences, identity crises, etc. – the spiritual journey is also existential: finding meaning (van Duerzen, 2012). In addition to meaning, spirituality could encompass the existential givens of freedom and isolation as well. In Ingersoll's (1998) theory of the 10 dimensions of spiritual wellness, he includes meaning, sense of freedom, and connectedness (which could be a corollary of isolation). As practices, spirituality and existentialism are quite similar. If one delves into the roots of her or his spiritual or existential self, she or he is essentially encountering the crux of the human condition, which is common to both concepts.

Having bridged these connections, though, it is important to differentiate between spirituality and existentialism as well. The best way to do this is by contrasting the tone of each concept. For lack of a better description, existentialism has a darker tone to it and has even been referred to as "pessimistic" (Sommers-Flanagan and Sommers-Flanagan, 2012, p. 133). Simply reviewing the tenets of the fathers of existential theory explains this perspective (Kierkegaard, Nietzsche, Heidegger, Sartre, Frankl, Yalom, etc.). Nietzsche assumed a nihilistic view on life, Heidegger explored death, and Frankl's focus on meaning stemmed from his time in a Nazi concentration camp (Bates, 2016). Furthermore, the titles of Yalom's (1980) givens of existence (death, freedom, isolation, and meaninglessness) carry a certain heaviness that likely isn't acknowledged in the everyday hustle and bustle of life. Even freedom, postulated from an existential lens, has a certain level of gravity to it. It is not necessarily the freedom associated with joyful exhilaration, but rather, the freedom associated with endless possibilities and responsibilities of one's life; such freedom can be incredibly anxiety inducing.

Spirituality, on the other hand, carries a ray of lightness. For example, Ingersoll's (1998) theory of the 10 dimensions of spiritual wellness includes the softer connotations of meaning, freedom, and connectedness. Furthermore, he includes such virtues as hope, present-centeredness, and forgiveness. Even his dimension of mystery is based on qualities of awe and wonder. Thus, both existentialism and spirituality explore the givens of what it means to be human. However, they each cast a different tone on the journey.

Nature of Spiritual Struggles

The nature of spiritual struggles, according to existentialists, centers on confrontations with Yalom's (1980) four givens of existence. For example, if a person feels depressed, an existentialist might postulate that (a) she or he has lost a sense of meaning, (b) she or he is coming to terms with isolation, (c) she or he is facing death (or the death of something or someone close), and/or (d) she or he is paralyzed by the expansive freedom in life. When people encounter these givens in an authentic manner, they cannot help but enter deep intra-personal conflict. Such internal chaos typically leads them to counselors and therapists who are not afraid to delve into these deep, unsettling conversations and use existentially oriented interventions.

Interventions

By its very philosophical roots, existentialism is not "technique-y," but rather, is nested inside the philosophical focus of the therapeutic stance. In fact, existentialists may deem quick-fix interventions as "phony" (Sommers-Flanagan and Sommers-Flanagan, 2012, p. 134). Furthermore, when speaking of techniques, Kottler (2002) stated, "You can *be* an existentialist, but you can't *do* it" (p. 77). Certainly, this becomes an issue when trying to teach new counselors how to practice existential counseling. Rather than leaving readers with an amorphous understanding of the theory, though, we strive to describe a few interventions that interweave both spiritual and existential tenets. Although the therapeutic relationship and existential discussions provide some foundation for existential counseling, the interventions included thereafter (spiritual lifemaps and expressive arts) are not inherently existential. Rather, existential perspective is simply used to enhance these interventions.

Therapeutic Relationship

The therapeutic relationship is one of the major factors in existential therapy (Sommers-Flanagan and Sommers-Flanagan, 2012). The relationship, as postulated by existentialists, is characterized by Martin Buber's (1958) *I-thou* connection, in which one honors another individual rather than objectifying her or him. Such a relationship may be characterized by *accessibility* and *expressiveness*, or a willingness to be impacted by the client and known to the client (Bugental, 1987). There's a certain sense of humility to this as well. Yalom (2002) noted the humanness of becoming a "fellow traveler" (p. 6) in the therapeutic relationship and acknowledging similar experiences/feelings or "sharing the shade of the shadow" (p. 215). Also relevant to the relationship, Yalom (2002) highlighted therapist authenticity, transparency, and empathy.

The existential relationship intersects with tenets of spirituality as well. Earlier, we used Young and Cashwell's (2011) definition of spirituality, which stated that spirituality results "… in greater self-other compassion and love" (p. 7). From this phrase, we begin to see how compassion for others can be a form of spirituality in and of itself. Furthermore, connectedness is noted as a dimension of spiritual wellness (Ingersoll, 1998), and deep moments in relationships (characterized by the concept of relational depth [Mearns and Cooper, 2005]) are deemed spiritual (Rowan, 2013). Thus, the relationship is not only an existential component, but its very essence may be considered spiritual as well.

Existential Discussions

Another existentialist "intervention" is simply engaging in discussions around Yalom's (1980) four givens: death, freedom, isolation, and meaninglessness. Such discussions may be uncomfortable; however, an existential counselor cultivates the courage to broach these types of issues. For example, imagine that a client is struggling with anxiety. Instead of working with cognitions and self-talk (as a cognitive counselor might do), an existential counselor might discuss anxiety related to death (as outlined in Yalom, 2002, 2008). The existential counselor might also inquire into the anxiety associated with freedom and possibilities. Perhaps the individual has just lost her or his job, and the freedom of selecting a new job is triggering substantial anxiety. Third, perhaps the anxiety is associated with a feeling of existential isolation. Here, a counselor might broach this discussion, emphasizing the reality of aloneness, while also highlighting the importance of connection. Finally, a counselor may invite discussions around meaning associated with anxiety. For example, perhaps the client is anxious because she or he is beginning to question religious teachings. In this context, the counselor may begin to discuss the meaning associated with religious beliefs. Such an existential discussion intersects with spirituality as well.

As existentially oriented individuals, we encourage counselors to actively broach discussions around Yalom's (1980) four givens. At the same time, it is important to know when this discussion is warranted and ethically appropriate. Counselors should take the counseling relationship, clients' needs, and clients' psychological readiness into account. Diving into such deep, perhaps unsettling and vulnerable topics may, understandably, rattle clients. Therefore, counselors need to be mindful and respectful when choosing this intervention.

Creative Interventions

Beyond the therapeutic relationship and existential discussions, there are certain types of interventions that have an existential flair to them. The ones that we describe are more creative ways of interweaving existential elements within various interventions. However, it is important to reiterate that existentialism is a philosophy and any techniques used are not inherent within the theory (Schneider, 2015).

Spiritual Lifemaps

One intervention that may be beneficial within the context of existentialism and spirituality is the use of spiritual lifemaps, first described by Hodge (2005). According to Hodge (2005), "Spiritual lifemaps are a pictorial depiction [sic] of consumers' spiritual journeys" (p. 78). These may be used as a stand-alone intervention or as a method of assessment for planning future counseling sessions (Dailey et al., 2011; Hodge, 2005). More concretely, these lifemaps often include a line depicting the linear journey of one's life, along with symbols or images that represent significant life experiences – both sacred and secular (Hodge, 2005). After creating the map, Hodge (2005) encouraged further processing based on an individual's spiritual beliefs and rituals, support from others, and overall relationship with her or his concept of "God."

Of particular relevance to this chapter, Hodge (2005) stated, "... life-maps are ideally suited for existential interventions as they intrinsically highlight the transitory nature of life and the inevitability of death..." (p. 84). Here, we touch upon the ways that spiritual lifemaps may intersect with Yalom's (1980) four givens of existence. For example, while creating a spiritual lifemap, a client may begin exploring those aspects of life that mean the most to her or him (Hodge, 2005), and she or he may be more closely oriented to the reality of death. Furthermore, life experiences of freedom and isolation (perhaps the disorienting feelings associated with the first year away at a new place) may emerge within the spiritual lifemap as well. In fact, spiritual lifemaps have been explored with populations who may be more inclined to existential approaches, such as hospice clients (Bushfield, 2010). Furthermore, if adapted, it may be a beneficial tool across various spiritual and cultural groups (e.g., Limb and Hodge, 2007; Limb et al., 2013).

Having explored some of the possibilities of using spiritual lifemaps, it is important to note some of the drawbacks as well. Participants who have been exposed to this intervention noted that Hodge's (2005) processing questions might need to be adapted for various cultural groups (e.g. Limb and Hodge, 2007; Limb et al., 2013). Furthermore, to increase the viability of the tool, practitioners may want to refer to it as a "Life Meaning Map" or "Core Values Lifemap" (Buser et al., 2013, p. 376). The lifemap also takes some time to complete, and thus, time may be a prohibitive factor (Bushfield, 2010). Some participants in both Buser et al.'s (2013) study and Bushfield's (2010) study questioned their roles in discussing issues of spirituality as well. Despite these barriers, the spiritual lifemap could be an advantageous tool for exploring the intersection of both spirituality and existentialism.

Expressive Arts

As identified earlier in the chapter, existentialism focuses on meaning making, connection, choice, and being. Portraying such abstract under-standings can be particularly difficult through verbal language alone (Gladding, 2011). However, it is possible, through the use of expressive arts, that individuals can gain a sense of meaning, increase their levels of self-awareness, and gain a sense of belonging (Atkins et al., 2003; Glad-ding, 2011; MacIntosh, 2003; Malchiodi, 2005; Murray and Rotter, 2002; Oaklander, 2001). If you have an interest in integrating various expressive methods into spiritual work with clients, be sure to refer to Chapter 12 within this text, specifically focused on expressive arts.

Case Study

The present case study involves the application of an existential framework to the case of Marian, a 62-year-old woman diagnosed with cancer. Please reference the full client profile description in the Introduction to this book. Working with Marian from existential and spiritual lenses, the goal of counseling is not to "fix" her, but rather, to walk with her as a "fellow traveler" (Yalom, 2002, p. 6). As such, it is important for the counselor to identify her personal experiences of brokenness, regret, panic, and groundlessness. Although painful and disorienting, the practice of connecting with these elements provides a launching pad for connection with Marian. As stated so eloquently by relational depth researchers, Mearns and Cooper (2005), "...we enter into our own 'depths' to meet our clients in theirs" (p. 137). In the spirit of this sentiment, the counselor strives for a stance of humility and open awareness in beginning her work with Marian.

We work to establish connection from a place of mutual openness. Adopting Bugental's (1987) notions of accessibility and expressiveness requires the counselor to be touched by the client's story of cancer, facilitating more of a personal, *I-Thou* relationship (Buber, 1958). Further, where appropriate and unassuming, the counselor authentically shares her personal reactions to the client's story as well. Being deeply present and empathic (although certainly not always perfect) sets the foundation for a relationship.

In the first session, the counselor simply enters as fully, as honestly, and as courageously as she can into the relationship. In our second session, the subject of death is broached by saying, "Marian, I realized after our last session that we seem to be dancing around the possibility that you could die from this..." It is important that the counselor encourages the client to sit with this comment and its implications. As the client begins to show stirrings of anxiety, she falters a little, pauses, and becomes slightly tearful. She states that she is feeling relieved that the subject of death has been broached, and that the counselor is willing to face the reality of this possibility with her. Marian further explains that in her everyday life, whenever death is mentioned, people swiftly interrupt her, prodding her to stay upbeat and positive. With a brief flash of anger in her eyes, she says, "But I don't feel positive. I feel tired and sick and nobody has the guts to look at death *with* me." Processing her feelings of anger (and underlying sadness) when others tell her to "be positive," allows the conversation to shift into her feelings of isolation. She admits feeling completely alone in facing death when others fail to consider the possibility with her. Here, the counselor strives for transparency, telling her that while processing the possibility of death with her is an important therapeutic task, in some ways, she *is* alone in confronting her death; we all are. While this proves difficult for the client to hear, it would be disingenuous, even patronizing to attempt to reassure her. It is in this moment when the counselor's awareness of her own desires to ease *personal* discomfort prevents unhelpful discourse. To be with her – to truly be *with* her – the counselor just remains present.

The following week, Marian shares that she feels a little different. She repeats a statement made in the earlier session; that we all confront our own deaths at one time or another. She reports that in a peculiar way, this made her feel less alone in the journey – that perhaps, she has begun integrating this reality into her own awareness. "In some ways," she adds, "I feel less of a panicked feeling, but in other ways, I feel a little more anxiety. If I really accept the notion that I am going to die – at least some day – then at that point, it's done. I can't go back and change the mistakes I've made…" This hints at regret and helplessness. She further adds that she doesn't feel a strong sense of spirituality around everything that has happened in her life.

Given that the client is in a reflective mood, the counselor introduces the idea of completing a spiritual lifemap together. "Marian, I wonder if it might be beneficial to create a lifemap depicting your experiences with spirituality throughout your life. Sometimes, these maps can help people make sense of decisions they've made and experiences that they've had, which could also help you explore those aspects of your life where you felt as though you made mistakes." The client initially responds with some hesitance, indicating that she does not consider herself to be artistic. She nevertheless agrees, after being assured by the counselor that artistic skill is not a requirement for the activity, and that she need not create the lifemap if she did not think it helpful.

The client uses paper and art materials to draw a line that represents her life. From there, we add symbols, pictures, words, etc. that denote meaningful spiritual events in her life. After finishing the drawing, Marian is invited to share the story of what she has constructed. Despite touching on many important life events, the client does not become solemn until discussing her first cancer diagnosis; at this point she sounds almost regretful. "I was 32 the first time that they diagnosed cancer – cervical cancer that time – and I had to undergo chemo immediately. After a couple rounds of the chemo, my ovaries were shot – no possibility for children; that was for sure." Despite the plain words, Marian's voice trembles slightly and she appears to be emotional.

This becomes an opportunity for some presence-focused reflections. The counselor reflects to the client that not being able to have children plays a role in her sense of regret, to which Marian readily agrees. Acknowledging the pain of this prompts the tears that threatened to emerge only moments earlier. She cries from a raw place not seen before in the therapy.

"My mom always told me that I'd be a good mom, and my co-workers at work told me the same thing. And I really love children, but after that chemo, I just couldn't. And I should have tried to adopt, but I didn't and then it was just all too late. Now when I think about dying, it's like there's nothing left. I don't have children to give my stuff to or pass along wisdom or anything. It's just me dying, and when I'm gone, it will be like I never existed." Her voice takes on a tone of desperation, corroborating the feeling that she is running out of time.

There are many ways the counselor could respond to this. She could reflect her emotions, ask more about what *does* give her life meaning, reassure her that she is important, refer back to the lifemap, or offer some type of platitude about life. Nevertheless, the counselor chooses to quietly respond as authentically as possible. "Marian, I'm struggling to find the words to respond. I just see how deeply this hurts." The counselor does not offer reassurances or quick-fix solutions as Marian continues to cry and express deep regrets about not being able to have children. Simply remaining present throughout this experience is critical to helping her to process her feelings

Toward the end of the session, Marian's tone shifts from regret and desperation to anger. "You know," she says, looking down at her spiritual lifemap, "it was after that first cancer diagnosis and all that chemo that I started questioning the notion of 'God.'" She continues, "How could any God allow this to happen to me? I believe that people can feel connected to each other and to nature and pets and stuff, and I guess that's my spirituality. Not 'God.'" "Actually," she says, pointing to a picture of an animal on her lifemap, "I credit my dog for bringing me through that time in my life. He provided more for me than anyone." The counselor and Marian continue to walk through her lifemap in a similar manner, exploring her emotions and creating meaning out of her spiritual journey.

At the next session, Marian says that she had thought about it over the week and decided that she wants to do something to help others. This serves as an indication that she is trying to make meaning for herself and for her life. On further inquiry, she discloses that she decided to become a "cuddler" at the local hospital's Neonatal Intensive Care Unit. She explains that a "cuddler" holds, rocks, and sings to premature babies during times when their parents cannot be there for them. She shares this with a gleam of bittersweet inspiration. In many ways, this endeavor might provide her with a sense of spiritual transcendence that she is seeking, a way to make her mark on the world. Furthermore, perhaps on a subconscious level, she is integrating the reality of her situation – that she might die soon and that she regrets not having had or adopted children of her own. By volunteering to be a cuddler, she chooses to give meaning to her life; passing along her gift of nurturance in a way that helps others. In other words, she completes the circle from death to life, and life to death, bringing hope and compassion to a new generation.

Summary

First, it is important to note that this case study seems deceptively simple. Marian is an insightful, self-aware, and "good" client, eager and willing to explore her life and assume responsibility for her future. Having noted that, this brief case study incorporates existential and spiritual interventions, including the establishment of the therapeutic relationship; discussions of existential issues such as death, meaning, and isolation; and creative interventions such as the spiritual lifemap. Through these approaches, the client is able to face some of her anxiety and regret, taking responsibility for creating meaning in her future endeavors.

References

Atkins, S., Adams, M., McKinney, C., McKinney, H., Rose, L., Wentworth, J., and Wentworth, J. (2003). *Expressive arts therapy*. Boone, NC: Parkway.

Bates, A. T. (2016). Addressing existential suffering. *British Columbia Medical Journal*, 58(5), 268–273.

Bodhidarma (1987) *The zen teaching of Bodhidarma* (R. Pine, Trans.). New York, NY: North Point Press.

Buber, M. (1958). *I and thou*. New York, NY: Scribner.

Bugental, J. F. T. (1987). *The art of the psychotherapist*. New York, NY: WW. Norton & Company.

Buser, J. K., Buser, T. J., and Peterson, C. H. (2013). Counselor training in the use of spiritual lifemaps: Creative interventions for depicting spiritual/religious stories. *Journal of Creativity in Mental Health*, 8(4), 363–380. doi:10.1080/15401383.2013.844659.

Bushfield, S. (2010). Use of spiritual life maps in a hospice setting. *Journal of Religion, Spirituality & Aging*, 22(4), 254–270. doi:10.1080/15528030.2010.509777.

Corey, G. (2013). *Theory and practice of counseling and psychotherapy* (9th ed.). Belmont, CA: Brooks/Cole.

Dailey, S. F., Curry, J., Harper, M., Moorhead, H. H., and Gill, C. S. (2011). Exploring the Spiritual Domain: Tools for Integrating Spirituality and Religion in Counseling. *VISTAS*. Retrieved from http://counselingoutfitters.com/vistas/vistas11/Article_99.pdf.

Eliason, G. T., Samide, J. L., Williams, G., and Lepore, M. F. (2010). Existential theory and our search for spirituality. *Journal of Spirituality in Mental Health*, 12, 86–111. doi:10.1080/19349631003730068.

Faller, G. (2001). Psychology versus religion. *Journal of Pastoral Counseling*, 36, 21–34.

Frankl, V. (1959). *Man's search for meaning*. Boston, MA: Beacon.

Gladding, S. T. (2011). *The creative arts in counseling* (4th ed.). Alexandria, VA: American Counseling Association.

Hodge, D. R. (2005). Spiritual Lifemaps: A client-centered pictorial instrument for spiritual assessment, planning, and intervention. *Social Work*, 50(1), 77–87. doi:10.1093/sw/50.1.77.

Ingersoll, R. (1998). Refining dimensions of spiritual wellness: A cross-traditional approach. *Counseling and Values*, 42, 156–165. doi:10.1002/j.2161-007X.1998.tb00421.x.

Kaut, K. P. (2002). Religion, spirituality, and existentialism near the end of life. *American Behavioral Scientist*, 46(2), 220–234. doi:10.1177/000276402236675.

Kottler, J. A. (2002). *Theories in counseling and therapy: An experiential approach*. Boston, MA: Allyn and Bacon.

Limb, G. E., and Hodge, D. R. (2007). Developing Spiritual Lifemaps as a culture-centered pictorial instrument for spiritual assessments with Native American clients. *Research on Social Work Practice*, 17(2), 296–304. doi:10.1177/1049731506296161

Limb, G. E., Hodge, D. R., Leckie, R., and Ward, P. (2013). Utilizing spiritual lifemaps with LDS clients: Enhancing cultural competence in social work practice. *Clinical Social Work Journal*, 41(4), 395–405. doi:10.1007/s10615-012-0404-3

MacIntosh, H. B. (2003). Sounds of healing: Music in group work with survivors of sexual abuse. *Art in Psychotherapy*, 30, 17–23. doi:10.1016/S0197–4556(02)00229–0.

Malchiodi, C. A. (2005). Expressive therapies: History, theory, and practice. In C. A. Malchiodi (Ed.). *Expressive therapies* (pp. 1–15). New York, NY: Guilford Press.

Mearns, D., and Cooper, M. (2005). *Working at relational depth in counselling and psychotherapy*. London: Sage.

Murdock, N. L. (2013). *Theories of counseling and psychotherapy* (3rd ed.). Boston, MA: Pearson.

Murray, P. E., and Rotter, J. C. (2002). Creative counseling techniques for family therapists. *The Family Journal: Counseling and Therapy for Couples and Families*, 10(2), 203–206. doi:10.1177/1066480702102010.

Oaklander, V. (2001). Gestalt play therapy. *International Journal of Play Therapy*, 10(2), 45–55. doi:10.1037/h0089479.

Rowan, J. (2013). The transpersonal and relational depth. In R. Knox, D. Murphy, S. Wiggins, and M. Cooper (Eds.), *Relational depth: New perspectives and developments* (pp. 208–216). New York, NY: Palgrave MacMillan.

Schneider, K. (2015). The case for existential (spiritual) psychotherapy. *Journal of Contemporary Psychotherapy*, 45(1), 21–24. doi:10.1007/s10879-014-9278-8.

Schneider, K. J., and Krug, O. T. (2010). *Existential-humanistic therapy*. Washington, DC: American Psychological Association.

Snodgrass, J., and Sorajjakool, S. (2011). Spirituality in older adulthood: Existential meaning, productivity, and life events. *Pastoral Psychology*, 60(1), 85–94. doi:10.1007/s11089-010-0282-y.

Sommers-Flanagan, J., and Sommers-Flanagan, R. (2012). *Counseling and psychotherapy theories in context and practice: Skills, strategies, and techniques* (2nd ed.). Hoboken, NJ: Wiley.

van Deurzen, E. (2012). Reasons for living: Existential therapy and spirituality. In L. Barnett, and G. Madison (Eds.), *Existential therapy: Legacy, vibrancy and dialogue* (pp. 171–182). New York: Routledge.

van Deurzen, E. (2002). *Existential counseling and psychotherapy in practice* (2nd ed.). London: Sage.

Vontress, C. E. (2008). Existential therapy. In J. Frew and M. D. Spiegler (Eds.), *Contemporary psychotherapies for a diverse world* (pp. 141–176). Boston, MA: Lahaska Press.

Walton, P. (2012). Beyond talk and text: An expressive visual arts method for social work education. *Social Work Education*, 31(6), 724–741. doi:10.1080/02615479.2012.695934.

Webb, J. R., Toussaint, L., and Dula, C. S. (2014). Ritualistic, theistic, and existential spirituality: Initial psychometric qualities of the rite measure of spirituality. *Journal of Religion and Health*, 53(4), 972–985. doi:10.1007/s10943-013-9697-y.

Yalom, I. (1980). *Existential Psychotherapy*. New York: Basic Books.

Yalom, I. (2002). *The gift of therapy: An open letter to a new generation of therapists and their patients*. New York, NY: Harper Perennial.

Yalom, I. (2008). *Staring at the sun: Overcoming the terror of death*. San Francisco: Jossey-Bass.

Young, J. S., and Cashwell, C. S. (2011). Integrating spirituality and religion into counseling: An introduction. In C. S. Cashwell and J. S. Young (Eds.), *Integrating spirituality and religion into counseling: A guide to competent practice* (2nd ed.) (pp. 1–24). Alexandria, VA: American Counseling Association.

Young, J. S., Cashwell, C. S., and Woolington, V. J. (1998). The relationship of spirituality to cognitive and moral development and purpose in life: An exploratory investigation. *Counseling & Values*, 43(1), 63–69.

6 Transpersonal Theory and Interventions

Scott L. Lipp, Carman S. Gill, and Ryan D. Foster

"Keep looking at the bandaged place. That's where the light enters you."
—Rumi

Introduction

Human beings have a strong tendency to seek transcendence. Questions such as, "Who am I?" "What else is out there?" and "Is there something more to life?" are essential to people's understanding of self (Smith, 1991). People often search for something more than just the tethered constraint of an ordinary conscience. Spiritual and religious settings are a historical venue for voicing these questions. As counselors became more aware of the search for meaning and transcendence within human experiences, they realized that these questions must be addressed through a theoretical approach based on an idea that everything is spiritual in nature. Therefore, if counselors have clients who are in search of understanding a higher state of being, or who are looking to incorporate their spirit into a collective conscience, then, a transpersonal approach is most certainly indicated.

Transpersonal theory has deep and diverse roots in the tenets of spirituality, philosophy, and psychology. In this chapter, a succinct account of major theorists that contributed to transpersonal theory in counseling and psychology will be afforded. Unique to a transpersonal perspective is that its foundation lies in the notion that transformation of the human spirit is not only possible, but is also part of the restorative process. The main objective of a transpersonal approach to counseling is to promote human growth, development, and to "heal traumas at all levels of development, including transpersonal levels" (Scotton, 1996, p. 4). The development, promotion, and unification of this practice have had numerous proponents over the years. Therefore, what follows is a review and summary of a few of the major and more recent contributors to a transpersonal approach in counseling.

Theoretical Development

Whereas the roots of transpersonal thought date back to the turn of the twentieth century, the origins of transpersonal theory as a distinct discipline stem from the turbulent era of the 1960s. In fact, the term was first used in a 1905 lecture by the prominent American philosopher and psychologist, *William James* (1842–1910; Vich, 1988). James' inquiry into transpersonal-related experiences was informed by many subject areas, including the mystical doctrines of Emanuel Swedenborg, American Transcendentalism, Theosophy, Christian mysticism, Sufism, Buddhism, Vedanta, and Yoga (Taylor, 1996). His investigation was further fueled by his own experiments with the mind-altering gas, nitrous oxide, which led James to conclude that humans possess untapped and unique states of consciousness (Daniels, 2015).

Following James' investigation into "special types of consciousness" (James, 1982), Swiss psychiatrist and psychoanalyst, *Carl Gustav Jung* (1875–1961) began his own journey into the transpersonal realm. After parting ways with Freud, Jung started to realize the potential of spiritual experiences. This was in stark contrast to Freud's view of such experiences, which he considered to be an expression of neurosis (Daniels, 2015). Jung considered spirituality to be a healthy "archetype" (i.e. universal pattern of experience) that occurs within the transpersonal world or what he deemed, the "collective unconscious." According to Jung, the goal of all human life is *individuation*, which can be considered a *psychospiritual* integration of both the psychological and human aspects of an individual (Storr 1991; Daniels, 2015). Furthermore, he regarded the human psyche as having a "transcendent" function, which helps to resolve conflicts from within, leading to the unification of unconscious and conscious matters (Daniels, 2015). According to Daniels (2015), the process of individuation can be fostered through the transcendent function via psychospiritual-transformative work (dream images, symbols, and myths). Ultimately, it is the belief in this transformative process that sparked a new epistemological force in various schools of thought, including the field of counseling.

Abraham Harold Maslow

American psychologist and proponent of health psychology, Maslow is considered to be one of the fathers of humanistic psychology or the *Third Force* in the field. In the early 1960s, a revolt of the reductionist perspective of the then popular Behaviorism, led to the rise of the humanistic movement within the United States (Daniels, 2015). Perhaps best known for his *Hierarchy of Needs*, Maslow's research on the *self-actualization* of the individual emphasized the positive qualities and the full potential of the human spirit (Maslow, 1968). Although Maslow recognized peak experiences as an irregular part of self-actualization, he asserted that "sacred in the ordinary" (Battista, 1996, p. 54), or plateau experiences, were more accurate and commonplace descriptors of self-actualization. A precursor to the now popular Positive Psychology movement, Maslow's work is still clinically relevant and highly applicable in counseling.

The groundbreaking research of Abraham Maslow showed that many individuals reported transcendent experiences, such as peak or ecstatic moments of *self-forgetting* (Daniels, 2015). Maslow considered these transcendent and transformational phenomena to be manifestations of the universal nature of human beings (Daniels, 2005). This interpretation is what, ultimately, lead to the transition from a third to a "Fourth Force" in the field of psychology.

Stanislav Grof

Stanislav Grof was a Czechoslovakian psychiatrist with multiple degrees in medicine, and an interest in the phenomenological effects of different substances. Early in his career, Grof researched the clinical uses of psychedelic substances at the Psychiatric Research Institute in Prague (Grof, 2017). As principal investigator of the program, Grof studied both the experimental and therapeutic possibilities of psychedelic substances ibid.). Most notable of his experimentation with these substances was that of lysergic acid diethylamide (LSD-25), or better known to the general public as "acid." Eventually, he brought his research to the United States, where he continued to pursue his psychedelic research at the prestigious Johns Hopkins University and the Research Unit of Spring Grove Hospital in Baltimore, Maryland ibid.). However, in the midst of growing legal suppression and governmental restrictions, Grof eventually decided to suspend his psychedelic research.

While conducting his LSD-25 research as Assistant Professor of Psychiatry at the Johns Hopkins University, Grof began to develop a theoretical framework, which he called *cartography*. Based on prenatal and perinatal psychology, along with transpersonal psychology, Grof proposed that psychedelic and other intense emotional experiences become mapped onto individual's encounters from early fetal and neonatal development (Rowan, 2005). Ultimately, cartography offers a comprehensive understanding and explanation of the inner dimensions of the human psyche.

Grof continued to develop his theory without the use of psychedelic substances, when in 1973, he discovered the powerful and therapeutic properties of a unique and innovative breathing technique (Cortright, 1997). This experiential psychotherapeutic intervention is known as holotropic breathwork, which was developed and trademarked by Grof and his late wife, Christina Grof. A powerful and transformative technique, Grof continues to hold holotropic breathwork trainings and workshops, while presenting on and promoting the restorative properties of this intervention throughout the world.

Stanley Krippner

Best known for his study and research into "anomalous experiences," American psychology professor and parapsychologist, Stanley Krippner has been associated with transpersonal theory for decades. In fact, he was one of the few voluntary participants in Timothy Leary's infamous psilocybin (psychedelic or "magic" mushrooms) research project at Harvard University in the early 1960s (Krippner, 2006). In the article, *Dancing with the Trickster: Notes from a Transpersonal Autobiography*, Krippner (2002) states "For a few moments, this experience was transpersonal" (p. 4). According to Krippner (2002), transpersonal experiences lead to a feeling of being more connected with reality, in which one's identity is extended beyond the "ordinary limits" of life. This definition of a transpersonal encounter seems to coincide with Krippner's research and personal experience in parapsychology and its related fields.

Krippner's quest into the transpersonal realm has led him to study and engage in various spiritual and cultural practices, including, shamanic traditions and Native American rituals. Throughout this journey, he has encountered and formed relationships with spiritual healers, medicine men, and religious leaders. Krippner has significantly contributed to the literature on altered states of consciousness (ASCs), dissociative states, dream telepathy, hypnosis, Shamanism, and parapsychology. Currently, his focus is mostly devoted to the study of dreams and hypnosis; especially, investigating the spiritual content of dreams (Krippner et al., 2001).

Ken Wilber

Deeply inspired by Eastern philosophy, Combs (2015) stated that Wilber's interest in psychological and spiritual development is due to a direct connection with the transpersonal. Still, Wilber is perhaps best known for the development of his own theory, the well-known, "integral" theory, which incorporates a synthesis of all human knowledge and experience (Rentschler, 2006). Wilber's metatheory is often used in conjunction with his self-designed four-quadrant grid or matrix, which is known as AQAL. The acronym means "all-quadrants, all-levels," which itself is short for "all-quadrants, all-levels, all-lines, all-states, and all-types" at any given period in time and circumstance (Rentschler, 2006). Both the theory and its model encompass various aspects that are directly related to transpersonal thought, as Wilber was highly influenced by transpersonal theory and its epistemology.

Wilber's highly acclaimed books, *The Spectrum of Consciousness* (1977) and *No Boundary: Eastern and Western Approaches to Personal Growth* (1979) were the first two of his many works. According to Combs (2015), as a "spectrum" of knowledge from various disciplines, Wilber's works helped to organize the entire field of Psychology into an integrative, theoretical framework. In fact, in the late 1970s and throughout the 1980s, Wilber's early publications helped to reconstitute the field of transpersonal psychology. As Combs (2015) explained, Wilber took transpersonal psychology from its humble "West Coast" Humanistic beginnings, and made it a more understandable form of psychological thought and practice.

Considered to be a one-time leader in the field of transpersonal studies, Wilber no longer identifies with the movement (Friedman and Hartelius, 2015). Ken Wilber is, without a doubt, considered to be one of the most influential figures and contributors to the evolution of transpersonal theory. Despite his lack of current affiliation with the field, it appears that Ken Wilber's legacy will forever remain an important influence on transpersonal theory.

Transpersonal Theory

Defining the term *transpersonal* and associated thoughts, experiences, and processes can be complex. The word "transpersonal" is sometimes referred to as the "personal plus" (Wilber, 1996, p. xviii). Known as the "fourth force in psychology," Daniels (2005) explained that the term "transpersonal" literally means beyond (or through) the personal. This refers to experiences, processes, and events in which our restricted sense of self is transcended, and there is a feeling of being connected to a larger, more meaningful and experiential reality (Daniels, 2005). Essentially, transpersonal theorists expand boundaries of ordinary psychological constructs and moves beyond and into profound aspects of human existence and experience. Relatedly, Fall, Holden, and Marquis (2010) defined transpersonal experiences as,

spontaneous, usually transient experiences involving perception and/or action that transcends the usual personal limits of space, time, and/or identity yet, paradoxically, are perceived as authentic or potentially authentic by the experiencer with consensus reality testing intact (p. 433).

Holden (2017) indicated that transpersonal experiences can be characterized as "intuitive, paranormal, and transmaterial" (p. 145), referring to a variety of ordinary and extraordinary events. According to Stanley Krippner (2002), transpersonal experiences lead to a more complete encounter with reality and a sense of identity that extends beyond ordinary limits to encompass the, sometimes, ineffable aspects of life. These can range from simple moments of joy and peace (e.g., plateau experiences), to a heightened sense of awareness of the supernatural or divine, to psychedelic or hypnotic states, and even to out-of-body and near-death experiences. In addition, Daniels (2017) stated that transpersonal practices and experiences include the following: spiritual healing, profound psychological transformations, transpersonal psychotherapy, spiritual discipline and training, vision quests, spiritual crises and emergencies, kundalini awakenings, possession, mediumship, and channeling. All of these experiences and processes can occur within both formal and informal settings. These events include religious and magical rituals, raves, religious festivals, along with other collective manifestations of spiritual participation and context (Daniels, 2017). Because all of these experiences cannot be described, ad nauseum, within the current text, more comprehensive discussions of such can be found in the works of Scotton, Chinen, and Battista (1996) as well as, Foster and Holden (2017).

Stanley Krippner (2002), an early proponent of transpersonal psychology and research, discussed how transpersonal and "anomalous" experiences are capable of taking humans to realms that mainstream science has yet to explore. Anomalous, exceptional human and transpersonal experiences can best be described as uncommon or inexplicable episodes (Cardeña et al., 2014). Categorically, there are apparently nine types of such episodes. These include (1) death related, (2) desolation/nadir, (3) dissociative, (4) encounter, (5) exceptional human performance/feats, (6) healing, (7) mystical, (8) peak, and (9) psychical experiences (White, 1997). Unfortunately, a thorough elucidation of all transpersonal experiences is beyond the scope of this chapter. Therefore, an explanation and review of some of the most researched transpersonal experiences will be included in the intervention section.

In an attempt to further define the field, Hartelius, Caplan, and Rardin (2007) conducted a 35-year retrospective analysis of 160 published definitions related to the field of Transpersonal Psychology. Their investigation revealed three themes, which include (1) beyond-ego psychology, (2) integrative/holistic psychology, and (3) psychology of transformation. This theme frequency analysis suggested that alternative states of consciousness (i.e. transpersonal experiences) extend into areas of human transcendence, wholeness, and transformation (Hartelius et al., 2007). Although the researchers attempted to render a perspicuous definition of this often-misunderstood subject area, unfortunately, it is still quite ambiguous to most. As Hartelius and colleagues (2007) so eloquently stated, "[a]rtistic inspiration is best expressed by creating art, rather than by making explanations…in this sense, transpersonal psychology, with its uplifting vision, has had difficulty defining itself" (p. 135).

Transpersonal Counseling

Transpersonal theory delves into aspects beyond the human psyche and helps to integrate individuals with their inner and outer experiences. Richly steeped in Humanistic and analytical approaches, therapy from a transpersonal perspective aims to explore human growth, while helping clients discover a deeper and more enduring self that supersedes or transcends the ego. The belief is that all pain and suffering is a result of, somehow, being disconnected from one's spiritual origins. Therefore, the goal of transpersonal counseling is the transformation and evolution of consciousness by reuniting clients with their "higher self"; ultimately, awakening within them that which has lain dormant (Sharma et al., 2009). Essentially, it takes fundamental psychological tenets and incorporates them into a spiritual framework that is extended both into, and beyond the person.

Theoretically, transpersonal counseling utilizes and combines aspects from traditional psychology, spirituality, and alternative schools of thought. The underlying assumption of the theory is that individuals are more than just the psychological "ego" or "self," and are rather "spiritual" beings (Sperry,

2001). Pulling on both psychological and spiritual traditions, this spiritually based theory creates a new and visionary approach to addressing spirituality and the "spectrum of the human consciousness" within a counseling context. The range of material addressed in this theory includes, (1) prepersonal to personal to transpersonal experiences; (2) instinctual to egoic to spiritual modes; (3) subconscious to self-conscious to superconscious structures; and (4) prerational to rational to transrational states (Wilber, 1996, p. xviii). The spectrum also includes a variety of pathological states (Wilber, 1996), all of which transpersonal psychotherapy and similar methods attempt to fully understand and sensitively treat.

An integrative and holistic approach, transpersonal counseling and psychotherapy involve the utilization of techniques that assist clinicians in addressing the spiritual side of clients' problems or difficulties, both individually and collectively. This technical expertise can be based upon a variety of relevant training, experience, and therapeutic approaches that include Jungian, person-centered, psychosynthesis, Buddhism, existential, holotropic, and integrative therapies (Daniels, 2017). For instance, Grof's technique, called *Holotropic Breathwork*, is derived from the Greek words, *holos* or "whole" and *trepein*, which means "to turn or direct toward a thing"; collectively meaning, "moving toward wholeness" (Mead Training Systems, 1994). A combination of deep breathing exercises, accompanied by evocative music and the assistance of a partner, this unique practice allows individuals to reach "nonordinary states of consciousness" in order to explore, heal, and provide insight into their inner psyche (Grof and Grof, 2010).

Throughout their work, transpersonal counselors attempt to examine states of consciousness and stages of human development that go beyond the bounds of the self, as customarily defined (Krippner, 2015). This is done scientifically, but is not bound by traditional materialist approaches, as the paradigm "integrates the entirety of human activity and experience, from the most pathological to the most sublime" (Tart, 2009; Krippner, 2015, p. xix). In order to fully understand and interpret these experiences, empirically based interventions are sensitively applied within the context of clients' situations. In addition to evidence-based approaches, other epistemological methods can be used to process transpersonal experiences. This includes gathering evidence and information about sensations as they relate to one's body, feelings, and intuition, which can provide further entry into experiential domains that conventional science is unable to understand, yet (Anderson and Braud, 2011). Ultimately, the goal of all transpersonal interventions is to integrate individuals with their experience(s) within the context of their social environment and conscious self.

Spirituality and Transpersonal Theory

Although not all transpersonal experiences are considered spiritual, all spiritual experiences are, in fact, transpersonal. By their very nature, spiritual experiences lead to a higher state of awareness, consciousness, and connection with the greater world. All of which meet the criteria for anomalous, exceptional human, and transpersonal experiences. In the field of mental health counseling, spirituality, according to Helminiak (2005), includes extraordinary experiences, mystical moments, and unusual happenings that are related to religious belief, deity, cosmic forces, and the like. By integrating the complexities of the human spirit and psyche, transpersonal counseling helps to explore and explain this type of "spirituality" in a pragmatic and scientific manner.

In transpersonal theory, spiritual experiences are considered to be the core of epistemology. Outside of a theoretical realm, this is best understood through the goals of transpersonal counseling, where spiritual experiences are not only relevant, but are fundamental. According to Vaughan (1991), "spirituality presupposes certain qualities of mind, including compassion, gratitude, awareness of a transcendent dimension, and an appreciation for life, which brings meaning and purpose to existence" (p. 105). Therefore, the primary purpose of counseling within a transpersonal context is to not only understand these spiritual experiences, but to also unify these subjective experiences within the client's mind, body, and spirit.

Spiritual issues are often intertwined with the topic of mental health (Vaughan, 1991). In fact, one could argue that today, more than ever before, spirituality is gaining traction in a variety of areas within the field of mental health services (Hartelius et al., 2015). However, Hartelius et al. (2015) elicit an important question. Is transpersonal counseling essentially spiritual counseling in the guise of a more unknown and less viable title? If so, this could explain the rise of spirituality in counseling, while transpersonal theory has seemed to wane since its genesis in the 1960s.

By some, transpersonal theory may be considered esoteric, technically abstract, and difficult to operationalize. However, not too long ago, the same was often said of spirituality, especially within the field of mental health. Fortunately, the antipathy toward spirituality has since dissolved, and both the term and its practice are widely accepted throughout the profession (Helminiak, 2005). Unfortunately, the same cannot be said for that of transpersonal theory and its methodology.

Proponents of a transpersonal approach to counseling argue that its future rests on a foundation of evidence-based research and scientific support. As explained by Stanley Krippner (1998), "there is an urgent need in today's fractious world for integrative transpersonal perspectives, especially if presented in ways that are self-critical and able to be linked to contemporary scientific and practical concerns" (pp. x–xi). This statement elucidates the important need for a transpersonal orientation in counseling today. Furthermore, it explicitly declares that the most legitimate and effective avenue for achieving this is through a positivistic course of action. According to Friedman (2002), "[w]ithout a rededication to science, the field is unlikely to progress or earn acceptance by the scientific and professional communities and, accordingly, it is likely to eventually stagnate and disappear" (p. 186). Therefore, the potential for transpersonal counseling, and its future, lies solely in the hands of its community of researchers and practitioners, slated with the task of making a concerted commitment to scientific endeavors.

Interventions

According to Kasprow and Scotton (1999), transpersonal theorists believe in developmental stages that extend beyond the adult ego and involve experiences of "connectedness" with phenomena considered outside the boundaries of the ego. For healthy functioning clients, these experiences can yield myriad benefits. However, for clients lacking healthy ego development, these experiences can mask or be symptomatic of potential psychosis (Kasprow and Scotton, 1999). Therefore, clinicians must be able to discern a positive transpersonal experience from potentially harmful psychotic symptoms, disguised as a transpersonal experience. Essentially, it is this clinical differentiation that is at the heart of all transpersonal counseling and its interventions.

As previously mentioned, the promise of transpersonal counseling depends on a strict adherence to evidence-based research and scientific inquiry. In regard to the research on transpersonal interventions, there are a few well-documented techniques and approaches to addressing the issues surrounding the many themes of spirituality. One such example is the experiential and psychotherapeutic intervention of *holotropic breathwork*. This regimen of deep breathing, in concert with evocative music, has been scientifically proven to induce non-ordinary states of consciousness without the use of substances. The research into these phenomenological states has shown that they have the capability to help individuals discover, recover, and transform their lives (Grof and Grof, 2010). Although there are other techniques and practices in the literature, what follows in this section is not an exhaustive account, but rather a representative list of transpersonal interventions that allow practitioners to competently address spiritual experiences.

Non-ordinary States of Consciousness

Unique to the field of transpersonal counseling is the therapeutic use of both substance-induced and non-substance induced, non-ordinary states of consciousness. In traditional counseling and psychotherapy, transpersonal clinicians tend to employ the latter. Whereas in the field of transpersonal psychiatry, the use of psychopharmacology and psychotropic medication tend to be the preferred course of treatment. Typically, these methods are beyond the scope of conventional counseling, and therefore, will not be discussed in great detail.

Substance-induced States. These states are best explored through the use of various psychedelic therapies under the care of a trained physician, who is qualified to administer and monitor the use of such substances. Generally, transpersonal drug therapy utilizes conventional psychotropic medication, including antidepressants, antipsychotics, mood stabilizers, and sedatives, in order to modulate the symptoms associated with a spiritual emergency, allowing patients to constructively explore the meaning of their experience (Kasprow and Scotton, 1999). The goal of treatment is not necessarily to subdue symptoms, but rather to control them to the extent which allows for individual evaluation and assimilation of the encounter. Other substances that are prescribed in transpersonal psychiatry include the controlled use of psychedelics, or hallucinogenic drugs. According to Roberts and Winkelman (2015), there are four main types of such treatment, as follows: (1) psycholytic, (2) psychedelic, (3) entactogenic, and (4) pharmacological. For the majority of these treatments, the main objective is to make unconscious or repressed memories become conscious or present. Then, the remainder of therapy is devoted to the processing of such revelations, allowing individuals to make sense and meaning of the information.

Non-substance Induced States. Also known as altered states of consciousness (ASCs), these experiences do not require the use of psychedelics or psychotropic medication and can be both highly therapeutic and transformative. Kasprow and Scotton (1999) defined an ASC as a profound alteration in thinking, feeling, and perception that is significantly different from one's typical state of consciousness. Effective transpersonal counseling with clients who leave their typical state of consciousness can be quite transformative, as it has the potential to help them form new and adaptive patterns of thinking, feeling, and behavior. Some of the activities that have been shown to produce ASCs include dancing, fasting, music, prayer, relaxation, and sex (Kasprow and Scotton, 1999). People from across the world in a variety of cultures have engaged in these practices for the purposes of ceremony, healing, ritual, and social activity. Recently, meditation and hypnosis have been given a great deal of attention in the clinical literature, and therefore, these two techniques will be our focus.

Meditation and Meditative States. Walsh and Shapiro (2006) defined meditation as "a family of self-regulation practices that focus on training attention and awareness in order to bring mental processes under greater voluntary control and thereby foster general mental well-being and development and/or specific capacities such as calm, clarity, and concentration" (pp. 228–229). In general, methods or techniques of meditation fall into two standard categories. These include methods that (1) use concentration on an explicit object of either internal or external meditation, and (2) cultivate undirected, receptive awareness or mindfulness (Kasprow and Scotton, 1999). Such mindfulness practices have been adapted and incorporated into transpersonal counseling since its inception (Lukoff and Lu, 2005). Meditation is just one example of a mindfulness-based practice that has become increasingly efficacious in contemporary counseling.

Meditation is now one of the most enduring, widespread, and researched of all therapeutic interventions, due in large part to its numerous therapeutic strengths and benefits (Walsh and Shapiro, 2006). Furthermore, meditation trains self-observation skills, which can be helpful for counselors who are looking to hone their skills in self-reflection and self-awareness (Lukoff and Lu, 2005). The overwhelming amount of physiological research on meditation provides strong indications that it positively contributes to ways in which the body and brain function (MacDonald et al., 2015). Therefore, the overall value of meditation and incorporating such states into clinical practice is endless.

Hypnosis and Hypnotic States. Hypnosis is often seen as a school of techniques that are used to disarm clients and break down their defenses, while integrating the mind and body connection. Regularly, Western society has struggled to understand and utilize this therapeutic phenomenon, and most modern-day citizens remain somewhat skeptical of its practice (Forrest, 1999). Yet, recent hypnotic and ASCs research have proven to be beneficial in the examination of anomalous experiences, parapsychology, and related phenomena (Wickramasekera II, 2015). Therefore, hypnosis and its associated states are worthy of investigation and deserve critical analysis.

There are four primary paradigms of hypnosis, including the following: (1) psychoanalytic, (2) Ericksonian, (3) socio-cognitive, and (4) health/medical approaches (Wickramasekera II, 2015). Of the four models, the Ericksonian approach to hypnosis seems to be most appealing to transpersonal practitioners. The reason being, according to Wickramasekera II (2015), that the Ericksonian tradition better lends itself to the discussion of anomalous experiences. Furthermore, Milton H. Erickson is considered to be one of the leading proponents and instructors of clinical hypnosis (Haley, 1993) and his lasting impact on the hypnosis community is still present in the practice of this intervention.

Recently, the most encouraging results in hypnosis research have occurred in the medical/health tradition to hypnosis. In fact, Covino, Wexler, and Miller (2010) stated that researchers have been able to reliably demonstrate the physiological benefits of hypnosis on the body. Although it still lacks scientific support, it has been known for quite some time now that hypnosis can alleviate pain in clinical contexts (Patterson and Jensen, 2003), remedy various maladies, reduce the utilization of medical services and drugs (Lang and Rosen, 2002), and support abstinence from a wide range of behaviors. It seems that, finally, research is starting to catch up with what hypnotists and those experienced in hypnotic states have known for hundreds of years. As for the future of hypnosis, developments in the areas of neuroscience and neurophenomenology seem to be promising (Wickramasekera II, 2015). These two fields are likely to attract many new researchers who are interested in exploring the exponential utility of transpersonal counseling and hypnosis.

When Clients Report Transpersonal Experiences

Although some clients may be open to transpersonal interventions in counseling, other clients may report a transpersonal experience with confusion, fear, worry, or curiosity. When clients report transpersonal experiences to their counselors, they may question the reality of the experience, their own perspectives, and the impact on their reality (Holden, 2017). All of these questions are ordinary questions regarding an extraordinary experience.

Was It Real?

One response to this question is, did it feel real? This question refers to the subjective nature of the experience. However, this answer is likely not good enough, because hallucinations and dreams can also *feel* real – and are real, from a phenomenological point of view – but clients often seek further validation. Sartori (2004) differentiated transpersonal experiences with experiences, such as hallucinations, and found them to have fundamentally distinguishing characteristics. In addition, the mounting experimental evidence confirming paranormal experiences (Beauregard, 2012; Targ, 2012; Tart, 2009) may provide counselors and clients with a high degree of confidence in both the subjective and objective *realness* of transpersonal experiences.

Am I Abnormal or Crazy?

Individuals may ask themselves, "Am I abnormal or crazy?" The answer, in short, is no, not necessarily. Transpersonal experiences, alone, do not indicate a mental health diagnosis nor psychopathology (Bates and Stanley, 1985; Greyson, 2003; Greyson and Harris, 1987; Lukoff et al., 1992; Noble, 1987; Noyes et al., 2009; Streit-Horn, 2011). However, the notion of *spiritual emergency* (Grof and Grof, 1989) – a condition in which a person experiences overwhelm due to frequency of or difficulty assimilating her or his transpersonal experience – may cause a person psychological dysfunction or disconcerting cognitive or affective reactions. In these cases, reality testing may be indicated. Counselors should attend to assessing the degree and method of client integration of transpersonal experience. A gradual integration tends to result in "kinder, gentler" (Holden, 2017, p. 150) management of this process.

Will I Change as a Result of This Experience?

Most people do change as a result of one or many transpersonal experiences. Changes can be short-term, such as a state of peace, calm, joy, love, or connectedness, as well as long-term. Longer-term changes may include increases or decreases in intrapersonal, interpersonal, spiritual, or religious functioning (Foster et al., 2009). The counselor's role in this process is to simply provide a safe space for clients to talk about their experiences. Some transpersonal experiencers have reported negative or unsupportive reactions from professionals with whom they have discussed their experiences, leading to psychological harm (Foster et al., 2009; Holden et al., 2014). Therefore, counselors should be prepared to provide an open and nonjudgmental space for clients who report these experiences, just as they would for any other client. For a detailed discussion of recommended approaches to client care when they report transpersonal experiences, please refer to Foster et al. (2009) and Holden (2017).

Case Study of Marian

Marian is a 62-year-old, heterosexual, White, cisgender female seeking treatment following a recent diagnosis of stage-three breast cancer, accompanied by ruminative worry, frequent thoughts about death, and panic attacks. The advanced stage of Marian's current condition has prompted her to feel a greater sense of fear regarding the outcomes. Given the circumstances, Marian has begun to evaluate the totality of her life, describing feelings of regret and loss about missed opportunities and mistakes. (For more information on Marian, please reference her client profile in the Introduction.) As her intake document is reviewed, it is noted that she wrote that she experienced "something strange" two weeks ago, but she did not bring it up during her verbal intake with you.

At this point in time, the transpersonal counselor has formulated a partial case conceptualization, and Marian has completed all initial assessments. Before coming to a full case conceptualization, the counselor understands that a discussion about Marian's "strange" experience is important. During the second session with Marian, the counselor asks her about her notation on her intake form. She states that she feels hesitant to share this information. However, she presses on. She states that following her diagnostic visit with her oncologist a few weeks ago, she arrived at home in state of worry. She states that she felt a burning sensation at the base of her spine, and this energy gradually rose up her spinal cord and rested in her head, behind her eyes. She immediately called her oncologist's office, and he stated that this seemed unrelated to her cancer diagnosis. Her experience lasted about half a day, and she has not had a similar experience since her initial one. She states that she feels frightened about the experience and her fear persists. Working from a transpersonal perspective, the counselor immediately recognizes her experience as kundalini, a spontaneous activation of chakra (Scotton, 1996), which can lead to spiritual or transcendent experiences and changes.

Following this discussion with Marian, it becomes clear that she does not present with any psychotic symptoms and does not meet the criteria for a psychotic episode. However, Marian does meet the criteria for an anxiety disorder due to another medical condition (American Psychiatric Association

[APA], 2013). More specifically, she meets the clinical diagnostic criteria for C50.91, malignant neoplasm of breast of unspecified site, female; 293.84 (F06.4) anxiety disorder due to malignant neoplasm of breast of unspecified site, female (APA, 2013). Therefore, there are no contraindications for initiating transpersonal counseling with Marian. Furthermore, treatment with Marian will be handled from a multidisciplinary perspective, in which the counselor is directly collaborating with the other members of her treatment team. This collaboration will ensure both a holistic approach and cooperation across the continuum of care for Marian's clinical treatment.

Currently, this is the third session with Marian, and the one during which transpersonal counseling will be applied to her current struggles with fear and her kundalini experience, regret, and death anxiety, related to her late stage cancer diagnosis. Further attention will be given to Marian's perspectives on faith and spirituality, while being culturally sensitive to her agnostic beliefs. The transpersonal intervention of meditation has been shown to be effective at increasing the immune function of cancer patients (MacDonald et al., 2015) and relieving condition-related stress. This intervention will enable Marian to become integrated with her current situation, through the use of ASCs via a combination of meditation and progressive muscle relaxation (PMR) exercises. These will initially be implemented in this session and will continue throughout Marian's treatment.

In addition, the counselor engages in consultation with a yogic teacher who is experienced and knowledgeable about kundalini. As part of a holistic treatment approach, the counselor becomes a supportive presence for processing psychological components of integration of her kundalini experience, and encouraging her through grounding interventions, such as reality-testing practices. For example, assisting Marian with getting in touch with her body through mindful eating practices or simply engaging in ordinary life tasks, such as cleaning her house and having surface conversations with others, becomes a focus of treatment. The objective here is to encourage Marian to engage with the mundane and to help ground Marian in a here-and-now state.

The intent of the interventions is threefold: (1) relief of Marian's anxiety-related symptoms, (2) integration of Marian's circumstance within her perspectives on faith and spirituality in order to make meaning of her current situation, and (3) assistance with managing her fear surrounding kundalini and potential management of kundalini awakening. Ultimately, the primary (first order) goal of treatment with Marian is to decrease her anxiety and related symptoms (e.g., rumination, obsessions, and panic attacks). Marian's secondary (second order) treatment goals include the following: (1) integration of self with religious and spiritual beliefs and (2) ego-transcendence, paying particular attention to the outcome of any potential of spontaneous transcendent experience related to kundalini awareness and management. The duration of treatment with Marian is expected to be longer term to support a patient, exploratory meaning-making process. If Marian adheres to the prescribed treatment protocol then it is expected that treatment may result in increased mind–body awareness, decreased death anxiety, and successful management of her anxiety symptoms. In line with transpersonal counseling, the counselor may find some difficulty measuring client change from a Western approach based in materialism (Tart, 2009), and would likely find some dependence on subjective, qualitative evidence from Marian's narrative report of her ongoing progress.

References

American Psychiatric Association. (2013). Anxiety disorders. In *Diagnostic and statistical manual of mental disorders* (5th ed.). Arlington, VA: American Psychiatric Publishing.

Anderson, R., and Braud, W. (2011). *Transforming self and others through research: Transpersonal research methods and skills for the human.* Albany, NY: State University of New York Press.

Bates, B. C., and Stanley, A. (1985). The epidemiology and differential diagnosis of near-death experience. *American Journal of Orthopsychiatry*, 55, 542–549. doi:10.1111/j.1939-0025.1985.tb02704.x.

Battista, J. R. (1996). Abraham Maslow and Roberto Assagioli: Pioneers of transpersonal psychology. In B. W. Scotton, A. B. Chinen, and J. R. Battista (Eds.), *Textbook of transpersonal psychiatry and psychology* (pp. 52–61). New York, NY: Basic Books.

Beauregard, M. (2012). *Brain wars: The scientific battle over the existence of the mind and the proof that will change the way we live.* New York, NY: HarperCollins.

Cardeña, E., Lynn, S. J., and Krippner, S. (2014). Introduction: Anomalous experiences in perspective. In E. Cardeña, S. J. Lynn, and S. Krippner (Eds.), *Varieties of anomalous experience: Examining the scientific evidence* (2nd ed., pp. 3–21). Washington, DC: American Psychological Association.

Combs, A. (2015). Transcend and include: Ken Wilber's contribution to transpersonal psychology. In H. L. Friedman and G. Hartelius (Eds.), *The Wiley Blackwell handbook of transpersonal psychology* (pp. 166–186). Malden, MA: Wiley Blackwell.

Cortright, B. (1997). *Psychotherapy and spirit: Theory and practice in transpersonal psychotherapy.* Albany, NY: State University of New York Press.

Covino, N. A., Wexler, J., and Miller, K. (2010). Hypnosis and medicine: In from the margins. In D. Barrett (Ed.), *Hypnosis and hypnotherapy* (Vol. 2, pp. 177–196). Santa Barbara, CA: Praeger.

Daniels, M. (2005). *Shadow, self, spirit: Essays in transpersonal psychology.* Charlottesville, VA: Imprint Academic.

Daniels, M. (2015). Traditional roots, history, and evolution of the transpersonal perspective. In H. L. Friedman and G. Hartelius (Eds.), *The Wiley Blackwell handbook of transpersonal psychology* (pp. 23–43). Malden, MA: Wiley Blackwell.

Daniels, M. (2017). Frequently asked questions about the transpersonal. Retrieved on July 31, 2017 from www.transpersonalscience.org

Fall, K., Holden, J. M., and Marquis, A. (2010). *Theoretical models of counseling and psychotherapy* (2nd ed.). New York, NY: Brunner/Routledge.

Forrest, D. (1999). *Hypnotism: A history.* New York, NY: Penguin Books.

Foster, R. D., and Holden, J. M. (Eds.). (2017). *Connecting soul, spirit, mind, and body: A collection of spiritual and religious perspectives and practices in counseling.*

Denton, TX: Aquiline Books and Alexandria, VA: Association for Spiritual, Ethical, and Religious Values in Counseling.

Foster, R. D., James, D., and Holden, J. M. (2009). Practical applications of near-death experience research. In J. M. Holden, B. Greyson, and D. James (Eds.), *The handbook of near-death experiences: Thirty years of investigation* (pp. 235–258). Santa Barbara, CA: Praeger/ABC-CLIO.

Friedman, H. L. (2002). Transpersonal psychology as a scientific field. *International Journal of Transpersonal Studies*, 21(1), 175–187.

Friedman, H. L., and Hartelius, G. (2015). Editor's introduction: The promise (and some perils) of transpersonal psychology. In H. L. Friedman and G. Hartelius (Eds.), *The Wiley Blackwell handbook of transpersonal psychology* (pp. xxv–xxxiv). Malden, MA: Wiley Blackwell.

Green, J. (2008). *Paper towns*. New York, NY: Dutton Books.

Greyson, B. (2003). Near-death experiences in a psychiatric outpatient clinic population. *Psychiatric Services*, 54(12), 1649–1651.

Greyson, B., and Harris, B. (1987). Clinical approaches to the near-death experiencer. *Journal of Near-Death Studies*, 6, 41–52.

Grof, S. (2008). Brief history of transpersonal psychology. *International Journal of Transpersonal Studies*, 27(1), 46–54.

Grof, S. *Biography*. (2017). Retrieved on July 10, 2017 from http://stanislavgrof. com.

Grof, S., and Grof, C. (Eds.). (1989). *Spiritual emergency: When personal transformation becomes a crisis*. Los Angeles, CA: Jeremy P. Tarcher.

Grof, S., and Grof, C. (2010). *Holotropic breathwork: A new approach to self-exploration and therapy*. Albany, NY: State University of New York Press.

Haley, J. (1993). *Jay Haley on Milton H. Erickson*. New York, NY: Brunner/Mazel.

Hartelius, G., Caplan, M., and Rardin, M. (2007). Transpersonal psychology: Defining the past, divining the future. *The Humanistic Psychologist*, 35(2), 135–160.

Hartelius, G., Friedman, H. L., and Pappas, J. D. (2015). The calling to a spiritual psychology. In H. L. Friedman and G. Hartelius (Eds.), *The Wiley Blackwell handbook of transpersonal psychology* (pp. 44–61). Malden, MA: Wiley Blackwell.

Helminiak, D. A. (2005). A down-to-earth approach to the psychology of spirituality a century after James's Varieties. *The Humanistic Psychologist*, 33(2), 69–86.

Holden, J. M. (2017). Transpersonal experiences: Responding therapeutically. In R. D. Foster and J. M. Holden (Eds.), *Connecting soul, spirit, mind, and body: A collection of spiritual and religious perspectives and practices in counseling* (pp. 145–153). Denton, TX: Aquiline Books and Alexandria, VA: Association for Spiritual, Ethical, and Religious Values in Counseling.

Holden, J. M., Kinsey, L., and Moore, T. R. (2014). Disclosing near-death experiences to professional healthcare providers and non-professionals. *Spirituality in Clinical Practice*, 1(4), 278–287. doi:10.1037/scp0000039.

Jalāl, D. R. (1995). *The essential Rumi* (C. Barks, Trans.). New York, NY: Harper Collins.

James, W. (1902/1982). *The varieties of religious experience: A study in human nature*. New York, NY: Penguin Group.

Jung, C. G. (1912/2003). *Psychology of the unconscious* (B. M. Hinkle, Trans.). Mineola, NY: Dover Publications.

Kasprow, M. C., and Scotton, B. W. (1999). A review of transpersonal theory and its application to the practice of psychotherapy. *The Journal of Psychotherapy Practice and Research*, 8(1), 12–23.

Krippner, S. (1998). Foreword. In D. Rothberg and S. Kelly (Eds.), *Ken Wilber in dialogue: Conversations with leading transpersonal thinkers* (pp. ix–xi). Wheaton, IL: Theosophical Publishing House.

Krippner, S., Jaeger, C., and Faith, L. (2001). Identifying and utilizing spiritual content in dream reports. *Dreaming*, 11(3), 127–147.

Krippner, S. (2002). Dancing with the trickster: Notes for a transpersonal autobiography. *International Journal of Transpersonal Studies*, 21(1), 1–18.

Krippner, S. (2006, June). The psychedelic adventures of Alan Watts. Paper presented at the Residential Colloquium, Saybrook Graduate School, San Francisco, CA. Retrieved on August 2, 2017 from http://stanleykrippner.weebly.com.

Krippner, S. (2015). Foreword. In H. L. Friedman and G. Hartelius (Eds.), *The Wiley Blackwell handbook of transpersonal psychology* (pp. xix–xxi). Malden, MA: Wiley Blackwell.

Lang, E. V., and Rosen, M. P. (2002). Cost analysis of adjunct hypnosis with sedation during outpatient interventional radiologic procedures. *Radiology*, 222(2), 375–382. Retrieved on October 5, 2017 from http://dx.doi.org/10.1148/radiol.2222010528

Lukoff, D., and Lu, F. (2005). A transpersonal-integrative approach to spirituality oriented psychotherapy. In L. Sperry and E. P. Shafranske (Eds.), *Spiritually oriented psychotherapy* (pp. 177–205). Washington, DC: American Psychological Association.

Lukoff, D., Lu, F., and Turner, R. (1992). Toward a more culturally sensitive DSM-IV: Psychoreligious and psychospiritual problems. *Journal of Nervous and Mental Disease*, 180(11), 673–682.

MacDonald, D. A., Walsh, R., and Shapiro, S. L. (2015). Meditation: Empirical research and future directions. In H. L. Friedman and G. Hartelius (Eds.), *The Wiley Blackwell handbook of transpersonal psychology* (pp. 433–458). Malden, MA: Wiley Blackwell.

Maslow, A. H. (1962/1968). *Toward a psychology of being* (2nd ed.). Princeton, NJ: Van Nostrand.

Mead Training Systems. (1994). *Holotropic breathwork: A conversation with Christina and Stanislav Grof, MD* [Video file]. Retrieved on July 17, 2017 from https://www.youtube.com/watch?v=LHaeH5MvdWg.

Noble, K. D. (1987). Psychological health and the experience of transcendence. *Counseling Psychologist*, 15(4), 601–614.

Noyes, R., Fenwick, P., Holden, J. M., and Christian, R. (2009). Aftereffects of pleasurable Western adult near-death experiences. In J. M. Holden, B. Greyson, and D. James (Eds.), *The handbook of near-death experiences: Thirty years of investigation* (pp. 41–62). Santa Barbara, CA: Praeger/ABC-CLIO.

Patterson, D. R., and Jensen, M. P. (2003). Hypnosis and clinical pain. *Psychological Bulletin*, 129(4), 495–521. Retrieved on October 3, 2017 from http://dx.doi.org/10.1037/0033-2909.129.4.495.

Rentschler, M. (2006). AQAL Glossary. *AQAL: Journal of Integral Theory and Practice*, 1(3), 1–39.

Roberts, T. B., and Winkelman, M. J. (2015). Psychedelic induced transpersonal experiences, therapies, and their implications for transpersonal psychology. In H. L. Friedman and G. Hartelius (Eds.), *The Wiley Blackwell handbook of transpersonal psychology* (pp. 459–479). Malden, MA: Wiley Blackwell.

Rowan, J. (2005). *The transpersonal: Spirituality in psychotherapy and counselling* (2nd ed.). New York, NY: Routledge.

Sartori, P. (2004). A prospective study of NDEs in an intensive therapy unit. *Christian Parapsychologist*, 16(2), 34–40.

Sharma, P., Charak, R., and Sharma, V. (2009). Contemporary perspectives on spirituality and mental health. *Indian Journal of Psychological Medicine*, 31(1), 16–23. Retrieved on July 19, 2017 from http://dx.doi.org/10.4103/0253-7176.53310.

Scotton, B. W. (1996). Introduction and definition of transpersonal psychiatry. In B. W. Scotton, A. B. Chinen, and J. R. Battista (Eds.), *Textbook of transpersonal psychiatry and psychology* (pp. 3–8). New York, NY: Basic Books.

Scotton, B. W. (1996). The phenomenology and treatment of kundalini. In B. W. Scotton, A. B. Chinen, and J. R. Battista (Eds.), *Textbook of transpersonal psychiatry and psychology* (pp. 261–270). New York, NY: Basic Books.

Scotton, B. W., Chinen, A. B., and Battista, J. R. (Eds.). (1996). *Textbook of transpersonal psychiatry and psychology*. New York, NY: Basic Books.

Smith, H. (1991). *The world's religions*. New York, NY: HarperCollins.

Sperry, L. (2001). *Spirituality in clinical practice: Incorporating the spiritual dimension in psychotherapy and counseling*. Philadelphia, PA: Brunner-Routledge.

Storr, A. (1991). *Jung*. New York, NY: Routledge.

Streit-Horn, J. (2011). *A systematic review of research on after-death communication (ADC)* (Unpublished doctoral dissertation). University of North Texas, Denton, TX.

Targ, R. (2012). *The reality of ESP: A physicist's proof of psychic abilities*. Wheaton, IL: Quest Books.

Tart, C. T. (2009). *The end of materialism: How evidence of the paranormal is bringing science and spirit together*. Oakland, CA: New Harbinger.

Taylor, E. (1996). *William James on the consciousness beyond the margin*. Princeton, NJ: Princeton University Press.

Vaughan, F. (1991). Spiritual issues in psychotherapy. *Journal of Transpersonal Psychology*, 23(2), 105–119.

Vich, M. A. (1988). Some historical sources of the term "transpersonal". *Journal of Transpersonal Psychology*, 20(2), 107–110.

Walsh, R., and Shapiro, S. L. (2006). The meeting of meditative disciplines and Western psychology: A mutually enriching dialogue. *American Psychologist*, 61(3), 227–239. Retrieved on October 2, 2017 from http://dx.doi.org/10.1037/0003-066X.61.3.227.

Walsh, R., and Vaughan, F. (1996). The worldview of Ken Wilber. In B. W. Scotton, A. B. Chinen, and J. R. Battista (Eds.), *Textbook of transpersonal psychiatry and psychology* (pp. 62–74). New York, NY: Basic Books.

White, R. A. (1997). Dissociation, narrative, and exceptional human experiences. In S. Krippner and S. M. Powers (Eds.), *Broken images broken selves: Dissociative narratives in clinical practice* (pp. 88–121). Washington, DC: Brunner/Mazel.

Wickramasekera II, I. E. (2015). Hypnosis and transpersonal psychology. In H. L. Friedman and G. Hartelius (Eds.), *The Wiley Blackwell handbook of transpersonal psychology* (pp. 492–511). Malden, MA: Wiley Blackwell.

Wilber, K. (1977). *The spectrum of consciousness*. Wheaton, IL: Quest Books.

Wilber, K. (1979). *No boundary: Eastern and Western approaches to personal growth*. Los Angeles, CA: Center Publications.

Wilber, K. (1996). Foreword. In B. W. Scotton, A. B. Chinen, and J. R. Battista, *Textbook of transpersonal psychiatry and psychology* (pp. xvii–xx). New York, NY: Basic Books.

7 Adler's Individual Psychology and Spirituality

Robert R. Freund, Andrew Z. Baker, and Paul R. Peluso

"Correction does much, but encouragement does more."

—Von Goethe

Introduction

The theory of Individual Psychology is one of the oldest among the helping professions. When he first founded the theory, Alfred Adler termed it "individual" in reference to the *holistic* nature of humans, though a more appropriate translation from the original German may be "indivisible" psychology." Adlerian theory is fundamentally holistic in nature; no individual person can be understood by fragmenting aspects of his or her existence and making generalizations (Peluso, 2006; Sweeney, 2009). A contemporary of Freud, Adler was similarly interested in the psychodynamic processes of human functioning, but rejected Freud's tenets of sexual drive and death instinct as the core elements of human behavior (Dinkmeyer et al., 1987). As a result, his theory is unique from Freud's (and even some modern theories). Adlerian theory (used interchangeably with individual psychology) is at its core oriented to the "psychology of use," in human behavior; that is, that all behavior is purposeful and goal directed (Carlson et al., 2006). By examining the larger systems of an individual's development, relationships, and functioning, we are able to derive the usefulness of seemingly 'irrational' behavior or beliefs. Lastly, Adler's theory views human functioning from a perspective of wellness, rather than pathology (Sweeney, 2009). This is profoundly humanistic in nature, allowing counselors to reframe problem behaviors as attempted solutions, and to recognize that connection, belonging, and thriving are natural orientations of human drives (Carlson et al., 2006).

Adler believed that because we live and function in a community, and because humans are fundamentally social creatures, the level of commitment to the betterment of others, the willingness to behave prosocially, and the flexibility one has in adapting to the needs of the environment, serve as a measure of psychological health. As a result, Adlerian therapy focuses on increasing a sense of community feeling and/or social interest (known as *Gemeinschaftsgefühl* in the original language), and decreasing perceptions of personal inferiority (Dinkmeyer et al., 1987). Rigid, self-interested, or isolating behavior, leads to psychological dysfunction or relational difficulty (Carlson et al., 2006). At the same time, Gemeinschaftsgefühl is not an orientation toward others that is unbounded or dismissive of one's personal needs. Rather, it is a form of social interdependence, where the needs of the individual are addressed and met in a reciprocal relationship with the community. In fact, a healthy level of community feeling would be more likely to prompt well-enforced boundaries between the self and society, and a level of assertiveness that is neither aggressive nor inappropriately deferential (Dinkmeyer et al., 1987; Carlson et al., 2006).

While social interest (or at least the capacity for it) is considered to be inherent in human beings, it must be encouraged by the family-of-origin, or the environment of the individual. At the same time, the child also develops a sense of their agency in life, or lack thereof, which contributes to *inferiority feelings*. Adler proposed that much of life is spent attempting to compensate for these feelings of inferiority that develop, much like community feeling, in childhood through significant relationships or experiences (Carlson et al., 2006). The drive for *superiority* (or, overcoming these inferiority feelings) shapes humans' perspective on self, others, and the world. In this theory, the term *superiority* is used in the sense of feeling self-confidence, self-efficacy, and the like, rather than self-aggrandizement as it may be used colloquially. Even though these feelings of superiority are built off of the subjective beliefs and conclusions of the client's developmental history, and as such are unattainable, they serve as a guidepost for his or her efforts in life.

The cognitive processes and self-talk that perpetuate these perspectives are not necessarily grounded in reality, forming a *private logic* that often sheds light on the utility behind maladaptive behaviors (Dinkmeyer et al., 1987; Carlson et al., 2006). In this regard, Adlerian theory is profoundly post-modernistic in that it speaks to the subjective individual experience of events, and the way that we derive unique meaning from them. These perspectives and meaning, also known as lifestyle convictions, form a constellation of beliefs that structure our unique experience and orientation to life. Generally speaking, lifestyle convictions speak to what Adler considered an existentially universal drive for meaning making and fulfillment. The behaviors that result from these convictions are known as the *style of life* (Peluso, 2006).

Lifestyle convictions and style of life are aimed at fulfilling five universal tasks that everyone must face. Adler proposed that these tasks serve as valuable domains for both assessment and intervention. The *friendships task* involves our connection with others, and the ability to maintain meaningful relationships with others in our community. Successfully navigating this task requires us to overcome isolation and forge connection, belonging, and acceptance with peers, groups, and other individuals (Ansbacher and Ansbacher, 1964; Carlson et al., 2006). The *work task* is met when we find fulfillment and satisfaction in careers and workplace contributions. The *love task* involves romantic partnership, intimacy, attachment, and procreation. It requires us to work toward being comfortable with our own sexuality, to have intimacy with others, and to have un-conflicted perception of our own or others' gender. In later years, Mosak and Dreikurs (1973) proposed additional life tasks that they considered to have been suggested, but not explicitly stated, in Adler's earlier writings. The *self task* requires us to learn to be self-accepting, to develop a healthy sense of agency, and to experience appropriate levels of esteem and efficacy (Sweeney, 2009). The second addition to the life tasks, the *spirituality task*, involves questions of purpose, existential concerns, and the metaphysical considerations of living, which will be elaborated on in the next segment of this chapter.

Adlerian treatment is generally divided into four phases (*establishing the relationship, assessment, insight,* and *reorientation*) that are tailored to the needs and characteristics of each client, couple, or family. Because Adlerian theory is fundamentally a theory of relationships (e.g. of behaviors to goals, between individuals, between groups of family members), the counseling process also revolves around this concept. Effective Adlerian therapy (or any therapy) cannot develop without a strong therapeutic alliance between the counselor and client. Continuing in this theme, the first stage of therapy is devoted to *establishing a relationship* with the client (Carlson et al., 2006; Sweeney, 2009).

Bordin's (1979) conceptualization of the therapeutic alliance is useful in breaking down this phase of treatment. The counselor and client must, first, establish a therapeutic bond. This is comprised of the interpersonal feelings of positive regard, respect, and trust that are the building blocks of any relationship, professional or otherwise. Counselors use empathy, warmth, and egalitarianism (among other skills,) to foster this bond in a very deliberate way. Though somewhat simplistic, this is a foundational part of the alliance (Ackerman and Hilsenroth, 2003). Without it, the two remaining elements cannot be effectively established. The second component of the alliance, mutual goal setting, helps counselors to ensure they are working in alignment with clients while also promoting shared ownership of the process. The last element of the alliance relates to how those goals are to be reached. Together, the counselor and client determine what kinds of therapeutic tasks are best in service of the client's dispositions, resources, and motivation. When the therapeutic bond, goals, and tasks are balanced in the initial phase of therapy, a productive relationship can be established (Carlson et al., 2006).

Once a strong therapeutic connection is established, counselors move into the *assessment phase* of counseling. Establishing the relationship and assessment can happen concurrently, or a therapist may move back and forth between connection and assessment (Carlson et al., 2006). The counselor brings an intense, targeted curiosity to the relationship, and scaffolds the client's investigative reflection of the problems they are seeking to address. This curiosity and interest serves as the foundation for empathy, and empathy further stimulates curiosity (Carlson et al., 2006; Sweeney, 2009). During this time, the counselor will use a variety of strategies to assess the client's style of life and family constellation. Clients discuss their family structure and dynamics between members; how an individual related to each person provides important information about how they approach life tasks (Dinkmeyer et al., 1987).

Adlerian counselors focus on helping clients to understand how all of their behavior is goal directed and purposeful, even if this is a subconscious process. The counselor consistently reminds clients that, though at times self-defeating, all behaviors are intended to address perceived inferiorities and promote a felt superiority (Carlson et al., 2006). In the *insight phase* of treatment, the client's behaviors are directly tied to the beliefs and private logic that stem from the client's lifestyle dynamics. The implicit nature of their functioning is made explicit, with the goal of helping clients to develop insight into the processes that fuel their behavior (Eckstein and Baruth, 1996). With this awareness, clients develop a new level of autonomy in being able to choose new ways of being. This can only happen when the clients experience a shift in how they understand their own thinking and experiences, which might promote style of life change.

Provided that clients are able to develop an explicit awareness of their thought processes, the psychodynamic influences that inform them, and the purpose of their behavior, he or she can then begin to set goals that are more adaptive and purposeful. This prepares clients for the *reorientation phase* of Adlerian therapy, which focuses on challenging maladaptive lifestyle convictions or faulty private logic (Carlson et al., 2006). At this point in the relationship, authentic trust and empathy has been established which allows for an increased level of transparency and sincerity. These challenges can be framed in many diverse interventions that will be discussed later. This stage cannot be effective without a strong relationship, solid assessment, and shared understanding of the style of life pattern. It is important to note these stages are not completely linear though, and it is possible for an experienced Adlerian therapist to move through these stages multiple times per session or to be in multiple stages simultaneously.

Spirituality and Adlerian Theory

As mentioned previously, the spirituality life task of was not initially included in Adler's theory of Individual Psychology. This construct was explicitly added to the theory by Mosak and Dreikurs in later writings despite the fact that themes of spirituality are deeply rooted in the philosophy of the theory since Adler's original writings (Cheston, 2000; Polanski, 2002). While psychoanalytic traditions rejected the significance and value of spirituality and religiosity, Adler embraced a holistic view of human growth and development, with meaning-making and teleological behavior as core elements of the human experience (Adler, 1943; Cheston, 2000). In fact, Adler viewed the Divine as a socially constructed model for living, describing the idea of God as, "… eternally complete, who directs the stars, who is the master of fates, who elevates man from his lowliness to Himself, who speaks from the cosmos to every single human soul, [and] is the most brilliant manifestation of the goal of perfection" (Walborn, 2014, p. 67). For Adler, the Divine, rather than being a reality, represented an ideal for living that ultimately helps individuals to foster social interest (Cheston, 2000; Walborn, 2014). The practices of self-reflection and deliberate pursuit of spiritual ideals are common to many world religions, and are consistent with the process for developing awareness of one's lifestyle dynamics (how they view themselves, others, and the world). In this way, religious and spiritual practice can be very helpful in moving individuals toward healthy awareness and growth. In the Adlerian tradition, spirituality serves as a means for organizing and expressing one's values, morals, and beliefs. This allows individuals to operate out of a sense of congruence and to put social interest into action (Eckstein and Baruth, 1996; Carlson et al., 2006).

Spirituality as a life task then represents a significant personal process for addressing and clarifying the meaning and purpose behind one's existence. The expression of spirituality and definition of existential meaning is then worked out through the holistic nature of all five life tasks. Counselors can implement this into practice by looking for opportunities to address spirituality within each of the other life tasks. Spiritual convictions and the private logic behind these processes are rooted in the early experiences of childhood, and as such, this provides an important area for exploration and reorientation.

Interventions

The Question

The question is simply asking your client what their life would be like without the symptoms or presenting concerns (Dinkmeyer et al., 1987). This can be phrased in a variety of ways depending on what you deem most appropriate (e.g. "Supposing you woke up tomorrow and the problem was gone... what would be different?" versus "Imagine I had a magic wand that would make this problem go away... what would be different?" etc.). It is predicated on the understanding that clients are often unaware of their ideal life. They may be able to articulate what they would like to have absent (e.g. "I don't want to feel sad anymore") but struggle to describe what could take the place of the problem or symptom (Carlson et al., 2006). There is a version of this intervention called "the miracle question" in Solution-Focused Brief Therapy (de Shazer and Dolan, 2007). Generally speaking, the client's response may indicate primarily psychological origins, somatic origins, or a combination of the two (Dinkmeyer et al., 1987). This provides useful information for treatment; it sheds light on the secondary gain of the problem, as well as encouragement for the client to see his or her life from an alternate, more positive perspective. It is a critical part of the assessment phase and provides excellent information for task-setting.

Early Recollections

Early recollections are a projective technique for assessing style of life patterns, and are a fundamental assessment tool in Individual Psychology. The childhood memories that individuals recall are selective; they reflect the beliefs, felt inferiorities, and lifestyle convictions of their current approach to life (Dinkmeyer et al., 1987). Individual approaches vary, however there are specific elements that counselors structure when conducting this assessment. Counselors should gather a minimum of three memories, though as many as can be remembered (10, maximum) are considered ideal for establishing patterns of movement (Eckstein and Baruth, 1996). Encourage clients to focus on episodic, personally experienced memories, rather than family stories or repeated rituals (e.g. "On Christmas we'd always...") These memories should come from when the individual was around six years old or younger. Valuable information to gather from these memories include: the individuals present, salient feelings and images, major actions and movements, and the most intense aspects of the memories (Carlson et al., 2006). Some counselors may also gather somatic feelings, title the memories, or other nuances (like recalling in the present tense, etc.) that elicit more descriptive information (Microtraining Associates, 2004). Processing the themes present across the memories can help clients and their counselors to better understand style of life dynamics. Given the nuanced nature of processing early recollections, we recommend that interested readers pursue further instruction on this intervention from one of the included resources for further reading.

Spitting in the Soup

Adler used to ask the following: *Imagine going to dinner with a friend. You are eating a nice, hot bowl of your favorite soup, and enjoying the time together. Suddenly, your friend leans over, slowly spits into your soup and says warmly, "Go on, keep eating."* Would you finish your soup? You could, but it won't taste as good. The same effect can be achieved using this paradoxical strategy with client symptoms. Many times, individuals continue in counter-productive or unhealthy behaviors without understanding the goal or utility of them. You must have a clear perspective on what the symptoms are providing your client (the secondary gains). More than this, you must also understand how these benefits fit the client's larger pattern and lifestyle dynamics. Once this is clear, explain the behaviors in this light (you might even compliment them for their ingenuity and skill!). You may then leave them with their "soup," or even encourage them to "keep eating." The client might continue in the behavior, but if this strategy is done effectively, the benefits of the symptoms may not "taste" as good. Clients' new awareness helps them to detangle the problems, benefits, and patterns and become free to explore other alternatives (Dinkmeyer et al., 1987; Carlson et al., 2006).

Push Button Technique

This intervention is used to help clients change the relationship of influence between themselves and their emotions. Oftentimes, individuals can begin to feel "stuck" in an emotion, and have the mistaken perception that the feeling or mood is in control of their experience. Using the push button technique, counselors can help clients to explore their autonomy and influence over his or her emotional and cognitive state. Invite your client to close their eyes and think of a time when they felt a strong positive emotion, focusing on mentally recreating the imagery accompanying this memory. The client then observes the feelings and thoughts that arise with this memory. When this is completed, invite the client to continue with closed eyes and think of a time when they felt a strong negative emotion, again observing the thoughts and feelings that emerge. Explore the contrast in experiences, and once again invite the client to think of another memory associated with positive emotions. In doing this, the client can explore the amount of control he or she has on their felt experience; that the emotions *don't* control them and in fact become strengthened by the erroneous belief that emotions simply *happen*, rather than serve a purpose (Dinkmeyer et al., 1987; Carlson et al., 2006). Practicing this exercise during the week between sessions can be an additional way for clients to explore the relationship between awareness, intention, and emotions.

Acting As If

An important element of an Adlerian counselor's work is encouragement. As clients become discouraged due to private logic and self-confirming experiences, it can be difficult for them to perceive another way of being or engaging with the world. The "acting as if," technique is one way of bypassing some of the initial resistance that arises when someone is attempting to think or behave outside of her or his entrenched patterns. This technique is useful when dealing with a specific behavior or relationship the client would like to change. As you discuss the situation with your client, invite them to identify someone who possesses the ideal qualities for dealing with that problem. Ask your client to explore how this individual (real or fictitious) might respond to the challenge at hand; what would their orientation to the problem be, and how would they be acting? Once you have processed this with your client, ask them to insert themselves into that identity and play out the situation "acting as if" they were that person. The client can then be encouraged to "act as if" they are that individual the next time they are confronted with the situation in real life (Carlson et al., 2006; Sweeney, 2009). Watts (2003) developed a modified version of this intervention called *Reflecting As If* that involves adopting the mindset and perspective of different individuals. Through scaffolding of thinking and behaving, clients can take manageable steps toward behavioral change (Watts et al., 2005).

Encouragement

Encouragement is supporting the client through identifying and/or reflecting their unique strengths, successes, efforts, and actions. It can be considered both an intervention and a therapeutic stance while practicing Individual Psychology. Through creative application of encouragement strategies, clients begin to understand alternative ways of approaching the life tasks. This intervention centers on increasing fulfilment of the life tasks, as well as community feeling and social interest. Encouragement is not false compliments or platitudes. Encouragement is not praise. Rather, it is a process of helping clients to foster an internal sense of empowerment and capability (Carlson et al., 2006).

Reorientation

The concept of reorientation, originating in Adlerian practice, is today ubiquitous to many counseling orientations. Many other approaches use this tried-and-tested intervention, but it is worth mentioning here. Also known as reframing, reorientation involves a re-interpretation of client's perspectives and behaviors. Because clients view circumstances within the framework of their private logic, maladaptive actions become reinforced (Dinkmeyer et al., 1987). The Adlerian therapist offers the client the same circumstances, but within the framework of an adaptive, purposive perspective (Carlson et al., 2006). For example, rather than the depression acting as an external 'black dog' that haunts the client, the counselor presents the symptoms as an elegant solution to a perceived problem. By being depressed, the client is able to elicit care from others while also minimizing their expectations for reciprocation. In this, the client can find belonging without confronting his or her fear of not being able to measure up to other's expectations. This reframe returns the agency to the client, and highlights two things: 1) the adaptive (and therefore destigmatized) nature of the behavior, and 2) the client's private logic.

Case Study

Engaging the Relationship

The present case study involves work with Cecily, a 42-year-old, Christian, African American woman struggling with depression; please see the Introduction for a description of her presenting problem. Cecily was wary of working with a secular counselor, but she states that she trusts her pastor, who had made the referral. She had evaluated the counselor's credentials, prior training program, and some publications before accepting his recommendation as well. It suggests that she is comfortable with being self-reliant and autonomous; though others could influence her, she will be making the final decisions. This is a likely predictor of how the therapy will progress, if successful.

The first several sessions are devoted to connecting with Cecily, and developing a sense of trust that serves as a foundation for the counseling work. During this time, she discusses her feelings of depression, hopelessness, and the interpersonal events surrounding this within her church; her "presenting problems." It is apparent that faith, community, and family are closely intertwined in her life. Cecily acknowledges that the devotion to her faith is due in large part to her family. "We've been settled in this town for five generations. My great, great grandfather was one of the founders of the church where I worship today." Her sad and drooping eyes flash with some pride as she says this.

After observing that faith and community seemed closely intertwined, Cecily corrects the counselor's language; "Not community; *fellowship.* There's a big difference between a group of people that get together every now and then and a *family.*" Cecily feels a sense of intimacy with her church family that comes from a shared ownership of the church itself (and by extension therefore, her faith). The counselor wonders if faith/family were factors in precipitating the feelings and beliefs that brought her to counseling. The guilt and feelings of letting God down may be a displacement of a family/church family dynamics process. What might Cecily be feeling guilty about? *How* exactly might she have let God down? This is something to pursue in the assessment phase of the therapy, once the relationship is established, so it is noted for later discussion.

During this phase of counseling, it is important that Cecily feels understood, validated, and respected. The counselor is careful to communicate empathy for her problems, as well as the significance of her spiritual relationships and struggles; rather than challenging or confronting her, it is important to ensure that the counselor understands what it is like to experience the world from her perspective. Using reflections and clarifying questions are invaluable resources in this process. The effectiveness of this shows in how Cecily warms over the sessions, taking on a more relaxed posture, showing greater affective variation, and offering more elaborative responses to questions. Merely the process of connection in the therapeutic relationship seems to alleviate some of her depressive experience, if only for the moment. This also provides useful information about the purpose Cecily's depression may be serving (an important consideration for an Adlerian counselor).

Following this relationship work is an exploration of the goals Cecily would like to work toward, and how we should do this. Her first and most pressing concern is to resolve her feelings of depression. "Not being depressed," is an ambiguous goal, so we spend time clarifying and reframing this goal. The Question is helpful in initiating this process. "Cecily, suppose that you went bed tonight and experienced a miracle. The depression is simply taken away. When you woke up the next day, how would you know this miracle had taken place? What would you notice is different about your life as you go through your day?" As a result, Cecily's desire to "not be depressed" becomes reinterpreted to include developing higher levels of emotional resiliency in relationships, being able to experience feelings of sadness or negativity without being overwhelmed, and to develop more frequent feelings of hope and inner peace. In addition to these emotional goals, Cecily expresses a desire to understand the causes and emergence of her feelings of depression. "If I know how it got here," she says, "I may be able to prevent it coming back." Lastly, Cecily states that she wants to feel a sense of connection with God once again. This is her chief goal, and she even shares that she could tolerate feeling depressed indefinitely if it meant that she could regain that sense of spiritual intimacy. This is difficult for her to articulate, and she relies heavily on descriptions of felt connection that is consistent with a Synthetic-Conventional phase of spiritual development (see Chapter 3 for Fowler's [1981] stages of faith).

In order to reach these goals, we agree that it would be useful to develop a greater awareness of her approach to life and the events that shaped this. An additional task will be to build awareness of her emotional experience and explore opportunities for modifying it. Lastly, Cecily agrees that it would be useful to bring each of these discussions throughout the therapy back to her understanding of her relationship with God, in order to clarify and better assess or grow that sense of felt connection.

Assessment

Several things are critical in understanding Cecily's depression and sense of spiritual disconnection. Adlerian clinicians believe that all behavior is purposive; it serves some purpose for the individual that may not always be healthy, but is intended to be adaptive. This means that Cecily's depression is (perhaps indirectly) an attempted solution to a perceived problem or inferiority. She lacks the sense of encouragement and capability to handle whatever this may be. It is possible that it helps her to meet or avoid complications in one or more of the life tasks. On face value, the depression helps Cecily to avoid addressing spiritual concerns; it gives her something to focus on that would be more manageable than the existential issues of spirituality. It is also possible that both issues help her to deal with problems related to her community. In order to assess this, we engage in a lifestyle assessment, evaluating her functioning in the five life tasks, exploring her past and current family dynamics, and early recollections.

Cecily shares that she is functioning well in her work; she is a lab manager for a university microbiology lab, and finds this to be stimulating, engaging, and fulfilling (the work task). She is married to a man who is a successful financial manager, and she states that they have a well-grounded, happy marriage. Her frequent tearfulness and low mood have negatively affected their intimacy of late, as she is disinterested in many of their shared activities, including sex. She describes them as "equal partners in life," and that this is very important to her, particularly since they have two high school–aged children (the love task). Cecily casually mentions that her relationship and work were somewhat counter to the culture of her church, which favors more traditional gender and marital roles. Other relationships are professional and limited in intimacy; she tends to be friendly with all at her work, but does not often engage with them beyond that environment. She shares that she is more likely to spend social time with people from church, but does not often share a sense of intimacy with them either (the friendship task). Cecily states that she likes herself, but often feels conflicted about the split between herself as a religious person, and some of her personal views that differ from the church (the self task). Lastly, Cecily discusses again the feelings of guilt and shame that pervade her sense of relationship with God. She talks of her need for more faith, of greater trust in God's will for her life, and that she wants to feel a greater sense of spiritual belonging (the spiritual task).

In exploring her family of origin dynamics, Cecily shares that she is the middle of three children. Her father was a pastor of the church where she currently worshipped, while her mother was a homemaker and the church organist. Her eldest brother (by three years) followed in the footsteps of her father, and became a pastor of a church on the west coast. Her younger brother (by two years) became a teacher. Service to the community, faith, and moral uprightness were strongly held values for her family, and Cecily recounts many times when her parents modeled these growing up. They were a close-knit, loving family, and Cecily describes her childhood with fondness. She describes her father as strict but warm, and very dedicated. Her mother, she says, was quiet and submissive but also very dedicated. As a child, Cecily clashed most often with her mother, and was closest to her father; however, in adolescence she began to have more frequent conflict with her father over issues like autonomy and generational differences. Cecily shares that in high school she took an interest in science which was nurtured by a teacher that became her mentor. Her parents encouraged this until college, when Cecily's career interests conflicted with the family's traditional values. "I had to find a way to make both work," she says, "honoring my parents, and honoring who I wanted to become. There's a tension that still exists between the two, but I've learned to make it work." Cecily met her husband in college, and was relieved to find a partner that was also a person of faith while still supporting her interests and career.

Following an exploration of the family dynamics, we engage in an assessment of her early recollections. The counselor asks Cecily to close her eyes, and to share whatever memories came up from her life prior to around six years old. He is careful to specify that these be first-person, single event memories; something that she recalls experiencing and was not a family story or something that was recurring. As she shares each memory, the counselor gathers specific information, including the most salient part of the memory, the feelings that arose with it, the significant people, and her own placement within it.

The first memory Cecily shares is from her third birthday party. She recalls going to the bathroom, and coming out into the backyard to see kids running around and playing with one another. She most vividly remembers the brightly colored party hats, streamers, and the sounds of the children laughing and talking. She describes herself in the memory off to the side of the door, observing everything going on around her. Despite it being her party, Cecily recalls feeling that it was important that all of the other children were having a nice time. "It sounds silly to say, but it felt nice to give them a reason to come together," she says. When asked about the salient emotions that emerge during this memory, Cecily says that she feels calm, content, and wistful. The last emotion, wistfulness, she attributes to a passing wish that she was a part of all the fun going on around her, rather than simply watching it. She titles the memory, *The Observer*.

Cecily's second memory is from her time in first grade. Roughly the age of six, she remembers getting a perfect score on a spelling test. She describes the intense effort that she put into studying for the test, and the over-whelming feelings of pride and satisfaction that came with knowing her hard work paid off. The most vivid part of the memory is watching her mother pin the test to the refrigerator door with a magnet. Her younger brother's artwork was moved to the side of the refrigerator to make room, "front and center," for her test. Cecily emphasizes this in the retelling, and added a feeling of superiority to the list of emotions that came up. She titles the memory, *High Marks Higher than Mark's*. She smiles at the wordplay, as her younger brother's name is Mark.

The last memory that Cecily shares is from her time in Sunday School at the church. She is unsure of her age, but supposed that it must have been prior to attending public school (around five years old). She recalls her teacher telling the story of Jesus's birth using cut out images on popsicle sticks. When the teacher began to talk about Jesus being God's son, Cecily says that she interrupted her to ask if Mary was God's wife. She remembers being confused by the teacher's explanation that Mary was just Jesus's human mother, and a special "vessel" for the son of God, who had decided to be born in human likeness so that he could bring salvation to humanity. Cecily remembers asking several questions about when Jesus was spiritually born if he was God's son, as the teacher described, and if so, who God's wife was. "I really flustered her," she says with a wince. "I must have seemed like such an obnoxious brat, asking all those questions, and she just wanted to get through the story!" After several minutes, she says the teacher got impatient, gave her a stern look, and told her that not every question needed an answer, because that was what faith was for. Cecily describes this as the most vivid part of the memory; the look on her teacher's face as her peers looked at her. A warm flush rises up her neck. She says she felt frustrated, ashamed, and angry, titling the memory, *Too Many Questions*.

Cecily shares that in the retelling, she feels all of the feelings coming back, noting similarities with the experience of her present depression.

Taken together, we can formulate Cecily's lifestyle dynamics in a cohesive way. Cecily found her place in the family along two important dynamics: being the "middle child," and being "the girl." First born children tend to directly align with the goals, values, and expectations of their parents. Cecily's older brother lived out the family's spiritual and occupational narrative by becoming a pastor like his father. Consequently, Cecily became an intellectual, pursuing academics and a career in science. As a girl in a traditionally Christian family, she was valued but trained to believe that her place in a natural order was second to others, particularly men. This theme is present in her first memory of the birthday party. As the observant birthday girl, Cecily helped people to come together in a safe and positive way (a family value). Even so, she didn't feel entitled to be a true part of that environment. This pattern holds in her professional career (as a lab manager who is aloof from coworkers) and spiritual world (feeling disconnected from her church family). Cecily also learned that if she works hard and applies herself, she is intellectually capable of succeeding, *and* of superseding her brothers (her demonstration of superiority). However, this intellectual superiority comes with a cost to her sense of belonging; by embracing her role as an analytical person she risks the castigation and exclusion of those closest to her (as demonstrated by the Sunday school teacher memory). Cecily then perceives a necessary balance between being worthy of love and belonging (conforming to socio-spiritual expectations) and personal authenticity (embracing and demonstrating her intellectual strengths).

Insight

During the insight phase of the treatment, Cecily explores and is made aware of the value that the ambivalence and depression bring to her life. The themes from her childhood and family are tied to her present situation; first through associative exploration, and then with more targeted questioning. Adopting a "not-knowing" stance with the client allows her to construct the meaning behind the experiences. Critical areas for personal exploration in this case are her beliefs about belonging and authenticity; specifically, her conviction that if she engages with her church community as an intellectual, and is willing to evaluate her faith from an intellectual perspective, that it will result in social rejection. Once Cecily is aware of these, it becomes beneficial for her to understand the protective nature her depression plays in preventing what she perceives as an inevitable outcome. Similarly, it is important that Cecily examine her sense of connection or disconnection from her God within this perspective. The push-button exercise is very useful in this phase of treatment as well, to help Cecily explore the purposive nature of her experiences. Using this tool with feelings of happiness vs. depression as well as with spiritual connection vs. spiritual disconnection can be an important part of Cecily's process of developing insight as well as agency for future behavior.

Reorientation

In order to help Cecily incorporate her knowledge and insights into practical action, we implement the "reflecting as if" and "acting as if" interventions using significant spiritual and intellectual models (including biblical and contemporary figures). These individuals embody the duality of spirituality and science, and allow Cecily to experiment with new ways of thinking and behaving. The idea behind this is to help Cecily to be comfortable not always having the answers to difficult questions, to connect with others in an authentic way, and to allow herself to "live in the gray" of both her faith and culture. Given her analytical nature, bibliotherapy and connection with other like-minded academics of faith are also strong empowering factors for Cecily. As she gains encouragement and applies her new perspectives to her situation, Cecily begins to take on leadership roles within her church congregation, offering her unique perspectives in Bible studies, and going on to establish a mentoring and discussion group for young parishioners attending college. With each progressive act of courage, Cecily's depression lessens, and her sense of connection to the Divine shifts as well. Cecily now reports that she realizes that connection with God is both feeling and action; while she may not feel connection at all times, she can honor that through action and cherish the felt spiritual moments when they happen. In summary, Cecily transformed her identity from someone who feels she must be either an intellectual *or* a person of faith, to someone who is an intellectual *and* a person of faith. As she embraces her own sense of identity she is able to enjoy the felt connection of her communities, while embracing those qualities that make her uniquely herself.

Recommended Readings

Carlson, J., Watts, R. E., and Maniacci, M. (2006). *Adlerian therapy: Theory and practice*. Washington, DC: American Psychological Association.

Dinkmeyer, D. C., Dinkmeyer, D. C., Sperry, L. (1987). *Adlerian counseling and psychotherapy*. (2nd ed.). Columbus, OH: Merrill Publishing Company.

Eckstein, D., and Baruth, L. (1996). *The theory and practice of life-style assessment*. Dubuque, IA: Kendall/Hunt Publishing Company.

References

Ackerman, S. J., and Hilsenroth, M. J. (2003). A review of therapist characteristics and techniques positively impacting the therapeutic alliance. *Clinical Psychology Review*, 23, 1–33.

Adler, A. (1943). *The science of living*. Garden City, NY: Star Books.

Ansbacher, H. L., and Ansbacher, R. R. (1964). *The individual psychology of Alfred Adler: A systematic presentation in selections from his writings.* New York, NY: Harper & Row.

Bordin, E. S. (1979). The generalizability of the psychoanalytic concept of the working alliance. *Psychotherapy: Theory, Research & Practice,* 16(3), 252–260.

Carlson, J., Watts, R. E., and Maniacci, M. (2006). *Adlerian therapy: Theory and practice.* Washington, DC: American Psychological Association.

Cheston, S. E. (2000). Spirituality of encouragement. *The Journal of Individual Psychology,* 56(3), 296–304.

de Shazer, S., and Dolan, Y. (2007). *More than miracles: The state of the art of solution-focused brief therapy.* New York, NY: Routledge.

Dinkmeyer, D. C., Dinkmeyer, D. C., Sperry, L. (1979). *Adlerian counseling and psychotherapy.* (2nd ed.). Columbus, OH: Merrill Publishing Company.

Eckstein, D., and Baruth, L. (1996). *The theory and practice of life-style assessment.* Dubuque, IA: Kendall/Hunt Publishing Company.

Fowler, J. W. (1981). *Stages of faith: The psychology of human development and the quest for meaning.* San Francisco, CA: Harper & Row.

Grey, L. (1998). *Alfred Adler, the forgotten prophet: A vision for the 21st century.* Westport, CT: Praeger Publishers.

Hanna, F. J. (2006) Community feeling, empathy, and intersubjectivity: A phenomenological framework. In S. Slavik and J. Carlson (Eds.), *Readings in the theory of individual psychology* (pp. 423–430). New York, NY: Routledge.

Jones Jr., J. V., and Lyddon, W. J. (2003). Adlerian and constructivist psychotherapies: A constructivist perspective. In R. E. Watts (Ed.). *Adlerian, cognitive, and constructivist therapies: An integrative dialogue* (pp. 38–58). New York, NY: Springer Publishing Company.

Mansager, E., Gold, L., Griffith, B., Kal, E., Manaster, G., McArter, G., Powers, R. L., Schnebly, L., Schneider, M. F., and Silverman, N. N. (2002). Spirituality in the Adlerian Forum. *The Journal of Individual Psychology,* 58(2), 177–196.

Microtraining Associates (Producer). (2004). *Adlerian Early Recollections: Live Demonstration Including DCT Assessment* [Video file]. Retrieved from Alexander Street database.

Milliren, A., and Clemmer, F. (2006). Introduction to Adlerian psychology. In S. Slavik and J. Carlson (Eds.), *Readings in the theory of individual psychology* (pp. 17–32). New York, NY: Routledge.

Mosak, H., and Dreikurs, R. (1973). Adlerian psychotherapy. In R. Corsini (Ed.), *Current psychotherapies.* Itsaca, Ill: F. E. Peacock Publishers.

Peluso, P. R. (2006). Style of life. In S. Slavik and J. Carlson (Eds.), *Readings in the theory of individual psychology* (pp. 189–206). New York, NY: Routledge.

Polanski, P. J. (2002). Exploring spiritual beliefs in relation to Adlerian theory. *Counseling and Values,* 46, 127–136.

Sweeney, T. J. (2009). *Adlerian counseling and psychotherapy: A practitioner's approach.* (5th ed.). New York, NY: Routledge.

Von Goethe (2016). *A treasury of wisdom: Expounding the Bhagavad Gita, and epitome of all teachings and learnings* (R. Pal Baran, Trans.). East Midnapore, WB, India: ·Partridge.

Walborn, F. (2014). *Religion in personality theory.* Boston, MA: Elsevier.

Watts, R. E., and Shulman, B. H. (2003). Integrating Adlerian and constructive therapies: An Adlerian perspective. In R. E. Watts (Ed.). *Adlerian, cognitive, and constructivist therapies: An integrative dialogue* (9–37). New York, NY: Springer Publishing Company.

Watts, R. E., Peluso, P. R., and Lewis, T.F. (2005). Expanding the acting "as if" technique: An Adlerian/Constructive integration. *Journal of Individual Psychology*, 61(4), 380–387.

8 Spiritual and Religious Interventions in "Third Wave" Cognitive Behavioral Therapies

Vassilia Binensztok, Tiffany E. Vastardis, and Carman S. Gill

"The mind is everything. What you think you become."

—Buddha

Introduction

Long considered a mainstay in the world of psychotherapy, Cognitive-Behavioral Therapy (CBT; Beck, 1976) is an effective treatment for many counseling issues (Butler et al., 2006). The practice of CBT has served as a foundation for the emergence of modern "third wave" therapies, such as Mindfulness-Based Cognitive-Behavioral Therapy (MBCT), Dialectical Behavioral Therapy (DBT), and Acceptance and Commitment Therapy (ACT). These new therapies, considered to be modernized versions of CBT, yield promising results when used to treat a variety of client issues (Forman et al., 2007). Mindfulness and meditation, ideas imbedded in Eastern spirituality, are also practical, effective intervention strategies when working within the spiritual domain (Hayes et al., 2012). Third wave Cognitive Behavioral Therapies integrate these concepts, traditionally seen in spiritual practices, and are heavily influenced by ideas from religions like Buddhism (Waller et al., 2010). Furthermore, many of these treatments incorporate values-based interventions that are strongly associated with spirituality and spiritual issues (Hayes et al., 2012). Spiritual concepts such as hope, well-being, and a focus on values and virtues, are reflected in DBT, MBCT, and ACT.

Because religious conceptualizations of the self and the mind are similar to those present in third wave therapies, comparisons can be drawn between them. For instance, in the Sufi tradition, the self is said to be made up of four elements – heart, spirit, soul, and intellect. These elements can be linked to CBT components like emotions, behaviors, thoughts, and reflection (Haque, 2004; Mirdal, 2012). Similarly, Pentecostal Christians conceptualize three levels of body, soul, and spirit (Porterfield, 2005). Both Buddhist and Christian doctrines value the concept of acceptance, and Jewish and Christian faiths similarly value the deferral of problems to God (Mull, 2015). Additionally, third wave therapies use interventions similar to

Humanistic and Existential therapies, with their focus on client values and context (Brown et al., 2011). In this chapter, we briefly describe MCBT, DBT, and ACT, and tie these modalities to elements of spirituality and spiritual/religious issues which may arise in treatment. Descriptions of practical interventions relating to spirituality are also detailed. We integrate ACT into a case example, describing more in-depth interventions and outcomes.

Introduction to Mindfulness-Based Cognitive-Behavioral Therapy

An offshoot of Kabat-Zinn's (1979) Mindfulness-Based Stress Reduction (MBSR) program, which was piloted at the University of Massachusetts Medical Center, Mindfulness-Based Cognitive-Behavioral came to fruition during the 1990s as a deterrent to episodic relapse in chronically depressed patients (Shapiro and Carlson, 2009). As MBSR applications across institutional and clinical settings continued to gain increased empirical support, proponents of traditional Cognitive-Behavioral Therapy began to recognize the utility of mindfulness practice in treatment. With the support of Kabat-Zinn, Segal et al. (2002) fused MBSR with CBT in the creation of what is now formally deemed MCBT (Shapiro and Carlson, 2009; Segal et al., 2002).

Mindfulness-Based Cognitive-Behavioral Therapy is most often administered in a therapeutic group forum, incorporating Mindfulness-Based Stress Reduction techniques extrapolated from the principles embedded within Eastern religions, such as Hinduism (Williams and Kabat-Zinn, 2013; Shapiro and Carlson, 2009). For example, the counselor may ask the group to engage in a mindfulness activity that requires them to attend to the present moment, focusing on self-awareness and self-acceptance. Though a descendent of Mindfulness-Based Stress Reduction, MCBT can be considered more didactic in focus, much like traditional Cognitive-Behavioral Therapy, a component of psychoeducation geared toward mental health hygiene management is included in the approach. Of primary interest in MCBT practice is to engender mindful awareness of variables associated with mental health symptomology, including irrational ideas such as persistent patterns of dichotomous thought and negative attribution styles. As such, at times, the counselor may educate clients regarding irrational beliefs and positive self-talk (Segal et al., 2002; Shapiro and Carlson, 2009). Furthermore, in keeping with traditional CBT, behavior-based "homework" is incorporated into the protocol and clients may be asked to engage in daily mindfulness activities and other interventions described below.

Religious Spirituality and Mindfulness-Based Cognitive-Behavioral Therapy. The general practice of mindfulness is heavily based upon the fundamentals of Eastern philosophy and religion. Merging tenets of various sects of Hinduism and Buddhism, mindfulness tactics reflect both journey and destination, through attention to and acceptance of all of that which is present in a given moment. The process of attaining a state of mindfulness involves both awareness and practice, the former pertaining to one's "way of being" and the latter representing the application of related skills in the pursuit of attaining one's chosen "way." This pursuit is scaffolded by a focus on self-awareness, self-exploration, and self-regulation. Affective grounding, for example, can be achieved via mindful meditation practices (Williams and Kabat-Zinn, 2013; Shapiro and Carlson, 2009).

The spiritual foundations of MCBT can be expanded to align with various religions extrinsic to those upon which the practice is based. For example, the Judeo-Christian practice of Centering Prayer can be considered a mindfulness practice which can fluidly integrate into the MCBT approach. Attention to such consistencies may make MCBT more applicable to a greater audience, including individuals who object to explicit Eastern philosophy (Blanton, 2011). In essence, the Centering Prayer in Western practice very closely parallels components of mindful mediation. Consider that the "illusion of the self," based in Buddhism, implies that "[…] while the self purports to think up the thoughts, the thoughts, in fact, help think up the self" (Albahari, 2016, p.xii). This delineation may be difficult to comprehend; and hence, to embrace by those who are engaged in a belief system that endorses individualist principles. In fact, Christian models of mindfulness, which shift meditative focus from the Buddhist "illusion of self" to the devotion to and appreciation of the wonderment of the powers and influences of the "the Divine," is currently being applied in MCBT practice (Symington and Symington, 2012; Tan, 2011). In efforts to reach a broader client base, further amendments to formal MCBT are in practice, slightly shifting the vernacular of acknowledgment of the universality of principles across religions, such as recognition of the "sacredness of the present moment" (Tan, 2011, p. 72). Furthermore, a burgeoning body of both professional and dissertation research is dedicated to the investigation of the integration of MCBT into models of both secular and non-secular therapeutic approaches (Thomas et al., 2016; Karigan, 2016; Newman, 2014).

Interventions. Techniques specific to the practice of Mindfulness-Based Cognitive-Behavioral Therapy are quite similar to those inherent to indfulness-Based Stress Reduction; however, they are formally streamlined in order to better fit psychotherapeutic orthodoxy. For example, the focus on love and compassion embedded within MBSR guided mediation is replaced by attention to experience and emotion in MCBT. MCBT also deviates from traditional Cognitive-Behavioral Therapy in that cognitive replacement is not of importance to practice, but rather, a mindful awareness of the existence and nature of intrusive thoughts is the therapeutic goal (Shapiro and Carlson, 2009). Here, the client is encouraged to passively tend to such intrusions by means of acknowledgment and acceptance; in turn, rather than intervening by means of restructuring as in CBT, the role of the MCBT practitioner shifts to one of which is Psychoeducational, guiding the client toward the understanding of how such thoughts operate in the client's daily life.

Introduction to DBT

Developed by Marsha Linehan (1993), and consistent with spiritual elements common to many major world religions, Dialectic Behavioral Therapy is a multimodal third wave cognitive treatment inspired by her work with individuals suffering from Borderline Personality Disorder (BPD) (McKay et al., 2007). In efforts to assist struggling clients in better regulating emotional impulses, especially those pertaining to chronic suicidality, Linehan (2015, 1993; Linehan et al., 2006) began to integrate cognitive approaches into broad-based treatment plans, including individual psychotherapy, group skills training, telephone coaching, and therapist consultation teams who collaborate on a regularly scheduled basis for the purposes of case conceptualization, treatment modification, and progress monitoring. DBT was the first evidence-based psychotherapy to exhibit effectiveness in the treatment of BPD (Linehan, 2015). Though initial studies evaluating the efficacy of DBT focused, primarily, on the treatment of BPD, numerous studies have since been conducted indicating DBT's utility across various presenting problems and diagnoses, and their inherent symptomological presentations (Linehan, 2015; McKay, 2007).

The crux of the Dialectic Behavioral Therapy approach is to facilitate emotional regulation by means of strengthening "a person's ability to handle distress without losing control or acting destructively" (McKay et al., 2007, p. 1). In addressing issues of *emotional dysregulation*, such as a lack of impulse-control, DBT aims to redirect cognitive and behavioral patterns that serve as saboteurs to stability and prosocial functionality. DBT client skills training "is based on a dialectical and biosocial theory of psychological disorder that emphasizes the role of difficulties in regulating emotions, both over and under control, and behavior" (Linehan, 2015, p. 3). DBT samples numerous notions and applications from the traditional Cognitive-Behavioral Therapy approach; however, in order to best address the often urgent needs of severely disturbed populations, several modifications to standard CBT practices, some directly related to spirituality, were integrated into the DBT approach, including:

1　Synthesis of acceptance with change.
2　Inclusion of mindfulness as a practice for therapist and a core skill for clients.
3　Emphasis on treating therapy-interfering behaviors of both client and therapist.
4　Emphasis on the therapeutic relationship and therapist self-disclosure as essential to therapy.
5　Emphasis on dialectical processes.

6   Emphasis on stages of treatment, and on targeting behaviors according to severity and threat.
7   Inclusion of a specific suicide risk assessment and management protocol.
8   Inclusion of behavioral skills drawn primarily from other evidence-based interventions.
9   Treatment teams as an integral component of therapy.
10   Focus on continual assessment of multiple outcomes via diary cards.

(Linehan, 2015)

At the time of DBT's inception, such tenets of practice constituted notable additions to Cognitive-Behavioral practice; however, over the past several years, many of the above interventions have been adopted by practitioners of such a school of thought.

Dialectics. The philosophical scaffolding of Dialectic Behavioral Therapy synthesizes a *dialectic* worldview with the biosocial model of severe emotional dysregulation, the latter of which forms the basis for the treatment approach. Here, the term *dialectic* refers to perceptions of the fundamental nature of reality, and relates to persuasive dialogues and relationships aimed at promoting positive change. In regard to the former, DBT supports the following three polarities: (1) reality is whole and interrelated, where evaluation of a system assumes a top-down approach, lending little meaning to the analysis of the individual component, (2) reality is fluid and composed of internal forces that are diametrically opposed, wherein the fusion of such forces begets a new "sub-set" of opposition, (in other words, existential paradoxy is inevitable to the human condition), and (3) the maintenance of personal integrity and validation of one's own personal viewpoints regarding their state-of-being serves to facilitate the emergence of wellness, as skill-building, alone, does not necessarily lend to longitudinally stable life gains, such as perceived self-efficacy (Linehan, 1993, 2015; Bandura, 1997).

Biosocial Theory of Emotional Dysregulation. In efforts to best conceptualize cases and meet the needs of severely disturbed clients expressing high rates of suicidality, as was the case with those for whom Dialectic Behavioral Therapy was originally designed, Linehan developed a biosocial theory based upon the notion that a great deal of psychiatric distress, namely that which is experienced by those who suffer from Borderline Personality Disorder is a by-product of emotional dysregulation. For example, in Neacsiu et al. (2014), Linehan's team posits that suicidality is a direct function of an inability to regulate emotions and control their accompanying impulses. Based upon the biosocial theory, issues such as affective stability and relational harmony are tarnished as a result of emotional dysregulation influenced by both social factors and biological diatheses, such as the neurochemical imbalances proposed to underlie conditions like Major Depressive Disorder (MDD) and Schizophrenia Spectrum Disorders (Linehan, 2015).

Religious Spirituality and DBT. Much akin to the fundamentals of Daoism and Zen Buddhism, the epistemological framework of Dialectic

Behavioral Therapy heavily emphasizes the mindful awareness and acceptance of the polarities inherent in the life experience. In fact, such a focus on dialectics lends credence to DBT's classification as a third wave behavioral therapy, in that such a cornerstone hallmarks the approach's deviation from previous therapies. Furthermore, Linehan (2015; 1993) has been noted to credit her personal experiences with Buddhism as highly influential in the development of DBT (Van Gelder, 2006); hence, "the connections between DBT and spirituality are obvious" (Johnson, 2013, p. 60). The innate bent of open-mindedness and non-judgment within the DBT approach aligns with principles universal to most major world religions. It is also purported that dialectical acceptance of one's reality and present situation lends to an increase in coping abilities, better emotional regulation, and a decrease in negative attributions (Johnson, 2013). As an abundance of literature suggests that healthy religious spirituality, in and of itself, increases resiliency (Amato et al., 2017; Kick and McNitt, 2016; Phillips et al., 2009), the integrity of DBT outcome research reporting high-yield client gains across a number of diagnoses and presenting problems can be assumed to be valid (Linehan, 2015; Mohr, 2011). For example, DBT readily merges with the 12-Step approach to addiction treatment. While based upon Judeo-Christian principles, the 12-Step emphasis on existential acceptance mirrors that which is embedded in the DBT approach, and the modality's focus on distress-tolerance is reported to decrease the likelihood of relapse by addressing the internal struggles that one may face throughout the process of recovery (Platter and Cabral, 2010).

In addition to incorporating the mindful acknowledgment of the interconnected nature of awareness, presence, and acceptance into traditional Cognitive-Behavioral Therapy, Dialectic Behavioral Therapy also aims to facilitate recognition of various levels of consciousness. In parlance to the DBT lexicon, targeted levels of consciousness are labelled: *reasonable mind, emotional mind,* and *wise mind,* which refer to states of logical, affective, and integrative consciousness, respectively. The latter of these, the wise mind, is considered to transcend the former two, as it constitutes an amalgamation of both, and is integral to maintenance of grounding and centeredness (Johnson, 2013). "The theory assumes that all individuals have access to wise mind, which is connected to deeper truths about reality and successful living" (Johnson, 2013, p. 60). As an abundance of world faiths strive to indoctrinate their followers with the tools necessary to strive for such pursuits, DBT can be considered a worthy companionate to traditional religious and spiritual counseling approaches.

Interventions. The Dialectic Behavioral Therapy treatment approach relies heavily upon the development of skills geared toward attaining and maintaining emotional regulation. "The overall goal of skills training is to learn skills for changing unwanted behaviors, emotions, thinking, and events that cause misery and distress" (Linehan, 2015, p. 127). Specific practitioner's scripts, handouts, and worksheets were designed to complement each skill targeted within the DBT treatment mainframe. DBT skills classifications include: general skills aimed at orienting and analyzing behavior, interpersonal effectiveness skills geared toward assigning meaning to and improving relationships with others, emotion regulation skills designed to help clients better recognize and manage variables of affect which impact well-being, distress tolerance skills which target the function and utility of clients' repertoires of behavior, and mindfulness skills focused on examining the previously mentioned levels of consciousness nestled within the heavily spiritual components of DBT (Linehan, 2015).

While all of the above domains may be considered attentive to religious spirituality (R/S), it is within the latter three arenas – emotional regulation, distress tolerance, and mindfulness – that skills lending to spiritual discovery and development are most prominent. For example, within the emotional regulation skills training module, a thematic training block relates to "build mastery" and "cope ahead" skills, which emphasize the value of daily purposive action in gaining a sense of accomplishment in one's life, and planning effective coping in the face of anticipated difficulties. Such virtues are highly correlative with those which are imbedded in various religious orientations, such as Islam, Judaism, and Christianity. Distress Tolerance tasks are also reflective of dialectic behavioral therapy's spiritual groundwork, as the embodiment of radical acceptance, willingness, clarity of mind, alternative rebellion, and adaptive denial are the focal points of skills training within this designation. Finally, it is within the mindfulness skills training modules that both Linehan's personal experiences and DBT's overall spiritual bent become most evident. Within the mindfulness training modules, traditional eastern-influenced mindfulness tasks, such as meditation and centering prayer are included, as well as skills emphasizing the importance of "practicing loving kindness" and "walking the middle path." Despite the Eastern origins of mindfulness practice, the universality of the above topical foci is apparent across the majority of well-known world religions (Linehan, 2015; 1993).

Introduction to Acceptance and Commitment Therapy

Acceptance and Commitment Therapy (ACT), is founded in the theory of functional contextualism, in which events and actions are seen as interactions between setting and purpose. In other words, context gives meaning to actions and psychological events are seen as interactions between "whole organisms" and "whole contexts." Applied to religious and spiritual issues, it can be understood that the meanings individuals give to their experiences and actions are influenced by the religious/spiritual context. Additionally, ACT considers language to be integral to human functioning and the process of change. Linear and logical language is used to help clients establish psychological flexibility by means of helping clients understand language in context. Whereas psychological flexibility is a central goal of the ACT process, psychopathology is viewed to stem from psychological rigidity, in which client language limits "behavioral repertoires" (Hayes et al. 2004, p. 25). Psychopathology is understood to be the result of the narrowing effects of language in three areas: *cognitive fusion, experiential avoidance,* and *disengagement. Cognitive fusion* occurs when an individual interacts with situations in relation to their verbally assigned functions, as opposed to their objective functions. *Experiential avoidance* refers to client avoidance of perceived negative consequences of events, regardless of actual potential for harm. Finally, *disengagement* constitutes an inability to engage in the present moment due to cognitions, such as: negative self-references, misguided beliefs, and a pessimistic worldview (Hayes et al., 2004).

The six core processes of Acceptance and Commitment Therapy are *acceptance, cognitive defusion, connection with the present moment, viewing oneself in context, values clarification,* and *committed action.* These core processes guide the focus of counseling sessions, during which the client is first challenged to identify the valued direction in which he or she would like to move, and then identify barriers to that values-driven goal attainment. Identification of values involves the following processes: values clarification, goal setting, committed action, skills training, and constructive problem-solving. Standardized instruments, such as the *Values Clarification Checklist,* are used to help clients identify and prioritize key areas upon which to focus (Harris, 2013). Barriers to values-driven goal attainment are then identified through evaluating the client's levels of internal barriers, such as, cognitive fusion vs. cognitive defusion, experiential avoidance vs. self and situational acceptance, and disengagement vs. connection with the current moment (Harris, 2013). While it is the client's duty to identify these barriers, the counselor can scaffold this process using several ACT interventions to help increase client awareness.

Religious Spirituality and ACT. Issues in Acceptance and Commitment Therapy (ACT) have been studied in spiritual traditions like Buddhism and Christian Mysticism. Hayes, credited with the development of ACT, himself, wrote that ACT's central goal of understanding and ameliorating human suffering is spiritual (Hayes et al., 2012). Similar to Buddhism, ACT views suffering as a product of how individuals view their experiences, rather than as an inherently internal or external experience (Santiago and Gall, 2016). ACT views acceptance of painful experiences as necessary for living in accordance with one's chosen values. Again, this is tantamount to various spiritual traditions that value openness and acceptance. Buddhism, for example, utilizes meditation for developing mindfulness and understanding (Bodhi, 2005), and Christianity fosters openness and acceptance through contemplation in order to develop an understanding of the self and God (John of the Cross, trans. 2008). Both ACT and various spiritual traditions work to help individuals come to terms with inner experiences through openness and acceptance to alleviate suffering. Additionally, ACT refers to transcendence, expansiveness, and interconnectedness of consciousness, which aligns with central tenets of many religious traditions. ACT's idea of self-as-context is reflective of transcendence, and can be seen as the behavioral translation of spiritual theories of mind, body, and spirit. The ACT counselor works to help the client defuse judgment and accept inner experiences; which, in turn, increases self-compassion and a sense of understanding that can lead to greater interconnectedness with the self, others, and the Divine (Santiago and Gall, 2016). Finally, the therapeutic posture consistent with ACT values equality, compassion, sincerity, and sharing, all of which are values equally common to spiritual and religious traditions (Luoma et al., 2007).

Counselors can use Acceptance and Commitment Therapy to treat various spiritual struggles, as it addresses the psychological processes that underlie spiritual struggles, particularly psychological inflexibility. Psychological inflexibility can affect one's relationship to the Divine in many ways, while ACT concepts of psychological flexibility can mollify these struggles. An example of psychological inflexibility in spiritual struggles can be seen with some Buddhist practitioners. Practitioners may become self-critical or dissatisfied for not following spiritual instruction "correctly," or failing to be mindful in all interactions (Phillips et al., 2009). Cognitive fusion may be displayed through an individual's judgment of God and rigid thinking about how the Divine should be. Individuals in very closed religious systems may also experience fusing with the rules and ideals ascribed by those systems. Conversely, cognitive defusion may foster openness to the Divine and a deeper understanding. Experiential avoidance can lead to mixed feelings about the Divine, and anger at God. Acceptance, on the other hand, can include acceptance of thoughts, ideas, and emotions about the Divine. Inflexible attention can lead to fixated expectations of God as well as preoccupation with disappointments in God. Present-moment awareness, however, allows the individual to experience the divine in the present as opposed to through fixated expectations. Attachment to the concept of self can lead to a rigid understanding of God and what one deserves from him. Self-as-context allows the individual to recognize the transcendent self in relation to the Divine. Inaction, compulsive action, or impulsive action can lead to rumination about the Divine or complete disengagement. Committed action could ameliorate this predicament by helping the individual engage in a more enriching experience with God. Finally, absent or fused values can lead to limited understanding of the Divine's values (i.e. forgiveness) and an imposition of one's values onto God. Chosen values, however, allow the individual to develop a more values-driven understanding of God (Santiago and Gall, 2016).

Struggles can also form when one's self-concept comes from an attachment to the negative aspects of the self-as-context. The individual, then, filters all experiences through this lens. For example, an individual who views herself as suffering from spiritual distress may generalize that notion to mean that she is entirely distressed and hopeless. This could, potentially, snowball into a sense of detachment from God and loss of spiritual connection (Santiago and Gall, 2016).

The ACT counselor focuses on processes and behavior, paying particular attention to the individual's relationship to religious and spiritual values and beliefs, rather than the literal content of those values and beliefs. This constitutes a defusion from the client's beliefs, as well as the counselor's values. When treating interpersonal spiritual struggles, the ACT therapist helps the client analyze personal interactions to identify periods of inflexible attention or attention to self-concept. For example, an individual may demonstrate inflexible attention when holding on to resentment over past interactions or may be attached to self-concept by striving to act in a stereotypical way (i.e. as the "Good Christian") (Santiago and Gall, 2016). Personal interactions can be explored to find the client's psychologically inflexible communication styles and replace them with more flexible styles.

Interventions. Therapeutic tools within ACT can include counselor modeling of pro-social behaviors, reinforcement of client progress, encouraging workable behavior between sessions by asking the client to commit to engagement in specific activities, and engaging in differential reinforcement by attempting to eliminate unworkable behavior through interruption of that behavior and replacement with more workable behavior (Harris, 2013; Hayes et al., 2004). Techniques such as "dropping anchor," help ground clients in sessions and break persistent behavioral patterns. Additional interventions aimed at moving from cognitive fusion to defusion, addressing problems of self, and experiential avoidance are fully described in the following case study.

Case Study

Susanna has been coming to counseling for three sessions (please see the client profile description in the Introduction to this book). Following the initial assessments and case conceptualization processes described in Chapters 2 and 4, the counselor knows that she is heavily committed to Mormonism, her family's religion, and that her belief system is moderately closed. The ecomaps provide the therapist with information regarding her family patterns and her relationship to them and to the Divine. Further, the counselor recognizes that this client's pattern centers around punishing herself when she fails to be perfect. The counselor determines that a diagnosis of nonsuicidal self-injury, Adjustment Disorder with depressed mood, Religious or Spiritual Problem (V62.89), and an obsessive-compulsive personality style is indicated.

Performing an Acceptance and Commitment Therapy–oriented assessment, the counselor finds numerous factors related to psychological inflexibility and cognitive fusion, including Susanna's behavior of abandoning intimate and socio-sexual exploration as a result of conflicts between religious beliefs and self-identified same-sex attraction. Further, she suppresses this exploration by investing her attention in her academic work and; as result, she is fusing with negative cognitive patterns and harsh self-judgment, which emerges in her pattern of punishing herself when she fails to be perfect. Susanna is also fusing with her rigid beliefs and self-references intrinsic to her moderately closed belief system. Finally, she is fusing with negative memories of past experiences, as she describes being "tortured" by romantic thoughts of her former friend and the messages that she has received about morality. Her guilt, confusion, fear, and anger resulting from her feelings of same-sex attraction lead to avoidance behavior, as displayed through her excessive dedication to school and faith-based activities (Harris, 2013).

Treatment goals include: reducing her presenting symptoms of depressed mood and related symptomatology (guilt, confusion, fear, anger), reducing frequency and severity of self-harm episodes, and establishing stability in daily life. Additional goals involve shifting her maladaptive pattern, from punishing herself in response to not feeling perfect, to being flexible and kind with herself as she processes her conflicting feelings. Whereas third wave CBT modalities are a good "fit" for this client, because of the significant role that Susanna's faith plays in her presenting problems, Religious/Spiritual interventions are also indicated.

In keeping with ACT's principle beliefs, treatment addresses psychological inflexibility in three target issues – 1) moving from cognitive fusion to defusion, 2) addressing Susanna's self-identified problems of self, and 3) reducing experiential avoidance.

Toward the goal of moving from cognitive fusion to defusion, two areas are addressed – Susanna's religious-based rigidity, which causes a clash between her religious-self and sexual-self, and her perfectionistic rigidity. Moving her toward psychological flexibility, the counselor includes interventions such as "Acceptance: 'Open Up," wherein Susanna learns to make room for self-acceptance, reducing perfectionism. This does not, necessarily, mean agreeing with things as they are; but rather, allowing life to occur as it is actually experienced. In this exercise, Susanna practices accepting how she feels and what she thinks. She begins labeling feelings externally. For example, "I am sensing some sadness and confusion." This intervention addresses Susanna's non-suicidal self-injurious behaviors, her spiritual struggle, and her perfectionistic pattern (Harris, 2013; Hayes and Strosahl, 2004).

Susanna also learns to cultivate wisdom as part of this process, meaning that she learns to take actions that will ultimately be fulfilling and helpful, rather than taking actions that are only immediately rewarding. For example, she decides to explore her feelings about her friend now, rather than avoiding the situation, the latter of which may feel more comfortable in the moment, but will lead to more confusion and guilt. Susanna cultivates willingness to view thinking as thinking and feeling as feeling, as well as a willingness to explore and act wisely.

The counselor leads Susanna through a process aimed at helping her to defuse from judgment and challenge her judgment process and her harshly conceptualized self, using the ACT intervention "Defusion: Watch Your Thinking." The first step in accomplishing this is for Susanna to recognize the effects of verbal dominance, meaning that she will understand how words affect lives. Susanna learns the ways in which saying, "I'm depressed," for example, can affect her mood and understanding of her experience. She defuses from verbal dominance by practicing techniques like covering her ears, speaking words out loud in a different accent, and interrupting thoughts with the reminder that words are just words. Susanna defuses from her harsh self-judgment by practicing, out loud, "I am having a thought...." and then stating the current thought. Helping Susanna treat the thought as merely a thought addresses her cognitive fusion and depressive symptoms (Harris, 2013; Hayes and Strosahl, 2004).

A final tool in the direction of moving toward defusion is "Contact with the present moment: be here now" (Harris, 2013; Hayes and Strosahl, 2004). This intervention helps Susanna become more mindful of the present, instead of interacting with intrusive memories and destructive thoughts and feelings. The counselor helps her in the cultivation of mindful awareness with the goal of becoming aware of and separate from thoughts and sensations. She practices noticing her thoughts and sensations and labelling them as they come through. For example, she notices, "I am having thoughts about deadlines approaching at school," and "I notice a tightness in my stomach."

Toward the second goal of helping Susanna resolve conflicts between her religious-self and her sexual-self (labelled self), as well as her lack of socio-sexual development related to her religious faith (underdeveloped self), the counselor addresses the lack of contact with her present self, lack of personal values development, and lack of goals. Interventions based in ACT begin with "Self-as-context: flexible perspective taking" (Harris, 2013; Hayes and Strosahl, 2004). Susanna practices observing her memories and experiences as she moves from the position of "I," who has been experiencing, to the position of "the observer," allowing her a more flexible perspective of herself and her experiences.

Susanna identifes and prioritizes her personal values using an intervention called "Values: know what matters." This begins with a psychoeducation piece, to help Susanna learn the difference between rules and values, then moves toward a more values-oriented approach. Susanna is able to differentiate that the rules of her religion state that same-sex attraction can occur, but same-sex relations are forbidden. She explores the context in which rules were taught and then probes deeper for the value underlying the rule. This helps Susanna understand how her rigid adherence to religious rules may not be congruent with her personal values. The counselor then moves to the intervention, "Committed action: do what it takes," using values checklists and Socratic questioning to help Susanna identify her values and develop values-driven goals (Harris, 2013; Hayes and Strosahl, 2004). Using the ACT values clarification checklist, Susanna identifies two of her values as family and achievement (Harris, 2013). Susanna sees that she can be committed to the value of family without adhering to every religious rule. She also determines that she can have the value of achievement by doing things that she finds satisfying instead of solely focusing on grades and other similar markers. This allows her to make decisions about her faith and her behaviors that are congruent with her values. Based on her values, Susanna decides she will commit to her value of 'family' by attending church functions with her family and by exploring her own romantic feelings, so that she can have her own family one day. She also decides to do her best on her school assignments and focus on what she would like to learn, so that she can meet her own achievement goals. Susanna completes an ACT bullseye, so that she can track her committed action goals and progress toward them (Harris, 2013).

The final area of focus with Susanna is her Experiential Avoidance. Issues of importance in this area include Susanna's lack of intimate relationship experiences and her suppression of intimate and sexual feelings by means of academic engagement, which only further perpetuates her perfectionistic tendencies. A key intervention here is "Values – know what matters" (Harris, 2013; Hayes and Strosahl, 2004). In this intervention, Susanna explores the values that she holds about intimate relationships. She learns to set goals driven by these values, rather than the rules of which she has been taught by her family's closed religious system. The counselor helps her link these values to actions, using the "Committed action: do what it takes" intervention (Harris, 2013; Hayes and Strosahl, 2004). This helps Susanna identify meaningful activities that align with her values. Susanna chooses meaningful activities in which to engage, so that she can continue to move in a flexible and values-driven direction, facilitating motivation toward attaining that which she deems personally important and a deeper connection with herself-in-context.

Markers of effective treatment include elimination of non-suicidal self-injury and depressive symptoms. Increased psychological flexibility is evidenced through Susanna's movement toward a more adaptive pattern of being reasonably conscientious, rather than that which is overly driven toward perfectionism. Susanna's ability to better grapple with conflicting feelings relating to religious devotion and same-sex attraction, resolving her spiritual struggle is evidence of improved cognitive defusion. Furthermore, Susanna's increased mindful acceptance and here-and-now awareness mark the resolution of her Adjustment Disorder, movement toward a more open belief system, and a shift away from her maladaptive pattern.

References

Albahari, M. (2016). *Analytical Buddhism: The two-tiered illusion of self.* New York, NY: Springer.

Amato, J.L., Kayman, D.J., Lombardo, M., and Goldstein, M.F. (2017). Spirituality and religion: Neglected factors in preventing veteran suicide? *Pastoral Psychology*, 66, 191–199.

American Psychiatric Association. (2013). *Diagnostic and statistical manual of mental disorders (DSM-5®).* Arlington, VA: APA.

Bandura, A. (1997). *Self-efficacy: The exercise of control.* New York, NY: Freeman.

Bergeman, E. R., Siegel, M. W., and Belzer, M. G. (2013). Mindfulness awareness, spirituality, and psychotherapy. *APA Handbook of Psychology, Religion, and Spirituality,* 2, 207–222.

Beck, A. T. (1976). *Cognitive therapy and the emotional disorders.* New York: International Universities Press.

Blanton, P. G. (2011). The other mindful practice: Centering prayer & psychotherapy. *Pastoral Psychology,* 60, 133–147.

Bodhi, B. (Ed.).(2005). *In the Buddha's words: An anthology of discourses from the Pali Canon.* Somerville, MA: Wisdom Publications, Inc.

Brown, L. A., Gaudiano, B. A., Miller, I. W. (2011). Investigating the similarities and differences between practitioners of second- and third-wave cognitive-behavioral therapies. *Behavior Modification,* 35(2), 187–200.

Buddha (2016). *A treasury of wisdom: Expounding the Bhagavad Gita, and epitome of all teachings and learnings* (R. Pal Baran, Trans.). East Midnapore, WB, India: Partridge.

Burns, K. (2016). *Henri Nouwen: His life and spirit.* Cincinnati, OH: Franciscan Media.

Butler, A. C., Chapman, J., Forman, E., and Beck, A. (2006). The empirical status of Cognitive-Behavioral Therapy: A review of meta-analyses. *Clinical Psychology Review,* 26, 17–31. doi:10.1016/j.cpr.2005.07.003

Forman, E., Herbert, J. D., Moitra, E., Yeomans, P. D., and Geller, P. A. (2007). A randomized controlled effectiveness trial of Acceptance and Commitment Therapy and Cognitive Therapy for anxiety and depression. *Behavior Modification,* 31(6), 772–799.

Haque, A. (2004). Psychology from Islamic perspective: Contributions of early Muslim scholars and challenges to contemporary Muslim psychologists. *Journal of Religion and Health,* 43, 357–377.

Harris, R. (2013). *Getting unstuck in ACT: A clinician's guide to overcoming common obstacles in Acceptance and Commitment Therapy.* Oakland, CA: New Harbinger.

Hayes, S. C. (2004). Acceptance and Commitment Therapy, Relational Frame Theory, and the third wave of behavioral and cognitive therapies. *Behavior Therapy,* 35, 639–665.

Hayes, S. C., and Strosahl, K. D. (Eds.) (2004). *A practical guide to Acceptance and Commitment Therapy.* New York, NY: Springer.

Hayes, S. C., Strosahl, K., and Wilson, K. G. (2012). *Acceptance and commitment therapy: The process and practice of mindful change* (2nd ed.). New York, NY: Guilford Press.

Johnson, R. (2013). *Spirituality in counseling and psychotherapy: An integrative approach that empowers clients.* Hoboken, NJ: Wiley.

Karigan, K. J. (2016). Integrating emotional regulation strategies and religiosity/ spirituality in counseling sessions: Perceptions of counselors in Christian school settings. *ProQuest Dissertations and Theses,* ProQuest Number 10012851.

Kick, K. A., and McNitt, M. (2016). Trauma, spirituality, and mindfulness: Finding hope. *Social Work & Christianity,* 43(3), 97–108.

Linehan, M. M. (2015). *DBT skills training manual* (2nd ed.). New York, NY: Guilford Press.

Linehan, M. M. (1993). *Cognitive-Behavioral treatment of Borderline Personality Disorder.* New York, NY: Guilford Press.

Linehan, M.M., Comtois, K.A., and Murray, A.M. (2006). Dialectic behaviour therapy reduces suicide attempts compared with non-behavioural psychotherapy in women with borderline personality disorder. *Archive of General Psychiatry,* 63, 257–266.

Luoma, J. B., Hayes, S. C., and Walser, R. D. (2007). *Learning ACT*. Oakland, CA: New Harbringer.

McKay, M., Wood, J. C., and Brantley, J. (2007). *The Dialectical Behavioral Therapy skills workbook*. Oakland, CA: New Harbinger.

Mirdal, G. M. (2012). Mevlana Jalal-ad-Din Rumi and mindfulness. *Journal of Religion and Health*, 51, 1202–1215.

Mohr, S. (2011). Integration of religion and spirituality in the care of patients with severe mental disorders. *Religions*, 2, 549–565.

Mull, A. A. (2015). Acceptance and Commitment Therapist Views on the Sacred (Doctoral dissertation). Retrieved from http://digitalcommons.du.edu/cgi/view content.cgi?article=1016&context=capstone_masters

Neacsiu, A. D., Bohus, M., and Linehan, M. M. (2014). Dialectical Behavioral Therapy: An intervention for emotional dysregulation. In J. J. Gross (Ed.). *Handbook of emotional regulation* (2nd ed., pp. 491–507). New York, NY: Guilford Press.

Newman, C. (2014). The relationships between spirituality and religiosity, trait mindfulness, and health outcomes in a Jewish community sample. *ProQuest Dissertations & Theses*, UMI 3662301.

Phillips, R. E., Cheng, C. M., Pargament, K. I., Oemig, C., Colvin, S. D., Abarr, A. N., Dunn, M. W., and Reed, A. (2009). Spiritual coping in American Buddhists: An exploratory study. *The International Journal for the Psychology of Religion*, 19(4), 231–243.

Platter, B. K., and Cabral, O. (2010). DBT meets the 12-steps. *Addiction Professional*, 8, 4, 20–24.

Porterfield, A. (2005). *Healing in the history of Christianity*. Oxford: Oxford University Press.

Santiago, P. N., and Gall, T. L. (2016). Acceptance and Commitment Therapy as a spiritually integrated practice. *Counseling and Values*, 61, 239–254.

Segal, Z. V., Williams, M. G., and Teasdale, J. D. (2002). *Mindfulness-based Cognitive Therapy for depression: A new approach to preventing relapse*. New York, NY: Guilford Press.

Shapiro, S. L., and Carlson, L. E. (2009). *The art and science of mindfulness: Integrating mindfulness into Psychology and the Helping Professions*. Washington, DC: APA.

Symington, S. H. and Symington, M. F. (2012). A Christian model of mindfulness: Using mindfulness principles to support psychological well-being, value-based behavior, and Christian spiritual journey. *Journal of Psychology and Christianity*, 31(1), 71–77.

Tan, S. (2011). Mindfulness and acceptance-based Cognitive-Behavioral therapies: Empirical evidence and clinical applications from a Christian Perspective. *Journal of Psychology and Christianity*, 30(3), 243–249.

Thomas, J., Raynor, M., and Bakker, M. C. (2016). Mindfulness-based stress reduction among Emirati Muslim women. *Mental Health, Religion & Culture*, 19(3), 295–304.

Van Gelder, K. (2006). Interview. In Lichtenstein, B. (2006). *Back from the edge: A landmark documentary-style short film*. United States: Lichtenstein Creative Media.

Waller, R., Trepka, C., Collerton, D., and Hawkins, J. (2010). Addressing spirituality in CBT. *The Cognitive Behaviour Therapist*, 3, 95–106.

Williams, M. and Kabat-Zinn, J. (2013). *Mindfulness: Diverse perspectives on its meaning, origins, and applications*. London: Routledge.

9 Addressing Spiritual Themes with Narrative Therapy

Andrew Z. Baker and Robert R. Freund

"The whole is more than the sum of its parts."

—Aristotle

Introduction

Personal and collective history are best understood as narratives. Humans process information like no other species, in large part, because of our ability to comprehend existence in a storied form. Our brains have developed to consume information via stories (Cron, 2012). In a book aptly titled *The Storytelling Animal*, Gottschall (2012) says, "We are, as a species, addicted to story. Even when the body goes to sleep, the mind stays up all night, telling itself stories" (p. xiv). Because of this obsession, the human experience is often defined by stories from many sources. Guiding stories fill sacred texts from every religious tradition, and people derive significant purpose and value from narratives of personal spiritual experience. Familial narratives, sociocultural messages, various forms of media, and even personal memories can drive present and future feelings, thoughts, behaviors, and ways of being. One study observed parents interacting with their children and they told a story an average of once every seven minutes. These stories were often themed with teaching life lessons and morals (Kottler, 2015). Meaning is often *made* for people in a passive or unconscious way from earlier in their lives.

Narrative Therapy

Eliciting and telling stories, meaning-making, and collaboration, are significant elements of many therapeutic approaches. In therapy, clinicians focus on the narrative of clients from the outset, often asking, "What brings you here today?" In simple terms, this is just a way of asking someone to tell you a story. Clients fill the session with similar communication, telling about six stories per session at about five minutes per story (Luborsky et al., 1992). As such, it would be folly to assume highlighting these concepts in therapy only began when founders Michael White and David Epston released *Narrative Means to Therapeutic Ends*

(1990). However, this is where narrative therapy as a separate and individual psychotherapeutic theory was truly rooted (Combs and Freedman, 1996). White and Epston (1990) posited clients present to therapy sharing a "problem-saturated" story of how they came to their current situation. These dominant narratives have been created by themselves and co-created with others in their lives. Clients often note various themes of failure or inadequacy. Narrative therapists seek to help clients "unpack" or "deconstruct" these narratives to create "thicker" or "richer" narratives, which allows them to change their relationships with their stories (Combs and Freedman, 1996; White, 2007). Better understanding personal narratives sequentially through the perspectives of the identity, actions, and the interaction of both gives clients power to shift their perspective and create a more meaning-driven life (White, 2007). Founders and proponents of narrative therapy focus on creating an explicit meaning-making process through processing narratives, which is what allows for this powerful re-authoring (White and Epston, 1990; Combs and Freedman, 1996; White, 2011; Madigan, 2011; Kottler, 2015).

To understand narrative therapy, it is important to understand the philosophical and paradigmatic foundation. In brief, the following concepts create the theoretical framework: reality is co-constructed between the observer and the observed; there are no "truths" only multiple perspectives (social constructivism); power and equality are important to assess and attend to in all systems and relationships (feminism); language is important in making meaning from life, so interpreting and studying language has utility (Hermeneutics); power and knowledge are often inseparable in society and power attempts to control knowledge (postmodernism); and labels and categories have limited utility (post-structuralism) (Combs and Freedman, 1996). This extremely abridged version of the theoretical underpinnings is meant only to serve as a scaffold for the philosophical base of narrative therapy. In essence, narrative therapy is a philosophical system as well as a therapeutic approach. This approach seeks to examine and uncover the relationship between power and knowledge in psychotherapy, and in doing so, challenges the status quo of diagnostic, problem-focused, top-down therapeutic practice. A quote from Chödrön (2002) illustrates the issue all-to-common within many counseling relationships: "Pity or professional warmth is easily mistaken for true compassion. When we identify ourselves as the helper, it means we see others as helpless. Instead of feeling the pain of the other person, we set ourselves apart" (p. 103). The most central concept to the philosophy of narrative therapy is that the therapist seeks a position as collaborator or consultant in the relationship.

One of the benefits of social constructivist approaches is that they are both "individual-acknowledging and system-acknowledging" (Cottone, 2012, p. 94). This is a benefit when considering application with diverse presentations; inclusive of religious, spiritual, gender, sexual orientation, cultural, political, socioeconomic, and other dynamics involving power differentials. The social constructivism paradigm focuses on the "relationship of the observer to the observed" (Cottone, 2012, p. 95), and because the client is the "observer" and the story is "the observed" the possibility of values imposition is decreased dramatically if executed appropriately. The therapist is both observer and participant within the therapeutic relationship. The therapist has inherent power over the therapeutic process, but a narrative therapist will purposefully focus on equalizing the power in the process as much as possible. This is to empower the client to hold the meaning-making and change processes. This is especially critical when attempting to deconstruct or unpack spiritual and religious themes from a client's story, as these themes are often central to the way people view their identities and the choices they make.

Spirituality and Narrative Therapy

As detailed in Chapter 2, there are many definitions of spirituality, but most tend to carry themes of meaning-making, values, identity, connection, beliefs, and concept-creation. If these concepts were framed as reflective questions they would convey the core implicit questions a narrative therapist may use to guide their curious exploration with a client. How do I make meaning with my actions? What are my values? What is my identity? One would be hard-pressed to answer these questions without reflecting purposefully on their lives as a storied existence. The thought experiments of theoreticians, the musings of philosophers, and the parables of religious figures were storied attempts to answer questions of such depth. Who we consider ourselves to be and the way we move through our lives is often led by a sense of belief. If these guiding concepts of meaning or belief, often labeled spirituality, were expressed; they would be conveyed in a narrative. Spirituality and story are inseparable. Stories are not told in isolation, and create shared meaning when discussed (White, 2011).

The first known story was designed to pass meaning to future generations – a cave drawing in the Chauvet Cave in the south of France, which depicts a group hunting, that is thought to be 30,000 years old (Kottler, 2015). Tracing back to the beginning of cultures, stories were (and are) important in the generational movement of information. There are dominant stories in all cultures, and often these narratives conflict with the individual narratives of clients (White, 2011; Kottler, 2015). Many cultures and religious traditions have their foundations in stories. Predominant religious and spiritual texts relay important meaning and messages to future generations which carry the values and morals of the system. These texts also serve to perpetuate the systems of which they are a part. Narrative therapy honors these systemic stories while also giving the client space to examine and change their relationship to these stories. It is critical to be able to help clients tease apart these dominant narratives from their own narrative, and examine the stories in their life from which they derive significant meaning. This process serves as a way to work with a host of cultures and diverse populations while remaining mindful and respectful of the different perspectives present.

Narrative Interventions and Techniques

The role of the psychotherapist in this theory is to help clients understand how they make meaning, and examine that meaning-making process collaboratively (Cottone, 2012). There are many techniques and interventions in various narrative forms of therapy, but only a small selection is summarized here. As Michael White is largely considered "the father of narrative therapy" (Combs and Freedman, 1996; Madigan, 2011), many of the interventions he discussed as "maps" (White, 2007) will be outlined. Although, it is important to note White stated, "I will emphasize here that the maps of this book are not the maps of narrative practice or a 'true' or 'correct' guide to narrative practice, whatever narrative practice is taken to be" (2007, p. 5). Because of the constructivist underpinnings of narrative therapy it is important to keep in mind that the client's perspective is what is most important and there is not one set "truth," but rather multiple and different viewpoints.

It is also important the therapist remain mindful of the privilege it is to hear rich stories, some of which have never been told to another human. As "Not only are we story*tellers* but also story*holders*" (Kottler, 2015, p. 12). As discussed earlier, and will be discussed further, the stance or posture of the therapist is as significant as any specific intervention or "map" (White, 2007). The process of therapy in the narrative tradition could potentially be sequential as discussed in this section, although any intervention discussed could be employed at any point throughout a course of therapy. The interventions that will be discussed are: externalizing conversations, conversations that highlight the unique outcomes, scaffolding conversations, re-authoring, re-membering conversations, definitional ceremonies, and using outsider witnesses (White, 2007).

Externalizing conversations are often discussed among narrative therapists using the expression, "you are not the problem, the problem is the problem," although it is not attributed to any one person (Combs and Freedman, 1996). This intervention also sets the stage for how a therapist is to approach the work. It is not a technique; it is a stance. This is best explained by White (2007) in the following metaphor:

> Although investigative reporters are not politically neutral, the activities of their inquiry do not take them into the domains of problem-solving, of enacting reform, or of engaging in direct power struggles with those who might be perpetrating abuses of power and privilege.
>
> (pp. 27–28)

This metaphor (true to narrative form) succinctly minimizes many concerns about the ability to utilize this therapy with diverse populations as it effectively shows that appropriate narrative practice requires setting personal and systemic power agendas aside during treatment. A high level of reverence is indicated when discussing concepts that surround how clients make meaning of their lives and their existence.

Externalizing a problem is a conversation which helps the client identify and define a problem, and create space between their identity and the problem. Upon creating this separation, a client-defined metaphor is often co-created. White (2007) offers a long list of examples, a few being: "Walking out on the problem," "Taming the problem," or "Harnessing the problem" (pp. 32–33). Clients often totalize their problem, and view it as completely negative (White, 2007). If a client can externalize the problem from their identity, they are often able to view their behaviors as purposeful and goal-oriented. Being able to deconstruct the externalized problem and carry forward the useful parts decreases the power of the less useful parts (White, 2007).

Externalizing spiritual or religious problems that the client perceives as fused to their identity could be helpful in creating enough space for the client to decide what parts of the problem they may want to keep. If a client has values that are clashing with their religious or spiritual beliefs the client has many choices: accept the incongruence, shift their religious identity to accommodate their values, change their actions to fit the culture or their values, and many other options. It is difficult to move through potential ambivalence if the client feels they do not have choices. Externalizing the problem will highlight these choices and disconnect the problem from the client's religious or spiritual identity which would allow for a thicker spiritual story (White, 2007).

Re-authoring or re-storying is the core therapeutic strategy in narrative therapy (White and Epston, 1990; Combs and Freedman, 1996; White, 2007, 2011; Kottler, 2015). While this concept can be thought of as an intervention, it can also be considered the driving force of all narrative conversations. Maintaining a curious perspective is of the utmost importance in narrative practice of any kind, as this allows the client to thicken their stories and allows the therapist to seek unique outcomes from which to build. Clients typically present to therapy with stories of problems, failures, or shortcomings. Realistically, if someone perceived everything to be going well in their life they probably would not be seeking the help of a professional. Re-authoring conversations are meant to assist the client in shifting their dominant (and often problem-saturated) story to something more strength- or solution-oriented. If one is able to raise the position of the more subordinate narratives of success or competence in their lives, they would be able to use these experiences to create further success and growth. As people change their relationships to their stories in this way, their identities and actions change as well (White, 2007).

Conversations that highlight unique outcomes (or exceptions), and scaffolding conversations are two interventions typically framed within re-authoring, although these can also be used as stand-alone interventions as well (White, 2007). Seeking unique outcomes centers on attending to subordinate and dominate narratives within the broader story someone is relaying. The client's dominant narrative is what is heard most and is likely how a client perceives themselves, others, and the world. If a client says,

"I am…", they are probably about to discuss the more dominant part of their narrative. For example, one person might say, "I was walking down the street and tripped on a curb, like always. I'm so clumsy." Another person might say, "I was walking down the street and tripped on a curb, which is strange because I'm usually so aware of my surroundings." In the first story, the narrator's dominant narrative may be that they are clumsy, unaware, or even inadequate at taking on life's challenges. This would then indicate their subordinate narrative is they are adequate and can handle life's challenges, which is what may be heard less often. The dominant narrative in the first version of the story is the subordinate narrative in the second version, and vice versa.

Beginning a conversation seeking unique outcomes would focus on noticing subordinate narratives of success, and asking questions that would develop these narratives further. Clients are able to shift their perspective by including these unique outcomes or exceptions into their dominant narrative (White, 2007). If a client's dominant narrative consists of a major theme of "weakness," a narrative therapist might listen for (or ask for) times the client was "strong" or "assertive." Examples of spiritual themes of strength may include times when the client was "faithful," "courageous," or "connected." These unique outcomes would serve to thicken a more preferable dominant narrative. As the client and therapist take notice of subordinate (and often strength-based) narratives, it comes to shift the client's perception of themselves and their ability to cope with life's challenges.

Scaffolding conversations are meant to bridge the gap between what is known and familiar and what could be in regard to the client's actions and identity (White, 2007). White (2011) based this intervention on Lev Vygotsky's concept of the zone of proximal development. In short, if one is to learn anything new there is a space that exists between what they already know, and what is possible to know. If this space is structured, a client can come to bridge this gap more quickly. Meaning is often made by the world, expectations, or others, whereas scaffolding conversations focus on the client making their own meaning, and the therapist's role is to help bridge this gap between the familiar and unfamiliar (White, 2007). If a unique outcome of "strength" was found and defined previously, counselors can scaffold by asking how the client was able to do something "strong" and what other "strong" actions may look like.

Further developing this conversation could be accomplished by asking the client what it means to be "strong" or what it would say of them if they were "strong" or acted in a "courageous" manner. Often though, one only has to listen for these exceptions to build on and follow up with questions rather than asking directly. The more a client guides the process, the more powerful the intervention, and more likely they will integrate change in their identity and accomplish actions. After scaffolding unique outcomes, re-authoring conversation can focus on defining landscapes of identity and landscapes of action (White, 2007). As the sequential narrative on each of these spectrums is defined and connected, future action and identity can be further developed.

Re-membering conversations are similar in shifting focus from the client's understanding of themselves to the people and connections in their life (White, 2007). To begin, encourage the client to consider life as a club of membership, and give them opportunity to change positions and importance of members (White, 2007). This often happens organically and only requires simple scaffolding questions on the part of the therapist. For example, a bully may be a main character in the bullied client's narrative, but a re-membering conversation could shift a good friend into a higher position of importance and shift the bully into a smaller role; asking a question like, "What might your friend think of you and what you're going through?" Focusing on the friend's perception could open up new possibilities and decrease the bully's perceived power over the client. The story could be viewed from multiple characters or member's perspectives in the client's life, and the client can learn novel strengths and solutions from these different views. Guardians, mentors, and supportive members of the client's life may be increased in position through considering their perception of the client. This also serves to externalize the problem as the narrative belongs to many different people in the client's life, but the narrative with a negative theme (in this case something like: "I'm too weak to defend myself") is the client's perspective so only they can change their relationship to it.

Definitional ceremonies and using outsider witnesses is another intervention for helping the client see their stories from multiple perspectives, and often serves to highlight themes, experiences, identities, and relationships (White, 2007). Potential outsider witnesses (e.g. family members, friends, clergy, or previous clients that went through a similar issue) would be prepared in lines of questioning and listening prior to the session (White 2007, 2011). The conversation would consist of the client telling the outsider witness their story, and the witness seeking themes and retelling the narrative. Then the client would retell the retelling as they heard it, which would allow for processing the narrative in an externalized way. This intervention serves to view the story from many perspectives and learn from the resulting thicker narrative (White, 2007).

Case Study

A fictional case example is used to illustrate how a narrative therapist may approach a conversation that is spiritually themed. Susanna is a 15-year-old, cisgender, Mexican American female; readers should reference the case of Susanna in the Introduction for a full description of her presenting problems. In introducing himself to the client, the counselor makes a mental note that he is a white male, who is large in stature and who is cast in a position of power as her therapist. His very presence may intimidate this client or lead her to feeling she cannot be genuine, so he takes particular care in assuming the perspective of an investigative reporter as White (2007) has discussed. He listens intently to the words the client chooses, and how she frames her reality. Further, he attempts to attend to how she feels others have shaped her story compared to where she feels she has more power in creating her own story.

She states her parents identify as part of the Mormon faith. The counselor notices how the client stated that her parents identify with that faith, but she doesn't include herself. She then shares she has been active in her church culture from a young age, and that she finds value in the sense of community, lessons on encouragement, and the moral structure that it provides. The counselor reflects how she seemed interested in what the community had to offer, and asks her about her personal beliefs. Upon discussion, the client reveals that she is not really sure how she identifies religiously, but described believing in God in the way that it has been discussed in her community. He asks the client how her own religious understandings influence her sense of spirituality. She begins, "I guess I never thought about the difference." After spending some time considering these differences, the client develops some ideas about her sense of connectedness to herself, the world, and others. The counselor asks, "How do your parents religious beliefs impact the way you see these concepts?" Susanna speaks about how she tends to view her beliefs and her parents as needing to be the same. The counselor notes the information and moves on.

She then begins to talk about why she is in therapy, and says that her guidance counselor wanted her to come in because she has been cutting herself and isn't spending time with friends anymore. The guidance counselor had informed the counselor that she has always been friendly, outgoing, and high achieving. She says she was just "stressed out" as she has always gotten good grades but is having trouble getting high scores like she used to. The counselor wonders aloud what it says about her if she doesn't get good grades; the client responds by saying it means she "isn't good enough." They spend time thickening this part of the narrative. In talking about other areas where she feels this applies to her, the client speaks about feeling it is another place where she is the "black sheep." "You see yourself as the odd one out," the counselor reflects. She says this is how she has felt since she could remember. They spend much of the remainder of the session discussing how the client's views of herself may influence behavior and vice versa. White (2007) refers to these areas as the landscape of identity and landscape of action. Understanding personal narratives in these two arenas and how they interact gives critical information in guiding conversation. The counselor attends to times that Susanna was not the "black sheep," which was quite easy to do. Susanna connects naturally, and exceptions to her problem are noted, as she has close friends at school and in her church community, despite feeling different historically.

When Susanna returns for another session, she speaks about how she had considered her own beliefs a bit more and had thought a lot about the things she values in her life. The counselor inquires what felt important to discuss from her reflections. She begins to discuss that these problems truly began when her body started changing and she felt attracted to other girls; specifically, a female classroom friend who expressed she liked Susanna as more than a friend. Although she felt the same way, she stopped talking with the girl and tried to focus on school more. She expresses feelings of guilt, confusion, fear, and anger. Susanna says she had begun to withdraw from others as well when this happened, including her family and faith community. The counselor reflects that it sounds like she began acting more "sheepish" than usual. She looks up from her downward gaze for the first time since beginning her soliloquy about her attraction to her friend. She wears a mischievous grin, and the counselor shares it with her. They laugh together for the first time. The counselor follows up, "So when you feel like a black sheep, you tend to act sheepish?" She nods. He asks her to define what it means to "act sheepish." She speaks about withdrawing, not feeling or being "herself," and feeling odd and not enough for others.

Susanna and the counselor have an externalizing conversation. They discuss if her attraction toward females is a problem for her, or if it is a problem of her church, her parents, or others. They spend sessions creating space for her preferred sense of self and deciding how she wants to relate to her problem of being "sheepish." They further discuss how she might change her relationship to this problem. Susanna comes to the conclusion that if being "sheepish" is the problem, being her true self is the solution. They begin to move deeper as therapy progresses. The counselor asks, "What does the church whisper into your ear?" and "What conclusions have you drawn about your relationship with the church because of these beliefs?" (Buchanan et al., 2001, p. 444). The counselor and Susanna then discuss what her true self whispers, and make meaning of that as well. Times that she acted in line with her true self serve as a beginning point to discuss how she might re-author the story of the "black sheep."

As conversations unfold the counselor focuses on understanding Susanna's dominant and problem-saturated story. More significantly, he looks for unique outcomes to the problems she discussed. They begin to discuss what this might mean for her in the near future, and she decides that continuing to cut herself and remain isolated would bolster her "sheepishness," so changing these behaviors is important. The counselor ends the session with Susanna by telling a story he had heard of Catholic priests who would punish themselves by walking up the stone steps of the cathedral on their knees until they would be bloodied. He tells her he isn't quite sure why it came to his mind, but that he thought it might be interesting to her. He asks her, "I wonder what the stone steps whispered in their ears?" and thanks her for being so authentic in the session. He shares with her that he values their relationship and the trust they have come to share.

The client begins to see improvements in grades, mood, and changes in her social and personal connectedness. At this point, the therapy shifts focus toward understanding her beliefs, sexuality, and the intersection of the two.

While this could have been addressed in prior sessions, the client's vulnerability and sense of safety were of greater importance to the therapy process. The counselor is careful to allow the therapy to develop at the client's pace, despite temptations to "dive in" when opportunities first arise. Once we hear such a problem it is the inclination of many of us to focus on the problem even if the client is not ready for such exploration. Knowing that Susanna will spend her whole life making meaning of what her spiritual and religious beliefs are, and how these intersect with her sexuality, the counselor thinks it prudent to take a few sessions (or more) for her to naturally bring them up. Buchanan et al. (2001) give wise suggestions for approaching these types of conversations:

> Are you comfortable with these religious (or spiritual) beliefs? Do you want them to guide your life? If yes, then what might your religious (or spiritual) beliefs tell you about your sexual identity? How might they encourage you to live? If no, then how would you like to modify or change your religious (or spiritual) beliefs? In what ways would you prefer that they support your sexual identity?... How is this way of looking at your sexual identity different from how you would have viewed yourself before? Who would be the first to notice if you viewed yourself in this way?... What does it say about you that you were able to look at your sexual identity in this way? What do you think your struggling with these issues tells me about you as a person? When you stand up against the oppression you feel, what type of person does that say you are?
>
> (p. 445)

Such questions allow for the ability to develop the client's preferred narrative and make meaning about how they view their own spirituality and sexuality. These questions allow for Susanna to do just that.

Susanna and the counselor later have a re-membering conversation in which they discuss the members in her life's club. Members include herself, her parents, the church, "Sheepishness," her friend whom she was attracted to, and so on. They discuss how these members contribute to her life and the importance each holds. Susanna shifts the importance or position of these members in her life and decides how she would like to view each member. To create even more richness in Susanna's process as she progresses in therapy, the counselor invites a past client who identifies as Mormon and who had come out as lesbian to a definitional ceremony in order to serve as an outsider witness. In this process, Susanna tells her story and the outsider witness is prompted to share the themes that stand out to her in retelling Susanna's story. Susanna then retells that retelling so she can make further meaning of her story through the externalizing conversational process (for more on re-membering conversations, definitional ceremonies, and outsider witness responses, see White, 2007). These sessions serve to further develop the richness of Susanna's re-authored understanding of herself and her problems.

Ideally in a course of narrative therapy, Susanna would go on to increase the position of her previously subordinate narrative that she is sufficient and anything unique about her identity would serve as strengths for her chosen actions. The counselor's goal is not simply to solve problems, nor to create specific outcomes, but to understand them in a broader context. Additionally, the counselor's goal is to have the awareness to notice the space between the known and familiar, and what could be. It is to highlight unique outcomes and scaffold the void between the dominant story of someone who is not enough, and the subordinate story of someone who is wholly sufficient. Re-authoring this story serves to create a richer, 'thicker' narrative and a deeper understanding of her preferred identity and reality. Throughout this process Susanna may come to develop the story of her identity further, as a young woman who is spiritual and religious, *and* attracted to the same sex. Moreover though, she may come to identify as sufficient, and her problems can be viewed as external. Her actions can become based on meaning, and reflect this new understanding of herself.

Further Reading

Combs, G. and Freedman, J. (1996). *Narrative therapy: The social construction of preferred realities*. New York: W. W. Norton.

Madigan, S. (2011). *Narrative therapy*. Washington, DC: American Psychological Association.

Morgan, A. (2000). *What is narrative therapy? An easy-to-read introduction*. Adelaide, S. Australia: Dulwich Centre Publications.

White, M. (2007). *Maps of narrative practice*. New York: W.W. Norton.

White, M. (2011). *Narrative practice: Continuing the conversations*. New York: W. W. Norton.

White, M., and Epston, D. (1990). *Narrative means to therapeutic ends*. New York: W. W. Norton.

References

Aristotle (2016). *A treasury of wisdom: Expounding the Bhagavad Gita, and epitome of all teachings and learnings* (R. Pal Baran, Trans.). East Midnapore, WB, India: Partridge.

Buchanan, M., Dzelme, K., Harris, D., and Hecker, L. (2001). Challenges of being simultaneously gay or lesbian and spiritual and/or religious: A narrative perspective. *The American Journal of Family Therapy*, 29(5), 435–449. doi:10.1080/01926180127629.

Chödrön, P. (2002). *The places that scare you: A guide to fearlessness in difficult times*. Boston, MA: Shambhala Publications.

Combs, G. and Freedman, J. (1996). *Narrative therapy: The social construction of preferred realities*. New York: W. W. Norton.

Cottone, R. R. (2012). *Paradigms of counseling and psychotherapy*. Cottleville, MO: Robert Rocco Cottone and Smashwords.

Cron, L. (2012). *Wired for story*. New York: Crown Publishing Group.

Gottschall, J. (2012). *The storytelling animal: How stories make us human*. New York, NY: Houghton Mifflin.

Kottler, J. A. (2015). *Stories we've heard, stories we've told*. New York: Oxford University Press.

Lopes, R. T., Gonçalves, M. M., Machado, P. P., Sinai, D., Bento, T., and Salgado, J. (2014). Narrative therapy vs. cognitive-behavioral therapy for moderate depression: Empirical evidence from a controlled clinical trial. *Psychotherapy Research*, 24(6), 662–674. doi:10.1080/10503307.2013.874052.

Luborsky, L., Barber, J. P., and Diguer, L. (1992). The meaning of narratives told during psychotherapy: The fruits of a new observational unit. *Psychotherapy Research*, 2, 277–290.

Madigan, S. (2011). *Narrative therapy*. Washington, DC: American Psychological Association.

McLeod, J. (2006). Narrative thinking and the emergence of post-psychological therapies. *Narrative Inquiry*, 16(1), 201–210. doi:10.1075/ ni.16.1.25.mcl.

Vromans, L., and Schweitzer, R. (2011). Narrative therapy for adults with major depressive disorder: Improved symptom and interpersonal outcomes. *Psychotherapy Research*, 21(1), 4–15. doi:10.1080/10503301003591792.

White, M. (2007). *Maps of narrative practice*. New York: W.W. Norton.

White, M. (2011). *Narrative practice: Continuing the conversations*. New York: W. W. Norton.

White, M. and Epston, D. (1990). *Narrative means to therapeutic ends*. New York: W. W. Norton.

10 12-Step Spirituality

Karrol-Jo Foster

"A journey of a thousand steps begins with a single step."

—Lao Tzu

Introduction

Addiction, whether it be to alcohol, drugs, food, sex, shopping, hoarding, work, gambling or the internet, is said to be one way that individuals try to fill an emptiness inside. While the etiology of addiction varies according to a diverse array of theories and a variety of factors, including heredity, environment, learning, stress, and behavioral frequency, one commonality among addictions is the pursuit of a promising pleasure. Furthermore, once the addiction becomes established, the energy and actions of the individual become destructive, demoralizing and compulsive in nature. This resulting excessive attachment not only impairs the addicted person's ability to perceive reality accurately, but also prevents the addicted person from living a balanced life (Sandoz, 2014). Such individuals are "restless, irritable and discontented" and "cannot after a time differentiate the truth from the false" (AA World Services, Inc., 2001). Destructive emotions such as anger, fear, and resentment compound these issues for the person struggling with addiction until they ultimately overpower the individual, forcing the admission of personal powerlessness and unmanageability. The solution to these internal effects of addiction, or the "spiritual malady," as described by Carl Jung, is the essential psychic change that takes place as the result of working the 12 Steps (AA World Services, Inc., 2001).

The 12-Step program outlined in the book *Alcoholics Anonymous* (AA World Services, Inc., 2001), more commonly referred to as the "Big Book," was groundbreaking for the treatment of alcoholism when it was first published in 1939, and has since been used as the program model for recovery from a multitude of addiction issues. *Alcoholics Anonymous* (AA) views addiction as an illness of the mind, body, and spirit that requires a commitment to abstinence and a working of the 12 Steps (Dermatis and Galanter, 2015). When AA refers to "working the 12 Steps," they are talking about spiritual practice (AA World Services, Inc., 2001). As such, the

12-Step model of recovery is a spiritual model that promotes a spiritual way of life. Even the first half of Step 1, "We admitted we were powerless over alcohol" is a spiritual experience (AA World Services, Inc., 1981, p. 21). In fact, scholars have gone so far as to describe 12-Step programs as spiritual programs of recovery that support the development of a new and transcendent meaning in the life of the recovery individual who is addicted (Cashwell et al., 2009).

Spirituality is virtually synonymous with 12-Step recovery, with underlying the substructure of each Step. In fact, the main mechanism of recovery and end goal of the entire 12-Step program is identified as a "spiritual awakening," or "vital spiritual experience" (AA World Services, Inc., 2001). The spiritual awakening is described in the Big Book as, "phenomena in the nature of huge emotional displacements and rearrangements. Ideas, emotions, and attitudes which were once the guiding forces of people's lives, are suddenly cast to one side and a completely new set of conceptions and motives begin to dominate them" (AA World Services, Inc., 2001, p. 27). This vital spiritual experience is discussed in depth in Appendix II of the Big Book, stating "with few exceptions, members find they have tapped an unsuspected inner resource which they identify with their own conception of a Power greater than themselves" (AA World Services, Inc., 2001, p. 567). Most believe this awareness is the essence of the spiritual experience. Yet, the spiritual experience in AA, and every other 12-Step derivative, is broad and varied, and for those who struggle with spiritual concepts, ongoing sobriety often brings the realization that, in some unforeseen and remarkable way, they have indeed experienced a spiritual change (AA World Services, Inc., 2014).

Bill Wilson, one of the co-founders of AA, describes spirituality in the Big Book's companion text, *Twelve Steps and Twelve Traditions* (commonly referred to as the "12 and 12"), stating,

> "[m]aybe there are as many definitions of spiritual awakening as there are people who have had them. But certainly each genuine one has something in common with all the others… When a man or a woman has a spiritual awakening, the most important meaning of it is that he has now become able to do, feel, and believe that which he could not do before on his unaided strength and resources alone."
>
> (AA World Service, Inc., 1981, p. 106)

The spiritual experience of the 12-Step model enables those who struggle with addiction to attain recovery physically, mentally, and spiritually. This chapter explores this 12-Step spiritual model. It includes a brief historical context, the role of spirituality in 12-Step addiction recovery and a full description of the 12 Steps, along with their goals and spiritual substructures. The chapter also provides evidence-based 12-Step interventions and a case example of the practical application of 12-Step Facilitation.

Historical Context

No commentary on the 12-Step model, especially with respect to spirituality, would be complete, nor can it be fully appreciated or understood, without the historical context of the 12-Step program that started it all: Alcoholics Anonymous (AA).

The 12-Step program of Alcoholics Anonymous (AA) is likely the most influential self-help organization in the world, and has enjoyed widespread acceptance as a *spiritual* approach to achieving recovery from addiction (Dermatis and Galanter, 2015; Kurtz and White, 2015; Sandoz, 2014). AA has been said to be the 'largest organization on Earth that nobody wanted to join' (Finlay, 2000). Current worldwide membership is estimated to be more than 2 million in 182 countries, with more than 100,000 active groups (AA World Services, Inc., 2015; McCrady and Tonigan, 2009). There are an estimated 53,665 AA groups and 1,213,269 members in the United States, alone (Schulz et al., 2009). The AA 12-Step model currently predominates in almost every substance abuse treatment and recovery program (Dermatis and Galanter, 2015; Walker et al., 2013), with 12-Step Facilitation empirically supported as an evidence-based practice (NIDA, 2017). The AA 12-Step program also has numerous derivatives, such as Narcotics Anonymous (NA), Cocaine Anonymous (CA), Sex and Love Addicts Anonymous (SLAA), Family Anonymous (FA), and Eating Disorders Anonymous (EDA). Suffice it to say, there is a 12-Step program for just about any issue, which speaks to both the popularity and utility of this model.

In addition to the contributions of AA co-founders Bill Wilson and Dr. Bob Smith, the origins of AA's 12-Step model, which serves as the benchmark upon which past and present self-help groups are measured (Kurtz and White, 2015), can be traced to some prominent influential figures; namely Dr. William Silkworth, William James, and Carl Jung. Furthermore, a significant contribution to the early evolution of the AA model came from the British-born Oxford Group movement, a non-denominational Christian evangelical group. Nonetheless, the 12-Step program, and its spiritual representation, *does not* promote nor affiliate itself with any religious organization (AA World Services, Inc., 2015; Friends in Recovery, 2012; Wilson, 1957), which can be a highly plausible testament to its world-wide success. Some basic knowledge of these major contributors and influences will provide substantial insight into the true technical merit of the 12-Step model, especially for those who struggle with the quasi-religious nature and underpinnings of the material presented in the Big Book.

Due in large part to Bill and Bob's participation in the Oxford Group, the Steps and the Big Book were written in the Judeo-Christian language of that group (Voxx, 2013). Consequently, a common misconception about AA is that it is a religious organization. Yet, in accordance with AA's primary purpose, "to stay sober and help other alcoholics to achieve sobriety" individuals need not subscribe to any particular belief system (AA World

Services, Inc., 2001). The word "God" is certainly there in the Steps, but it is purposely expressed in terms of a God or Higher Power of one's own understanding, that which anybody – anybody at all – can accept and try (Wilson, 1957).

In addition to the Oxford Group's influence, one of the three main individuals who also contributed to the development of AA was William D. Silkworth, MD. Dr. Silkworth was a neurologist and specialist in alcoholism, and responsible for providing Bill with the knowledge of alcoholism as an "allergy of the body" and an "obsession of the mind." Dr. Silkworth endorsed the AA program and contributed the first chapter to the Alcoholics Anonymous "Big Book," entitled "The Doctor's Opinion" (AA World Services, Inc., 2001). It is estimated that during his lifetime, Dr. Silkworth treated over 40,000 alcoholics and that perhaps no other physician has given so much individual attention to alcoholics (Wilson, 1957; Voxx, 2013).

Another hugely significant influence on the development of the 12-Step model was that of William James, a Harvard professor of psychology and philosophy. James wrote the book *Varieties of Religious Experience* (1902), which discusses various types of spiritual or religious phenomena and how it helps people live healthier lives. Bill received a copy of James' book during his final treatment for alcoholism at Towns Hospital in New York in 1934. James' beliefs about spiritual experiences and how they might totally transform a person's life provided Bill with many instrumental concepts that were later incorporated into the 12-Step program (Finlay, 2000).

Noted psychiatrist Carl Jung described the craving for alcohol as the equivalent of a spiritual thirst for wholeness, expressed in medieval language as, "the union with God"; his writings served to significantly influence the 12-Step program. Practitioners refer to his concept as "the hole in the soul." Though addictive behavior doesn't permanently fill the hole, this search for wholeness gives us a clue about spirituality. Jung said that alcohol in Latin is called "spiritus," and pointed out that we use the same word for higher consciousness experiences that we use for the most depraving poison. Jung believed that spirituality might be the best solution for an addicted person, and suggested that the most helpful formula, therefore, is: *spiritus contra spiritum* – the spirit against spirits (Cashwell et al., 2009; Covington, 2011). Many others concur with Jung's interpretation of addiction as a spiritual malady (Clinebell, 1963; Kurtz, 1979; Jellinek, 1952; Jellinek, 1960; Wilson, 1957).

Spirituality and 12–Step Recovery

Research supports spiritual growth as a change mechanism in 12-Step programs. In fact, among the change mechanisms specific to 12-Step recovery programs, none is more central to 12-Step philosophy or stressed as much in 12-Step practice as spiritual growth (Tonigan et al., 2013). This emphasis is made clear in the Big Book (AA World Services, Inc., 2001) which states, "the alcoholic at certain times has no effective mental defense against the first drink. Except in a few rare cases, neither he nor any other human being can provide such a defense. His defense must come from a Higher Power" (p. 43). Many recovering individuals point to their spiritual lives as being central to their sobriety (Cashwell et al,, 2009), with spirituality consistently ranked as one of the top factors in long-term sobriety (Foster, 2015).

An enduring challenge in 12-Step engagement (Brown et al., 2007) and spirituality research (Kelly, 2016) has been in adequately defining and measuring what constitutes the true meaning and nature of spirituality. The religious overtones of AA continue to raise concern and skepticism in the media and scientific arenas. Interestingly, in a general mental health context, spirituality has been defined as "a process of promoting opportunities to build meaningful personal connections, whether these are with oneself, others, nature, or a higher power" (Subica and Yamada, 2017). Definitions, however, vary greatly.

Based upon the role of spirituality in 12-Step recovery, adequately and competently addressing clients' understanding and potential misconceptions regarding spirituality and religion, within the context of their own personal belief system, practices and experiences, will be an important primary goal when working with individuals struggling with addiction. To that end, a helpful description has been presented by the psychiatrist, George Vaillant (2014). Vaillant describes spirituality as being biologically based, and religion as being entirely culturally based. According to this view, spirituality is similar to shining a white light through a prism to discover the spectrum of colors. Similarly, shining spirituality through a prism uncovers positive emotions such as gratitude, hope, forgiveness, compassion and empathy. These emotions lie within the biology of the human brain's limbic system and thus, are a universal reality of humankind. Vaillant (2014) further describes spirituality and religion using the metaphor of music and lyrics, with spirituality being like the music, and religion being like the lyrics. Many different sets of lyrics have developed over the centuries, manifesting as different religions.

Kelly (2016) extends Vaillant's words and music metaphor to AA members who choose or construct any form of belief system that makes sense to them. Even merely having a faith in the AA group appears to implicitly state that "you have the music within you"; but, instead of saying "here are the lyrics you must sing," AA's 12-Step model says "you get to write your own lyrics." Arguably, 12-Step models may be construed as religious, but certainly not as religions. Newcomers are recommended to attend 90 meetings in 90 days to encourage immersion in the program, but also as a way to try out many different meetings in hopes that the individual will find some that fit their style, and at which they experience a sense of being "at home" (Kurtz and White, 2015).

Professional counselors should not only be aware of the different styles of meetings offered within the AA 12-Step program (i.e. speaker, literature, discussion, gender-specific, etc.), but also be aware of the many diversified alternative recovery groups which exist relative to AA and the 12-Step recovery model. There are, essentially, two broad patterns of diversification within the history of AA. The first occurs when one or more members experience an incongruity between their personal beliefs and AA practices, prompting them to abandon AA and start an organization that offers an alternative to AA. This is represented in AA adaptations and alternatives such as Alcoholics for Christ, Millati Islami, Celebrate Recovery, Buddhist Recovery Network, Rational Recovery, SMART Recovery, and Moderation Management (Kurtz and White, 2015). The second occurs when individuals or subgroups seek and promote a different style of recovery within AA, itself. This trend includes adjuncts for AA members who wish to pursue spiritual growth through a particular religious orientation (Jewish Alcoholics, Chemically Dependent People and Significant Others or J.A.C.S.) and adaptations that seek to secularize or "Christianize" AA history and practice. The former including groups within AA (AA for Atheists and Agnostics) and the latter involving groups that promote a more religious focus within the meetings (i.e. the "Back to Basics" and "Primary Purpose" movements). Having a familiarity with these programs, other 12-Step alternatives (i.e. NA, CA, SLAA, FA, EDA), and where they exist within your community will be extremely helpful to the variety of clients you will serve.

The 12 Steps

Table 10.1 provides a complete listing of the 12 Steps, along with the corresponding goal, purpose and spiritual substructure. This is followed by a more detailed description of the Steps.

Steps 1–3 all focus on powerlessness and surrender (letting go), and build the spiritual foundation for the remaining nine steps. Sandoz (2014) refers to *Step 1* as the readiness and willingness to place oneself on the "spiritual conveyer belt," a process which he describes as ultimately moving one onto the path of change and transformation. *Step 2* is the gradual process of coming to believe in something greater than oneself as a resource for change. Early on, some people identify the AA group, itself, as this power for change. Therefore, meeting attendance and fellowship are critical. *Step 3* is a crucial and pivotal point in the program when the addicted person lets go of his or her ego and self-centered thinking, or "running the show," as it is referred to in the Big Book (AA World Services, Inc., 2001). During this step, the individual begins to seek the intuitive knowledge that God or a Higher Power provides. This is simplified by a three-fold procedure of *think, pray, act*; whereby, the newcomer thinks about the pain that is avoided through sobriety, prays for the willingness to continue with recovery, and takes action, in efforts to follow through with such intentions.

Steps 4–9 have been referred to as the "Action Steps" by members of the AA fellowship (AA World Services, Inc., 1981). *Step 4* is about becoming

Table 10.1 Goal of the Twelve Steps

Goal	Purpose	Step	Spiritual substructure
Peace with God, Universe, Higher Power	**Step One** is about recognizing our problem and the inability to solve it on our own (lack of sufficient power).	We admitted we were powerless over *the addiction/issue* – that our lives had become unmanageable.	**Honesty and Acceptance**
	Step Two is about the birth of faith that there is a Power sufficient to solve the problem.	Came to believe that a power greater than ourselves could restore us to sanity.	**Hope**
	Step Three involves a decision to let that Power be in charge and help guide our lives.	Made a decision to turn our will and our lives over to the care of God; *as we understand God.*	**Faith**
Peace with Self	**Step Four** involves self-examination.	Made a searching and fearless moral inventory of ourselves.	**Courage**
	Step Five is the discipline of admitting our wrongs.	Admitted to God, to ourselves, and to another human being the exact nature of our wrongs.	**Integrity**
	Step Six is the beginning of an inner transformation.	Were entirely ready to have God remove all these defects of character.	**Willingness**
	Step Seven involves the transformation of our character through the Power.	Humbly asked God to remove our shortcomings.	**Humility**
Peace with Others	**Step Eight** involves examining our relationships and preparing ourselves to make amends.	Made a list of all persons we had harmed and became willing to make amends to them all.	**Brotherly Love**
	Step Nine is the discipline of making amends.	Made direct amends to such people wherever possible, except when to do so would injure them or others.	**Self-Discipline**
	Step Ten is about maintaining progress in recovery.	Continued to take personal inventory and, when we were wrong, promptly admitted it.	**Perseverance**
Keeping the Peace	**Step Eleven** involves the spiritual disciplines of prayer and meditation.	Sought through prayer and meditation to improve our conscious contact with God as we understand God, praying only for the knowledge of God's will for us and the power to carry that out.	**Connection to Power**
	Step Twelve is about sharing the Power with others.	Having had a *spiritual awakening* as the result of these steps, we tried to carry this message to others, and to practice these principles in all our affairs.	**Love and Service**

Source: Adapted from *The Twelve Steps: A Way Out* (Friends in Recovery, 2012).

honest about actions and behaviors. Sponsors assist the newcomer in pre-paring an inventory of fears, resentments, and harms done to others. This takes courage, and is a place where many individuals are at risk for relapse, due to the process of having to take a hard and painful look in the mirror. *Step 5* involves the sharing of one's 4th Step list with another person. This process of telling one's story promotes self-knowledge and acceptance. *Steps 6 and 7* allow for changes in one's current identity and self-image, as one becomes more open to added growth and recovery. This step includes a willingness to get rid of personal shortcomings by asking God or a Higher Power to remove them. *Steps 8 and 9* are all about our personal relationships with others, and involve making amends to those harmed, either by personal apology or restitution. Critical to Step 9 is that no amends are made if it runs the risk of causing any additional harm in the process.

Steps 10–12 are considered "Maintenance Steps," but are steps that the newcomer is encouraged to begin to practice very early in recovery, they do not need to wait until they complete Step 9. *Step 10* represents the ongoing attention paid to actions, on a daily basis. *Step 11* is the practice of prayer and meditation. While the newcomer may not yet have had a spiritual awakening, in *Step 12*, they are encouraged to reach out and do service as quickly as possible. All three steps are reminders that one must continue to grow spiritually, or one will revert back to old habits; ways of thinking and behaving that could ultimately lead to death (Sandoz, 2014).

12 Step Interventions

Intervention, as described in this section, refers to a professionally delivered program or service designed to treat an individual's addiction issue. Empirically supported, evidence-based interventions which are specific to the 12-Step program model are presented, as well as, the spiritual sub-structure represented by this model. This requires a two-fold approach, as facilitating 12-Step participation is an evidence-based "intervention," in and of itself. Yet, there are also beneficial and empirically supported therapeutic interventions represented *within* the 12-Step model (i.e. prayer, meditation, gratitude) that can be employed to further foster spiritual growth as the primary mechanism for change.

12 Step Facilitation

According to the U.S. Department of Health and Human Services (US HSS, 2016), 12-Step programs are not, themselves, classified as medical treatments; but rather, fall under the category of Recovery Support Services (RSS). Conversely, there are numerous 12-Step *facilitation* interventions that are considered individual or group therapy models designed specifically to prepare individuals to understand, accept, and become engaged in Alco-holics Anonymous (AA), Narcotics Anonymous (NA), Cocaine Anonymous

(CA) and other similar 12-Step programs (Kaskutas et al., 2009; Walitzer et al., 2009). These 12-Step facilitation interventions not only produce significantly higher rates of abstinence post-treatment, but also result in lower health-care costs (Humphreys and Moos, 2001; Mundt et al., 2012).

Twelve-Step facilitation interventions differ from simply emphasizing and encouraging clients to attend 12-Step meetings. The interventions serve a conjunctive purpose with the philosophy and tenets to facilitate and build on what individuals learn by participating in meetings. It begins with systematically helping the individual gain a better understanding of the components of the 12-Step program model. Subsequently, their under-standing and acceptance of these principles will lead to greater engagement and better outcomes (Donovan et al., 2013).

Spirituality Facilitation

Key components of the 12-Step model include trusting in a higher power, finding strength through prayer and meditation, and connecting with others of similar beliefs (AA World Services, Inc., 2001). Many individuals struggle with the quasi-religious nature of the 12-Step model and will typically define and understand "God" and spirituality based upon prior religious experiences. As a result, in order to fully engage and participate in a 12-Step recovery program, many need assistance in order to understand spirituality and develop spiritual behaviors that either veer outside of the context of religion, or fit within their own religious framework. Research has shown that the practice of prayer and meditation has a positive correlation with length of sobriety, and that those individuals who remain sober for greater than two years expressed significantly greater levels of spirituality, as compared to those who had relapsed (Priester et al., 2009).

The 12-Step model, as a spiritual program of recovery, utilizes spiritual practice to promote recovery, yet there are no evidence-based program specifically designed to facilitate spiritual involvement. In a search of the literature, the only known formal *spirituality* intervention was developed by Brown et al. (2007). This seven-week behavioral spirituality intervention is called "Knowing Your Higher Power." The program is intended to be utilized in conjunction with the individual's 12-Step participation to facilitate integration of spiritual beliefs into their treatment plan. The intervention is based on social-cognitive theory, and is aimed to impact behavioral skills related to spiritual involvement, such as identifying a higher power, practi-cing prayer and meditation, and attending group spiritual activities (Brown et al., 2007). This is done through readings followed by facilitated group discussion, vicarious modeling through accounts of spirituality mediated sobriety success and skills training. In a study conducted by Brown et al. (2007), the sample showed significant increase in spiritual involvement and beliefs over the 12-week measurement period and significantly greater spiritual involvement and beliefs in those maintaining total sobriety,

Table 10.2 Focus and key features of four evidence-based 12-step facilitation interventions

12-Step Intervention Features	Twelve-Step Facilitation Therapy (TSF)	Systematic Encouragement and Community Access (SECA)	Making AA Easier (MAAEZ)	Stimulant Abuser Groups to Engage in 12-Step (STAGE-12)
Primary Focus	To increase likelihood of 12-Step engagement by increasing knowledge and understanding of 12-Step principles and steps.	To increase 12-Step engagement by linking the individual to 12-Step group through use of a 12-Step volunteer.	To increase likelihood of 12-Step engagement by reducing real or perceived barriers and addressing expectations.	To increase the likelihood of 12-Step engagement by linking the individual to 12-Step group through use of a 12-Step volunteer and increasing knowledge and understanding of 12-Step principles and steps.
Goal	Understanding and integration of the 12-Step concepts of acceptance and surrender.	Facilitation of participation in AA, NA, CA or other 12-Step program.	Facilitation of participation in AA, NA, CA or other 12-Step program.	Facilitation of participation in AA, NA, CA or other 12-Step program *plus* understanding and integration of the 12-Step concepts of acceptance and surrender.
Intervention Delivery	5 "core" and 6 "elective" individual or group sessions.	3 individual sessions	6 group sessions.	3 individual and 5 group sessions.

Source: Adapted from Donovan et al. (2013).

compared to those who relapsed. This intervention can be utilized and incorporated by the professional counselor in conjunction with any of the above referenced 12 Step Facilitation interventions.

Spiritual Practice

Without any formally "agreed-upon" definition of spirituality, the focus of the 12-Step model on gratitude, hope, forgiveness, and compassion can be considered spiritual, in essence (Kelly, 2016). Therefore, utilizing specific spiritual practice interventions such as gratitude, prayer, meditation, and self-forgiveness to enhance spiritual growth serves to further facilitate resilience and recovery from addiction (Kelly et al., 2011; Dermatis and Galanter, 2015; Tonigan et al, 2013).

Positive Psychology (Seligman et al., 2005) has been a popular approach to overall improved health and wellbeing. This approach can be useful in providing a rubric under which AA's *spirituality* can be framed to provide ancillary clinical interventions to clients struggling with addiction issues. One of the main conceptual domains of Positive Psychology is a "Meaningful Life" which Seligman (2005) describes as "belonging and serving something larger than oneself." This parallels the 12-Step model's concept of a "higher power." Positive Psychology is a beneficial resource for spiritual practice interventions that are empirically supported, such as: prayer, meditation, cultivating forgiveness, self-compassion, mindfulness, cultivating gratitude, gratitude journaling, identifying strengths, search for the Sacred, and "you at your best," to name a few.

One reason for the popularity and growth of the 12-Step model and its inherent focus on spirituality may relate to the disinhibiting effects of substance abuse on behavior; specifically, the often and regrettable deviations from an individual's personal values. This "Jekyll and Hyde" scenario, repeated over and over, can lead to a sense of profound moral failing and self-loathing, which is intensified and deepened by the reproach of affected loved ones. For many individuals struggling with addiction, the sense of "redemption" that is historically and implicitly embedded within 12-Step philosophy (AA World Services, Inc., 2001) may provide a compassionate framework for self-forgiveness (Kelly et al., 2011).

Case Study

The present study involves the case of Nassir, a 40-year-old man who practices the Islamic faith and is in recovery from an addiction to prescription pain medication (please see Nassir's client profile in the Introduction to this book). During one of the initial sessions with Nassir, a spiritual assessment was conducted to gather information regarding Nassir's spiritual beliefs, practices, and experiences. The counselor's goal is to identify what potential misconceptions he may have regarding spirituality, if any. Nassir reports that as a Muslim, he believes in Allah as the one God and follows the teachings of Muhammad. He says that he attended mosque religiously with his family growing up, and was still very involved in his faith community up until his surgery. He started to fall off with his religious practices soon after his surgery, and has not been able to return to the mosque at all since his overdose, primarily due to the shame. Nassir says that he believes Allah is all-powerful and the one and only God. He additionally states that he feels he has disappointed Allah and brought shame upon his family with his drug use and resulting overdose. He shares that he has always prayed on a daily basis, but that he hasn't been praying as much since his, "problem with his medication" took hold. He states that he generally only prays when he is in desperate pain; he is embarrassed to admit that at times he has cursed Allah for this pain. Nassir also reports having a hard time coming to terms with being identified as an "addict" and even though he knows in his heart that he is addicted to "these drugs that have taken over my whole life," he is still having a hard time accepting his situation and where it has taken him.

When asked specifically about spirituality, Nassir states that he considers his Islamic faith to be his spirituality and that all spirituality, and even faith, he once had and felt has been lost as the result of his drug use. He shares that he doesn't know if he will ever feel worthy again in the eyes of Allah. Conducting a formal spiritual assessment with Nassir provides the counselor the opportunity to educate him on spirituality outside the context of his religious beliefs and to gain a better understanding of spirituality as it relates to his beliefs, practices, and experiences. It also offers an opportunity to discuss spirituality in the context of his addiction. Nassir discloses that, as a child, he experienced feeling close to his higher power, but that he has not felt close to Allah in a "very long time." He further talks about his prayer life and not feeling as though his heart was in it for a very long time, even before his addiction took hold.

Twelve-Step Facilitation Therapy (TSF) is the main intervention selected for use with Nassir. It begins with educating him about the 12-Step program and helping him to engage in the 12-Step program of Narcotics Anonymous (NA). This proves especially beneficial for Nassir, as he believed 12-Step programs to be religious, and in direct conflict with his own specific belief system. By educating Nassir about the history and philosophy of the program, as well as, how it works, Nassir is able to gain a new awareness and understanding of the 12-Step model as a "spiritual" program, and not one that is religious. He also begins attending NA meetings; albeit, reluctantly, at first. After a few weeks, Nassir identifies a sponsor who practices Islam, and who has a similar history of struggles with medication and drug abuse as his own. After beginning his work with his sponsor, Nassir shares that he has started praying again on a daily basis (both morning and night), and has begun to practice meditation as well. Through the on-going relationship with his sponsor, as well as his work with his counselor, Nassir has come to accept his addiction and the steps he will need to consistently take in efforts to stay abstinent; healing physically, mentally, emotionally, and spiritually.

In addition to the daily practice of prayer and meditation as a part of his NA program, Nassir also benefits from the spiritual practice interventions of gratitude, mindfulness, cultivating forgiveness and self-compassion implemented by his counselor. Nassir's counselor gives him assignments to complete on forgiveness and self-compassion, specifically designed to address his shame. Nassir is also encouraged to start a daily gratitude journal.

After three months of following the NA program and working with his counselor to address his shame, Nassir is able to accept his powerlessness over his drug use and the unmanageability that it has caused in his life. He also expresses faith that through his relationship with his sponsor, attending meetings and working the Steps, that his life will get better. He is embarking on the process of self-examination to identify unhealthy patterns of behavior. As a result, Nassir is no longer on probation with his job as an insurance salesman.

After six months of sobriety, Nassir begins to work on healing the damaged relationships with friends and family members. He also begins attending mosque again for the first time in almost a year. Nassir reports a renewed connection to his faith and a more personal relationship with Allah. He talks about Allah's mercy and his gratitude for the strength and power he has been given through a relationship with Allah and others. He sees his ability to continue to move forward in his recovery, and interprets his ability to remain clean and sober as a sure sign of Allah helping him.

After nine months of sobriety, Nassir has completed nine of the 12 Steps of his NA program, and is feeling a novel sense of awareness and empowerment. He reports that he is feeling a sense of purpose in life that is "different this time." Even more importantly to Nassir has been the ability to come to forgive himself, and the overwhelming sense of gratitude he has for his life. He says that he no longer sees his addiction as a moral failure and feels that, through the process of recovery, he is starting to see himself as becoming a better version of himself than he was before the accident and his addiction took control. Nassir reports that his sales at work have been the best they have ever been, and says his sense of confidence has improved. He specifically credits his ongoing recovery, especially his *spirituality*, restoration of faith, and connection to his Allah.

Nassir continues to attend NA meetings and sees his counselor once a month to check-in, review his progress and address any ongoing issues. These sessions generally focus on continuing to build upon Nassir's strengths and his ongoing desire to develop healthy relationships. Nassir states that he is looking forward to becoming a sponsor, so that he can help others like those who have helped him. He has a home group, does service for NA, as well as in his faith community, and has built a solid support group of others in NA on a similar path with similar beliefs and religious practices to his own.

References

Alcoholics Anonymous World Services, Inc. (2001). *Alcoholics Anonymous* (4th ed.) New York, NY: Author.

Alcoholics Anonymous World Services, Inc. (2015). *A.A. Fact File*. New York, NY: Author. Accessed June 24, 2017, http://www.aa.org/assets/en_US/aa-litera ture/m-24-aa-fact-file.

Alcoholics Anonymous World Services, Inc. (1973). *Came to believe*. New York, NY: Author.

Alcoholics Anonymous World Services, Inc. (2014). *Many paths to spirituality*. New York, NY: The A.A. Grapevine, Inc.

Alcoholics Anonymous World Services (1981). *Twelve steps and twelve traditions* (3rd ed.). New York, NY: Alcoholics Anonymous World Services, Inc.

Allen, J. P., Mattson, M. E., Miller, W. R., Tonigan, J. S., Connors, G. J., Rychtarik, R. G., … Litt, M. (1997). Matching alcoholism treatments to client heterogeneity: Project MATCH posttreatment drinking outcomes. *Journal of Studies on Alcohol*, 58(1), 7–29.

Bevacqua, T., and Hoffman, E. (2010). William James's "sick-minded soul" and the AA recovery paradigm: Time for reappraisal. *Journal of Humanistic Psychology*, 50(4), 440–458. doi:10.1177/0022167810373041.

Brown, A. E., Pavilik, V. N., Shegog, R., Whitney, S. N., Friedman, C. R., Romero, C., Davis, G. C., Cech, I., Kosten, T. R., and Volk, R. J. (2007). Association of spirituality and sobriety during a behavioral spirituality intervention for twelve step (ts) recovery. *The American Journal of Drug and Alcohol Abuse*, 33(4), 611–617. doi:10.1080/00952990701407686.

Cashwell, C., Clarke, P., and Graves, E. (2009). Step by step: avoiding spiritual bypass in 12-step work. *Journal of Addictions & Offender Counseling*, 30(1), 37–48.

Centers for Disease Control and Prevention (2017). Fact sheets – Alcohol use and your health. Retrieved from https://www.cdc.gov/about/report/health-statistics. html Accessed June 24, 2017.

Clinebell, H. J. (1963). Philosophical-Religious factors in the etiology and treatment of alcoholism. *Journal of Studies on Alcohol and Drugs*, 24, 473–488.

Covington, S. (2011). *A woman's way through the twelve steps & a woman's way through the twelve steps workbook*. Center City, MN: Hazelden Publishing.

Dermatis, H., and Galanter, M. (2015). 'The role of twelve-step-related spirituality in addiction recovery. *Journal of Religion and Health*, 55(2), 510–521. doi:10.1007/s10943-10015-0019-0014.

Donovan, D. M., Ingalsbe, M. H., Benbow, J., and Daley, D. C. (2013). 12-Step interventions and mutual support programs for substance use disorders: An overview. *Social Work in Public Health*, 28(3–4), 313–332. doi:10.1080/19371918.2013.774663.

Finlay, S. (2000). Influence of Carl Jung and William James on the origin of Alcoholics Anonymous. *Review of General Psychology*, 4(1), 3–12.

Foster, A. (2015). An investigation of the program curriculum leading to successful sobriety in a substance abuse residential treatment center in florida (Doctoral dissertation). Retrieved from FAU database June, 2017.

Friends In Recovery (2012). *The 12 Steps: A Way Out*. Scotts Valley, CA: RPI Publishing, Inc.

Humphreys, K., and Moos, R. (2001). Can encouraging substance abuse patients to participate in self-help groups reduce demand for health care? *Alcoholism: Clinical and Experimental Research*, 25(5), 711–716.

James, W. (1902/1985). *Varieties of Religious Experience*. Cambridge, MA: Harvard University Press.

Jellinek, E. M. (1952). Phases of alcohol addiction. *Quarterly Journal of Studies of Alcohol*, 13, 673–684.

Jellinek, E. M. (1960). *The disease concept of alcoholism*. New Brunswick, NJ: Hillhouse Press.

Kaskutas, L. A., Subbaraman, M. S., Witbrodt, J., and Zemore, S. E. (2009). Effectiveness of making Alcoholics Anonymous easier: A group format 12-step facilitation approach. *Journal of Substance Abuse Treatment*, 37(3), 228–239.

Kelly, J. F. (2016). Is Alcoholics Anonymous religious, spiritual, neither? Findings from 25 years of mechanisms of behavior change research. *Society for the Study of Addiction*, 112, 929–936. doi:10.1111/add.13590.

Kelly, J. F., Stout, R. L., Magill, M., and Tonigan, J. S. (2011). The role of Alcoholics Anonymous in mobilizing adaptive social network changes: A prospective lagged mediational analysis. *Drug and Alcohol Dependence*, 114: 119–126.

Kurtz, E. (1979). *Not God: A history of Alcoholics Anonymous*. Center City, MN: Hazelden Educational Services.

Kurtz, E., and White, W. (2015). Recovery Spirituality. *Religions*, 6(1), 58–81.

Lao-tzu (1988). *Tao te ching: A new English version* (S. Mitchell, Trans.). New York: Harper & Row.

McCrady, B. S., and Tonigan, J. S. (2009). Recent research into twelve step programs. In R. K. Ries, D. A., Fiellen, S. C. Miller and R. Saitz (Eds.), *Principles of addiction medicine* (4th ed., pp. 923–938). Philadelphia, PA: Wolters Kluwer/ Lippincott Williams & Wilkins.

Mundt, M. P., Parthasrathy, S., Chi, F. W., Sterling, S., and Campbell, S. I. (2012). 12-Step participation reduces medical use costs among adolescents with a history of alcohol and other drug treatment. *Drug Alcohol Dependence*, 126(1–2): 124–130. doi:10.1016/j.drugalcdep.2012.05.002.

National Institute on Drug Abuse. (2017). DrugFacts: Treatment approaches for drug addiction. Retrieved from https://www.drugabuse.gov/publications/princip les-drug-addiction-treatment/evidence-based-approaches-to-drug-addiction-trea tment/behavioral-therapies. Accessed on June, 2017.

Priester, P. E., Scherer, J., Steinfeldt, J. A., Jana-Masri, A., Jashinsky, T., Jones, J. E., and Vang, C. (2009). The frequency of prayer, meditation and holistic interventions in addictions treatment: A national survey. *Pastoral Psychology*, 58, 315–322. doi:10.1007/sl11089–11009–0196–0198.

Sandoz, J. (2014) Finding god through the spirituality of the 12 steps of alcoholics anonymous. *Religions*, 5(4), 948–960. doi:10.3390/rel5040948.

Seligman, M. E., Steen, T. A., Park, N., and Peterson, C. (2005). Positive psychology progress: empirical validation of interventions. *American Psychologist*, 60(5), 410–421. doi:10.1037/0003–066X.60.5.410.

Schulz, J. E., Williams, V., and Galligan, J. E. (2009). Twelve step programs in recovery. In R. K. Ries, D. A. Fiellen, S. C. Miller, and R. Saitz (Eds.), *Principles of addiction medicine* (4th ed., pp. 911–922). Philadelphia, PA: Wolters Kluwer/Lippincott Williams & Wilkins.

Subica, A. M., and Yamada, A. (2017). Development of a spirituality-infused cognitive behavioral intervention for individuals with serious mental illnesses. *Psychiatric Rehabilitation Journal*, 41(1), 8–15.

Tonigan, J., Rynes, K., and McCrady, B. (2013). Spirituality as a Change Mechanism in 12-Step Programs: A Replication, Extension, and Refinement. *Substance Use & Misuse*, 48(12), 1161–1173.

U.S. Department of Health and Human Services (HSS), Office of the Surgeon General. (2016). *Facing Addiction in America: The Surgeon General's Report on Alcohol, Drugs, and Health*. Washington, DC: HHS.

Vaillant, G. E. (2014). *Spiritual evolution: A scientific defense of faith harmony*. New York, NY: Oxford University Press.

Voxx, A. (2013). *The five keys: Twelve step recovery without a God*. 1st ed. Maze Publishing.

Walitzer, K. S., Dermen, K. H., and Barrick, C. (2009). Facilitating involvement in Alcoholics Anonymous during out-patient treatment: A randomized clinical trial. *Addiction*, 104(3), 391–401.

Walker, R., Godlaski, T. M., and Staton-Tindall, M. (2013). Spirituality, drugs, and alcohol: A philosophical analysis. *Substance Use & Misuse*, 48(12), 1233–1245. doi:10.3109/10826084.2013.799020.

Wilson, W. G. (1957). *Alcoholics Anonymous comes of age*. New York, NY: Alcoholics Anonymous World Services, Inc.

11 Family Systems

Genograms and Socio-metric Assessments

Brian S. Canfield

"So I say to you, ask and it will be given to you; search, and you will find; knock, and the door will be opened for you."

—Jesus of Nazareth (Luke 11:9; NIV)

Introduction

Human behavior is best understood when there is an assessment of the context in which such behavior occurs. It is widely recognized that significant interpersonal relationships, notably current family and family-of-origin experiences, exert a life-long and profound influence in shaping attitudes, beliefs, and expectations (Canfield et al., 1992). Depending upon the nature of the issue that prompts a person to seek help from a professional counselor, the interconnected nature of family relationships, and religious and spiritual beliefs often emerge during the course of therapy.

For many, exposure to religious education and practices begins in childhood, and reflects family beliefs and core values. Invariably, a child born into a religiously observant family is cognitively and emotionally impacted by the religious beliefs of the family (Abbott et al., 1990). As such, it is often useful within the context of the therapeutic relationship for the counselor to explore thoroughly family religious and spiritual associations, and the influence these associations may play in understanding a client's needs (Mahoney, 2010). More important, is gaining an understanding of the meaning the client attributes to these issues. To advance this understanding, several family-based assessment tools and socio-metric intervention techniques for facilitating therapeutic change are presented in this chapter.

In examining the use of socio-metric interviewing techniques, this chapter also contains a perspective on the status and changing demographics of religious affiliation, both within American culture and around the world. Inclusion of this information reflects the isomorphic and concentric nature of religion and spirituality, and the impact it has on individuals, couples, families, communities, nations, regions, and the world-at-large. Insights into changing international demographics also parallel how religious identity and affiliation may change over the course of a person's life, and the potential impact resulting from such change. Over their life span, a person may become more or less observant in their religious practice, or change their religious belief and/or affiliation altogether. Socio-metric techniques provide a means for gathering this information and assessing the impact that the current status or changes in client's religious or spiritual beliefs may hold (Frame, 2000).

Family Systems and Spirituality

Regardless of the cause or nature of a client's concerns – whether "bio-genic," "psychogenic," or a combination of both – all problems are embedded within the context of interpersonal relationships. A family systems approach to counseling recognizes the impact and importance of such relationships in a person's life. In addition to a person's current family relationships, childhood family experiences (i.e. "family-of-origin" experiences) exert an emotional influence over their life span (Canfield et al., 1992). A person's self-identity, with regard to religion or spiritual awareness, often holds broad implications for shaping and maintaining a client's worldview on a wide range of issues. For many people, "family" conveys powerful messages with regard to religion and spirituality.

The role of religion and spirituality is an important aspect in the lives of many people. For billions of people around the world, religious identity and practice is a key defining cultural demographic and a central determinant of their worldview, as described in Chapter 2. For most people, their initial sense of spiritual awareness and religious identity stems from childhood family (family-of-origin) experiences (Canfield et al., 1992). As such, it is incumbent upon a counselor to explore these issues with clients, in order to gain an understanding of how these issues may contribute to the creation, maintenance, and amelioration of client concerns that emerge in therapy.

While often individuals are born into a religious culture, such identity is not fixed and is subject to change over the lifespan for many people. As noted by the Pew Research Center (2015):

> In some countries, including the United States, it is fairly common for adults to leave their childhood religion and switch to another faith (or no faith). For example, many people raised in the U.S. as Christians become unaffiliated in adulthood, and vice versa – many people raised without any religion join a religious group later in their lives. However, in some other countries, changes in religious identity are rare or even illegal.

In working with clients, it is essential that the counselor gain an understanding of the meaning the client and those with whom the client interacts assign to spirituality, religious identity, and belief, in order to avoid misleading assumptions or generalizations. In particular, an understanding of the meaning assigned to religion by the client's current family, as well as the client's family-of-origin, should be explored to gain an understanding of the client within significant relational contexts. While the client may, at present, demonstrate a weak or non-existent religious affiliation or practice, family-of-origin religious experiences often continue to exert a powerful (albeit, sometimes subtle), influence upon the client in either positive or negative ways (Canfield et al., 1992). For example, a person's Roman Catholic identity might play a central role, or it may be inconsequential and eclipsed by other more meaningful influences existent in the person's life. Gaining an understanding of the importance that the client places on religious or spiritual issues is essential. A counselor might ask: "Given that you were reared in a devotedly Catholic (Muslim, Baptist, Mormon, etc.) family, what place does spirituality or religion currently hold in your life?" For some clients born into a family of a particular religion (e.g. cradle Catholics), religious identity may be merely incidental, a historical vestige. However, for a devout believer, religious identity may be *the* central factor in social or cultural identity and sense-of-self.

While religious beliefs, values, ideas, and attitudes may change over the course of a person's life, as a result of education, subsequent life experiences and exposure to new ideas or belief systems, the religious beliefs held in a person's family of origin serve as the "reference point" by which subsequent values, beliefs, expectations, and ideas are compared (Becvar et al., 1997). Spiritual awareness and religious belief may intensify, diminish or change altogether. However, a person can never fully escape the profound influence of religious messages from early family experiences. Family-of-origin beliefs may be accepted and embraced, rejected, or modified, but they can never be erased (Canfield et al., 1992).

Regardless of whether a counselor considers spirituality and religion as a social construction, or as a dimension of the human condition relating to an independent truth (i.e. belief in the existence of a supreme being), the influence of spirituality and religion is ubiquitous and a profound influence in the lives of billions of people. All societies and communities have mechanisms for shaping and controlling the conduct of their members. Individuals are expected to conform to the general standards of the society in which they live. To ensure compliance with cultural norms, various mechanisms of social control exist. Social control is necessary to maintain a stable society, as it ensures that individuals within that society conform to expected standards of conduct. Beginning in early childhood, the primary instrument of social control is the family. Individuals who deviate from the standards and values of the community in which they reside are often punished.

In childhood, each person constructs a set of core beliefs – notions as to how things are or how things should be. For the vast majority of people, the construction of this personal belief system stems from the family of origin and is reinforced by one's current family. A person's core beliefs are continuously reaffirmed, modified, or altered; alterations influenced by new information and experiences. As described in Chapter 2, in childhood, a person's worldview is shaped by cultural customs, which for many are strongly influenced by religious identity, doctrine, belief, and practice. These beliefs include an array of social and moral rules pertaining to acceptable and unacceptable conduct and distinguishing right from wrong behavior (Canfield et al., 1992).

In many societies, religion is employed as an instrument of social control (Stark and Bainbridge, 2012). This reality presents a challenge for the counselor at practical, ethical, and moral levels. In many cultures, violations of religious laws or rules result in profound consequences that significantly impact family relationships and the person's standing within society (Bainbridge, 1999). This reality can have a powerful and lingering impact upon a client's welfare and their ability to bring about needed changes in his or her life. For example, a person struggling with a dysfunctional marriage may desire divorce, but their religious belief may prohibit or impede such action. The cognitive dissonance resulting in the contemplation or action to exit a troubled marriage may result in an overwhelming sense of guilt and symptoms of psychological distress (e.g. depression and anxiety).

Depending upon the context, religious rules may be codified into doctrine and law, or in a subtler manner, take the form of local community or social customs. The consequences of violating religious rules and expectations vary greatly, ranging from disapproval and admonishment, isolation or rejection, and various forms of punishment, including expulsion from the group and being ostracized by one's family (Nussbaum, 2012). In some cultural contexts, egregious violations of religious law (e.g. adultery and homosexuality) may result in criminal prosecution, including imprisonment or death (Neal and Corrigan, 2010).

Recognizing that clients who violate personal or societal rules may suffer, to what extent does the counselor work to protect and guide the client in order to avoid the consequences of such psychological distress? To what degree should the counselor align their work, in order to be of help to their client without directly or indirectly violating the religious and cultural mores of the client's community? Answers to these questions are often found while working with clients within the context of family relationships. It is obligatory that a counselor gain an understanding of and assess the impact that religion and spirituality may hold in a client's life, particularly within the context of the client's family and other significant relationships. Such inquiry should be standard practice with every client.

Genograms and Other Socio-metric Assessments and Interventions

The methods employed in systemic family counseling offer a means for helping clients – whether individuals, couples, groups, or families – and address a wide-range of mental health, relationships, and life-adjustment issues. A common task in the counseling process is how to best identify and assess the impact of religious and spiritual experiences, including differences and similarities that exist between the client and client's family, and how these factors might enhance or impede upon attaining the goals of counseling. Effective counseling requires an acquisition and understanding of the client's belief system. However, if approached awkwardly, inquiry about religious experiences can result in increased client distress and anxiety, particularly when such experiences have historically negative connotations. Critical to this task is the ability to discern those religious and spiritual beliefs that are central and significant, from those beliefs that are merely incidental.

Many counselors hold that employing a spiritual dimension in counseling or therapy should be a client-driven task (Anderson and Worthen, 1997). However, in maintaining sensitivity with the use of religious or spiritual language and/or practice within the counseling process, it is important not to avoid an inquiry and discussion of religious and spiritual issues. Regardless of the role that religion and spirituality play in a counselor's own worldview, a counselor must respect the religious and spiritual differences that may exist between themselves and his or her client (Abbott et al., 1990; Gottman, 2002: McGoldrick et al., 2005; Cashwell and Watts, 2010). While it is unethical for a counselor to utilize their own religious or spiritual beliefs to influence, proselytize, convert, or indoctrinate a client, it is appropriate – indeed desirable – to gain an understanding of the client's religious and spiritual belief system. Non-religious clients, including self-identified agnostics and avowed atheists should be understood and respected in their religious and spiritual identity (or lack thereof) (D'Andrea and Sprenger, 2007).

There are various ways in which a family counselor may focus on spirituality and religion, either as a primary or concomitant theme, in therapy. A client struggling with broader spiritual issues may benefit from discussing family-of-origin experiences pertaining to religious belief and practice (Canfield et al., 1992). One of the most expeditious, minimally invasive, and potentially helpful ways to facilitate such a conversation with a client is to utilize socio-metric techniques.

Socio-metric techniques are in-session procedures that serve to gather both historical and contemporary data for the purposes of expanding and modifying the client's understanding and meaning that they attach to significant relationships. When used effectively, socio-metric techniques serve to accomplish the following specific tasks:

- Gather current and historic demographic information about the client, the client's immediate family, extended family, and other significant relationships.
- Provide a visual and verbal illustration of significant client relationships that may expand insight for the client and others in the therapy room.
- During the initial session, or early stages of the counseling process, create a therapeutic, relational environment in which the "Question

and Answer" exchange of gathering information allows the counselor to inquire, and the client to provide information that "educates" the counselor, about the client. This "research posture" establishes the client in the role of "knowledgeable expert" about their life experiences and circumstances, and the counselor as the "inquiring helper," who wishes to better understand and assist the client in creating desired changes.

- The "real time" gathering of information and the meaning the client attributes to this information may result in new insights for the client and others in the therapy room, leading to cognitive shifts and changes to existing narratives, which lends to greater empathy or insights pertaining to significant others (e.g. parent, spouse, etc.).
- The process of counselor inquiry and client disclosure facilitates the process of "joining" with the client, which has been noted as an essential component in a successful therapeutic relationship (Kazdin, 2009; Laska et al., 2014).

Socio-metric Interviewing

A *socio-gram* provides a visual representation similar to a genogram (described below), but rather than gathering data about family relationships, the socio-gram gathers data on each individual family member. Placing the subject of the socio-gram at the center of an illustration, various influences are noted and drawn concentrically around the subject. Using phased questions similar to those employed in the genogram, the counselor gathers information about a best friend(s), neighbors, classmates, fellow sport team members, online friends, church youth groups, etc. The socio-gram allows other family members to gain a better understanding of the social and relational influences influencing each family member. It also provides an illustration of competing influences and opens a discussion among family members regarding possible solutions.

Similarly, a family constellation provides a visual representation of the various influences that impact the family (Toman, 1961). The counselor draws the family in a circle at the center of a concentric diagram with lines connecting to other influences. The influences described in the case study below would include the family's Jehovah's Witness community, school, any community organization in which the family participates, employers, etc. The depiction of the family constellation facilitates a discussion about the various direct and potentially competing influences with which the family must contend. Socio-metric interviewing facilitates family disclosure and therapeutic discussion about an array of primary or concomitant issues relating to religion or spirituality.

Genograms

One of the most commonly employed socio-metric techniques in family counseling is the "genogram." As with other social-metric techniques, a primary purpose of the genogram is to gather data from the client relating to various social and relationship contexts. The genogram also assists the counseling in gaining an understanding of the current and historical relationship structures and emotional connections and processes that family members and other significant persons exert upon the client (McGoldrick and Gerson, 1992; McGoldrick et al., 1999).

Bowen is credited with bringing the genogram into widespread use in the field of psychotherapy, particularly among family therapists and other relationally oriented clinicians (Hoffman, 1981). Reflecting upon Bowen's work, Hoffman recognized Bowen's use of the genogram as "a visual diagram of the family tree going back in time and extending collaterally, with an individual or a couple as the focal point" (Hoffman, 1981, p. 244). Similarly, Bitter defines a genogram as a "... family map that outlines both the structure and the emotional processes of the family" (Bitter, 2013, p. 73).

Socio-metric techniques, such the genogram, allow the counselor to accomplish multiple purposes. It is recommended that the various phases of inquiry move in a more or less sequential manner. However, the process is not rigidly sequential. The task outlined in the following case study illustrates how various processes may be accomplished, concurrently, in various phases of inquiry. As a general rule, questions should begin with basic demographic information requiring only concrete statements of fact on the part of the client. As the client becomes acclimated to the interview and comfortable with counselor queries, the counselor may pose more complex, subjective nature questions.

Case Study

Lin is a 34-year-old female who is a naturalized American citizen. Lin was born in China, but immigrated to the USA with her family at the age of six. She is married to Paul, a 37-year-old male, and native of California. Lin and Paul met at college and have been married for 16 years. Paul is employed as a software engineer. Lin does online consulting as an accountant for several companies, but works primarily as a stay-at-home mom (see the full family description in the Introduction for more information).

The couple is seeking help over concerns with their two biological children, Adam (14 years of age) and John (11 years of age.) The presenting issue relates to increasingly defiant behaviors that both Lin and Paul have observed with both Adam and John, and social adjustment concerns reported by the boys' school.

Lin and Paul identify as Jehovah's Witnesses. As a religiously observant family, they abstain from celebrating major holidays and birthdays, as well as certain patriotic activities, such as serving in the military or saying the pledge of allegiance. The family recently moved from southern California to their current community of Longview, Texas, for Paul's work as a software engineer. As a result of the relocation, the family lost a strong social support network and has struggled to adjust to the new environment that offers a smaller church community and no extended family support.

Lin shares that they have been careful to rear their sons in accordance with the religious teachings of their faith. The boys understand what behavioral expectations, consistent with the family's faith, exist for their conduct in school and home. Recently however, Adam and John have begun to protest not being able to participate in the school's Halloween celebration, where students dress up and trick-or-treat throughout the school. They state that they do not like being the "oddballs," in the school and that they were harassed by some fellow students for not participating in the daily pledge of allegiance. More recently, a friend invited Adam to the friend's birthday party. Adam insisted on attending, despite the parents' attempts to uphold the family's values regarding this issue. Lin and Paul share that the boys have become increasingly withdrawn and angry in recent weeks, have resisted completing household chores, and that Adam has, on occasion, refused to engage in family prayer. The parents state that they are at a loss for how to help their sons adjust to the new environment and also address the behavioral resistance without using force or escalating the conflict.

The Assessment Interview

Lin contacts the family systems therapist who recommends that all four family members attend the initial consultation session. Attendance of all family members is preferred, in that it places the counselor, from the start, in an equal role with all family members. Working with a single client family member, who is then joined by other client family members, is often problematic, as it creates the perception (real or imagined) that the counselor and initial family member have formed a bond or coalition. This potential problem is avoided by seeing all family members together during the initial session. Within the initial consultation session with the family, the counselor asks permission to draw a family map (i.e. a genogram) in order to better understand the relationships influencing the family members.

Phase 1 – Joining

The initial session is ideal for employing the genogram technique and gives the counselor an entry into the family system. Following an initial inquiry as to what prompted the family to seek help, the counselor continues by asking permission to gather demographic information about the client family, including the name and age of each person noted in the genogram. The counselor may elicit information from one family member, or may alternate questions among family members, to construct the genogram. It is essential that the counselor provide a "real-time" visual representation of what the client verbally discloses, which all participants in the session can view. For this purpose, a dry marker board, smart board, or a large paper tablet are essential. Visual presentation of information allows for immediate confirmation of accuracy. The following statements and questions are examples of how the counselor might begin the genogram activity, in order to join with the family and begin gathering information:

- *I would like to find out more about each of you and other members of your family. Would it be ok if I asked some questions, in order to draw a map of your family on the marker board?* (The term "genogram" is optional and need not be used, depending upon the dynamics of the client.)
- *I think it could be very useful in our work together, as it will help me learn everyone's name and his or her relationship to you.*

Phase 2 – Initial Inquiry

In this the initial inquiry phase, the goal is to gather basic demographic information about the family. Ideally, the genogram should cover a minimum of three generations, including parents, grandparents, and siblings. For each person, include the names, age, and relationship to the client. Stylistically, it is common practice is to depict males within a "square" shape and females within a "circle" on the genogram. Individuals of unknown gender are depicted in a "triangle." Transgendered individuals may be depicted by their identifying gender symbol, encompassing their biological gender, but this is entirely optional, based on the needs of the client. The inquiry may initially be directed to a single client, or questions may be posed, intermittently, between each parent and each child, as the counselor deems appropriate. Rather than having a parent provide all the information, it is often useful to initiate questions with a younger family member, or a family member who appears to be less assertive. Having multiple family members participate sets the tone for future counseling sessions to be collaborative among all family members and the counselor. Typical initial questions with this family might include:

- *Lin, if we could, let's start with you and Paul. How long have the two of you been a couple? How long have you been married?* (These questions allow Lin and Paul to offer information about dating, cohabitation, etc.)
- Turning to the youngest brother, *Your name is "Adam," is that correct? Adam, how old are you? And your brother is "John"? How old is John?* (The counselor would draw upon the board two squares containing the name and age of each brother).
- *Paul, is this your first marriage?* (This question allows for a disclosure and discussion of prior marriages and other significant relationships.)
- *What about you Lin, is this your first marriage as well?*
- *John, how long has your family lived in your current home?* (This question invites initial disclosure about the relocation, etc.)

- *Besides the four of you, who else lives in your household?* (Any family member can answer this question and allows for disclosure of an extended family household or atypical living arrangement.)
- *Paul, are your parents still around? Lin, are your parents still around?* (This question allows for Lin and Paul to disclose about parental divorce, death, or client-parent cut off without directly posing those questions.) *Where do they live? How old are they? Do they get around pretty well? (i.e., how is their health?).* Paul and Lin's parents are depicted in the genogram above them, with Adam and John below their parents. Stylistically, when drawing the genogram, it is best to depict persons of the same generation on the same horizontal plane.
- *Tell me about your Dad's (Mom's) education level?*
- *Paul, what type of work did your father (mother, grandfather, grandmother, etc.) do?* (Asking Lin similar questions provides data regarding socio-economic status similarities or differences.)
- *Lin, did your mother have any brothers or sisters? Names and ages? Where do they live? What type of work or career? Children? Their names and ages? Where do they live?* (Marital and parental status, career, etc. may be asked*). Do you have much contact with them? Are your grandparents still around?* (Asking if they are still around is preferred to still alive, as it is a less intrusive question and a more open-ended question.)
- *Paul, do you have any siblings? What are their names and ages? Where do they live? Married, single, divorced? Children? Does your sister work outside of the home? Paul, are your grandparents still around?* (Questions about Lin's and Paul's parents and siblings provide data for constructing a four-generation genogram).

Phase 3 – Detailed Inquiry

Utilization of the genogram allows each member of the family to expand their understanding of the issues that prompted them to seek counseling. With this family, related concerns are social adjustment to a new school/community, defiance, and how the family/parental religious beliefs clash with the new school/community environment. In the detailed phase of inquiry, the questions move from factual data, previously gathered, to questions of a more subjective and interpretive nature. However, preceding questions and discussion between the counselor and family have established a specific tone and comfort level, allowing the counselor to ask more detailed and potentially intrusive questions with less risk of heightening client anxiety. Detailed inquiry typically involves more probing questions that require a more subjective and reflective response in comparison to previous questions:

- *Paul, how did you and Lin meet?* (This question could be posed during the initial inquiry, as a logical matter of fact follow-up to the previous questions about the couple's relationship history, or brought forth at a later point.)

- *Lin, you shared with me that you have a degree in accounting; do you enjoy working out of your home? If it were possible, is there anything you would like to do differently concerning your work?*
- *Paul, you shared with me that you are an only child. Aside from your parents and grandparents, who were you closest to growing up?*
- *Lin, did your family have any particular religious affiliation when you were growing up? How active was your family in church or religious activities?* (The counselor could pose a similar question to Paul, uncovering similar or dissimilar religious experiences.)
- *How was it that the two of you came to embrace the Jehovah's Witness faith?*
- *What role does your religious affiliation currently play in your life?* (This is a very open question that invites disclosure about issues of shared or conflicting belief with one's spouse, family of origin, and current family.)
- *I understand there have been some challenges in moving to a new community and school. Who in the family do you think has been most impacted by this move?*
- *I understand your faith prohibits certain types of celebrations and activities and this has caused some problems at school for John and Adam. Can someone tell me more about this?*
- *Mom (Dad, John, Adam) what would you like to see change in the family?* (This question helps establish desired goals for counseling and illuminates that family members may have differing goals.)
- *Up to this point, what has the family done in an attempt to solve these problems? What has been helpful? What has not worked?* (This question identifies "attempted solutions" and sets the stage for changing parental and/or sibling behaviors that have failed to ameliorate problem concerns.)
- *Given that what you have been doing has failed to produce the desired results you seek, would you be willing to try something different that might produce better results?*

Phase 4 – Relational Inquiry

The relational inquiry phase shifts the conversation to questions that are potentially more intrusive in nature, requiring more disclosure of personal opinion and meaning. Examples of relational questions include:

- *How would you describe your current relationship with your mother (father, spouse, siblings, sons)?*
- Asking both Lin and Paul, using the genogram depiction as a backdrop: *Tell me about your childhood. What was it like for you when you were John's age?*

- *Paul (Lin), tell me about the family in which you grew up. How strict were your parents about religious rules and expectations? Can you recall an incident in which your parent(s) made an exception to a religious rule?*
- *Looking back on your religious upbringing in your family, how do you feel about this experience? Overall was it positive, negative, mixed? Lin (Paul) did you experience any conflicts with your parents over religious beliefs as an adolescent? Tell me more about this.* (This question allows the genogram inquiry to expand into the broader therapeutic conversation that prompted this family to seek help.)
- *How do you think your earlier life experiences in the church and its religious teachings have impacted your relationship with your wife (husband)? Your relationship with your sons? Tell me about this.*
- *Paul, as you look at the picture of your family on the board – parents, siblings, grandparents, aunts, uncles, cousins, – whom do you recognize or suspect as having struggled with a problem such as alcohol (or drugs, pornography, infidelity, money, violent behavior, etc.)? Is there anyone in your family who is currently struggling with an issue?* (This question allows the client to make concrete connections with various family themes and intergenerational problem issues. It also invites disclosure of family secrets – problems of which people are aware, but do not talk about.)
- *Tell me about the conflict between what you were taught by your faith and what you currently believe.*
- *Lin, you shared with me that you converted to the Jehovah's Witness faith when you and Paul were in college. Tell me about this adjustment in light of your Roman Catholic upbringing. How did you and Paul navigate these initial differences?*
- *Lin, since your religious affiliation and beliefs have changed, what impact has this had on your relationship with your mother (siblings)?*

Phase 5 – Client Integration and Discussion

Viewing the genogram that was collaboratively constructed in session by the counselor and client, the integration and discussion phase allows details disclosed in the genogram interview to be expanded into a much broader therapeutic conversation. The genogram serves as a medium for continued therapeutic conservation. Useful questions might include:

- *Lin (or Paul, Adam, John), as you look at this depiction of your family and all of the family connections, what "jumps out" at you? How do you feel this relates to the concerns which brought the family into counseling?*
- *John (or Adam) as you think about the current conflict between you and your parents over rules and expectations. how would you like for things to be different, if it were possible?*

Supplemental Readings

McGoldrick, M., Gerson, R., and Shellenberger, S. (1999). *Genograms: Assessment and intervention* (2nd edn). New York, NY: W.W. Norton and Company.

Wiggins Frame, M. (2000). The spiritual genogram in family therapy. *Journal of Marital and Family Therapy*, 26(2), 211–216.

Wiggins Frame, M. (2001). The spiritual genogram in training and supervision. *The Family Journal*, 9(2), 109–115.

References

Abbott, D. A., Berry, M., and Meredith, W. H. (1990). Religious Belief and Practice: A Potential Asset in Helping Families. *Family Relations*, 39, 443–448.

American Association for Marriage and Family Therapy (AAMFT). (2016). *AAMFT Code of Ethics*. Alexandria, VA. Author.

American Counseling Association (ACA). (2014). *ACA Code of Ethics*. Alexandria, VA: Author.

Anderson, D. A., and Worthen, D. (1997). Dimension: Spirituality as a resource for the couples therapist . *Journal of Marital and Family Therapy*, 23(1), 3–12.

Bainbridge, W. S. (1999). The politics of religious apostasy: The role of apostates in the transformation of religious movements. *American Journal of Sociology*, 105(1), 261–262.

Becvar, R., Canfield, B., and Becvar, D. (1997). *Group Work: Cybernetic, Constructivist, and Social Constructionist Perspectives*. Denver, CO: Love Publishing.

Bitter, J. (2009). *The Theory and Practice of Family Therapy and Counseling*. Belmont: Brooks/Cole.

Bitter, J. R. (2013). *Theory and Practice of Family Therapy and Counseling* (2nd ed.). Belmonte, CA: Brooks/Cole, Cengage Learning.

Canfield, B., Fenell, D. L., and Hovestadt, A. J. (1992). Family-of-origin influences upon perceptions of current family functioning. *Family Therapy*, 19, 55–60.

Cashwell, C. S., and Watts, R.E. (2010). The new ASERVIC competencies for addressing spiritual and religious issues in counseling. *Counseling and Values*, 55(1), 2–5.

Council for Accreditation of Counseling and Related Educational Programs. (2016). *CACREP Standards*. Alexandria, VA: Author. Retrieved from http://www.ca crep.org/for-programs/2016-cacrep-standards.

D'Andrea, L. M., and Sprenger, J. (2007). Atheism and nonspirituality as diversity issues in counseling. *Counseling and Values*, 51, 149–158. doi:10.1002/j.2161-007X.2007.tb00072.x.

Frame, M. W. (2000). The spiritual genogram in family therapy. *The Journal of Marital and Family Therapy*, 26(2), 211–216.

Gottman, J. M. (2002). *The Seven Principles for Making Marriage Work*. New York: Three Rivers Press.

Hoffman, L. (1981). *Foundations of Family Therapy*. New York: Basic Books.

Kazdin, A. E. (2009). Understanding how and why psychotherapy leads to change. *Psychotherapy Research*, 19(4–5), 418–428.

Laska, K., Gurman, A., and Wampold, B. (2014). Expanding the lens of evidence-based practice in psychotherapy: A common factors perspective. *Psychotherapy: Theory, Research, Practice, Training*, 51(4), 467–481.

Mahoney, A. (2010). Religion in families, 1999–2009: A relational spirituality framework. *Journal of Marriage and the Family*, 72(4), 805–827.

McGoldrick, M., and Gerson, R. (1992). *Genograms in Family Assessment*. New York: W.W. Norton.

McGoldrick, M., Gerson, R., and Shellenberger, S. (1999). *Genograms: Assessment and Intervention. (2nd Edition)*. New York, NY: W.W. Norton.

McGoldrick, M., Giordano, J., and Garcia-Preto, N. (2005). *Ethnicity and Family Therapy*. New York: Guilford Press.

Neal, L. S., and Corrigan, J. (2010). *Religious Intolerance in America: A Documentary History*. Chapel Hill, NC: University of North Carolina Press.

Nussbaum, M. C. (2012). *The New Religious Intolerance: Overcoming the Politics of Fear in an Anxious Age*. Cambridge, MA: Harvard University Press.

Pew Research Center (2015) The Future of World Religions: Population Growth Projections, 2010–2050. Retrieved from http://www.pewforum.org/2015/04/02/religious-projections-2010-2050.

Stark, R., and Bainbridge, W. (2012). *Religion, Deviance, and Social Control*. New York: Routledge.

Toman, W. (1961). *Family Constellation*. New York: Springer.

12 Addressing Spiritual and Religious Themes with Play, Creativity, and Experiential Interventions

W. Bryce Hagedorn, Elizabeth Pennock, and Laura Rendon Finnell

"The correct analogy for the mind is not a vessel that needs filling, but wood that needs igniting."

—Plutarch

Introduction

Unlike the others in this book, this chapter focuses on the therapeutic use of interventions that are not necessarily tied to a specific personality or treatment theory. The use of play and creative/experiential activities are a part of many clinicians' repertoires, regardless of their theoretical orientation. Even though play therapy hails from particular schools of treatment, its techniques are often utilized by counselors who do not identify themselves as play therapists. Therefore, it is our desire to briefly examine the foundations from which these interventions originate, and then focus primarily on their application to working with clients' spiritual and religion themes.

It is our assertion that the interventions and techniques discussed in this chapter are particularly relevant to working within clients' religious and spiritual domains for two primary reasons. First, treatment of the whole person necessarily involves the treatment of the whole brain (Ivey et al., 2012). Traditional models of brain functioning have indicated that the left and right hemispheres perform different functions, with the left side attributed to more analytical functions (e.g. those often addressed with talk therapy) and the right side lending itself to creative endeavors (Lindell, 2011). Here is where play, creativity, and experiential activities assume an important role, as they all access the right hemisphere, the same area that affords processing of the abstraction, mystical, and spiritual (Ivey et al., 2012). Therefore, when used in conjunction with talk therapy, the use of play, creative, and experiential activities can foster engagement with the whole brain.

The other reason that these techniques and interventions work so well is that the idea of *experience* (which is at the foundation of play, creativity, and experiential interventions) is a core component of both religion and spirituality (Evans and Atkins, 2007). There are various definitions of religion, but most revolve around the shared and corporate beliefs, practices, and *experiences* of a group of people. As explained in Chapter 2, spirituality is more difficult to define, but the search for meaning and purpose, along with a felt and profound connection/experience, seem to be common among spiritual definitions. Given the experiential components of religion and spirituality, it would appear evident that clients would have a certain comfort level using experiential activities to access their religious/spiritual selves, as well as to help them find meaning and purpose in their current circumstances.

The focus of this chapter will be on both play and creative/experiential interventions. First, an examination of play therapy, noting its background and the major theories that contain play is presented. Following that, an exploration of the underpinnings of creative and experiential interventions and the theories that utilized them will be noted. Next, a brief commentary on the role that religion and spirituality specifically play in these theories before jumping into explicit examples of play and creative/experiential activities will be presented. The chapter will conclude with an application of one such technique to a therapeutic case study.

Play and Play Therapy

Background

Play is a universal experience that serves several functions and purposes. Throughout infancy and childhood, play allows for physical, cognitive, emotional, social, and moral development. Although play is more commonly associated with childhood, it continues to serve valuable purposes across the life span. Whereas there are many definitions of play, for the sake of this chapter, it is most important to focus on the primary *characteristics* of play, which were noted by Henricks (2014). To begin, play is self-directed, meaning that it cannot be imposed on the person; but rather, must be chosen. Another characteristic is that the process is more important than the outcome. Play usually follows rules; however, those rules are developed by the players, rather than their being imposed upon them by others. Most importantly, play is imaginative, active, and pleasurable. Given that play is a natural phenomenon that occurs in childhood, it has been a powerful medium in analyzing and understanding children (Landreth, 2012).

Psychotherapists first began observing children's natural play in the late nineteenth century, and mental health professionals have continued this process by developing systematic approaches to using play in their work with children, now known as play therapy (Carmichael, 2006). Traditional psychotherapy requires the expression of thoughts and feelings through words, which is not necessarily appropriate with children who have not yet acquired the necessary vocabulary and/or cognitive abilities to do so.

Therefore, play therapy is a developmentally appropriate, child-centered approach based in theory and research. It has been used by mental health professionals for nearly 70 years, to work with children through their natural language of play. In addition to the use of toys, play therapy also incorporates expressive forms of therapy that include art, books, dance, movement, music, puppets, sandtray, and storytelling. Research has shown that play therapy is effective for a variety of behavioral, social, and emotional concerns and play therapists often give testimonies of the "power of play." Specifically, play therapy allows children to express themselves symbolically by allowing them to change their unmanageable reality to a manageable representation by using toys and a variety of other materials (Landreth, 2012).

Major Theories of Play Therapy

As with the numerous psychotherapeutic approaches to working with adult concerns, there is a vast amount of theoretical approaches to play therapy that stem from psychological and personality theories. Different approaches view the counselor's role as falling along a continuum of non-directive to very directive. However, there is consensus that the child's play should be natural for it to be therapeutic. It is important to note that play therapy techniques have been used successfully with adults for a variety of presenting issues (e.g., trauma, anxiety, depression, relational discord, and family therapy) (Doyle and Magor-Blatch, 2017; Schaefer, 2003; Schwartz and Braff, 2012). For the purposes of this chapter, the discussion will be limited to a brief description of three most widely used and evidence-based theories of play therapy.

Child-centered Play Therapy (CCPT). Child-Centered Play Therapy has the longest history of use and follows the major principles of person-centered therapy first developed by Carl Rogers. Virginia Axline was the first person to adapt and operationalize this approach for use with children in play therapy (Landreth, 2012). In CCPT, the relationship between the play therapist and child is paramount, with the belief that children are capable of directing their own growth. Ten major tenets in relating to children provide the framework for this approach. A few examples of these tenets are that children have an inherent tendency toward growth and maturity; children are capable of positive self-direction; and that children will take the therapeutic experience to where they need it to be (Landreth, 2012). In sum, the child is the one who directs what happens in session, with the play therapist taking a non-directive stance.

Adlerian Play Therapy (AdPT). Adlerian Play Therapy combines the concepts and strategies of individual psychology (described in Chapter 7) with the basic premises and techniques of play therapy. The five basic principles to which AdPT subscribes are: a) all behavior has social meaning; b) all behavior has a purpose and is goal-directed; c) all people are made up of a unified whole and have unique patterns of behavior that are used to meet their goals; d) people behave the way they do to overcome feelings of inferiority and move toward feelings of superiority; and e) behavior is a result of people's subjective perceptions (Kottman, 2001). The relationship between the play therapist and the child is also the foundation for the process, with both playing an equal role in directing what happens in sessions.

Cognitive-Behavioral Play Therapy (CBPT). Cognitive-Behavioral Play Therapy integrates the therapeutic foci of cognitive behavioral therapy with the foundations of play therapy to appropriately meet the developmental needs of clients. A major component of CBPT relies on the use of modeling to help children learn adaptive coping behaviors (Knell, 2009). Again, the relationship between the play therapist and the child is essential; however, the therapist takes a more directive stance with this approach.

Creative and Experiential Therapies

Background

Many theoretical schools of counseling and psychotherapy encourage or allow for the incorporation of creative and experiential interventions into the counseling process. In a narrow sense, the term experiential therapy is often used to refer to therapeutic approaches from the existential-humanistic tradition that emphasize working in the here-and-now, relational interaction, and attunement to the internal experiences of physical sensation and emotion (Gendlin, 1996; Perls et al., 1951; Yalom, 1980). Furthermore, the term experiential therapy also describes an approach used by systemic and family therapists which focuses on the moment-to-moment affective and relational experiences of family members and counselors (Kempler, 1965; Satir, 1988; Whitaker and Bumberry, 1988). In contrast to psychoanalytic and behavioral schools of thought, experiential therapies focus on the present, emotions, relational interactions, and a holistic view of well-being. With roots in existential philosophy, experiential approaches also lend themselves to exploring spiritual themes and experiences.

Experiential and Expressive Techniques

Experiential therapeutic interventions are also used by counselors from various theoretical backgrounds, in order to move beyond traditional talk therapy into the realm of engaging a client's emotions via action, creative expression, and interaction (Newman et al., 2004). Experiential interventions can include techniques from diverse fields such as: emotionally focused therapies, art therapy, sand tray therapy, animal-assisted therapy, music therapy, dance/movement therapies, psychodrama, yoga therapy, and play therapy. Residential treatment programs for substance abuse, eating disorders, and severe and persistent mental illness often utilize many of these techniques, in both group and individual therapy, as part of a holistic, integrative approach to treatment. Experiential interventions have been shown to have a positive impact on client outcomes (Kennedy et al., 2014). Additionally, experiential, body-focused, and expressive therapies are increasingly being utilized and researched within the field of trauma therapy (see Van der Kolk, 2014).

The Role of Spirituality and Religion in the Use of Play and Creative/Experiential Activities

One does not have to look far to see the enormous influence that religion and spirituality have on the creative and experiential arts. Walk into most any religious sanctuary, museum, government building, or historic dwelling and the impact of religion and spirituality on the historic lives of all peoples is evident, both past and present. The paintings, sculptures, music, dance, poetry, and literary achievements that have been inspired by matters of faith form much of the foundation of our aesthetic pleasures. Given these influences on how we have recorded history and expressed our deepest longings, it seems only natural to use experiential activities to access our clients' religious and spiritual themes during the therapeutic process.

As noted by the chapter's opening quote from Cameron (2016), there are clear connections between: (a) play and creative/experiential interventions and (b) spirituality and religion. Some, such as Miller (2011) assert that therapy necessarily involves an active engagement with the client's spiritual/ religious path, and go on to note that the two primary goals of counseling should be to promote personal growth and to reduce client suffering. A spiritual/religious approach addresses both goals (e.g. growth and meaning-making, which in turn can lead to pain reduction). Given that play and creative/experiential activities can serve as the vehicle for accessing the Sacred and spiritual, it seems prudent to use these to meet the two primary goals of therapy.

Diving deeper into the growth and meaning-making aspects of therapy, play and creative/experiential activities allow counselors access to the influences of their clients' spirituality, culture, values, and beliefs on the experience of their primary therapeutic concerns (Ginicola et al., 2012). Evans and Atkins (2007) noted the crucial role that experiential activities play in helping clients to discover depths of meaning that extend beyond what might be found through other means. They encouraged counselors to seek meaning along with their clients, with experiential activities serving as the bond between mutual meaning-seekers. Shepard Johnson (2003) agreed and stated that, "…the use of rituals and the expressive arts offers a vehicle through which the client can transform suffering into meaning through allegorical reflection and activity" (p. 235). When used appropriately, play and creative/experiential activities can help bring awareness and new meaning to cognitive, emotional, and/or spiritual processes that had heretofore been unavailable to clients (Rosen and Atkins, 2014); these in turn, can resonate in powerful ways between the client and counselor. Fitzpatrick (2002) artfully noted that the creative space in the therapy room becomes a sacred space where transformation occurs. Lord (2015) goes a step further by referring to the space where play and improvisational techniques lead to client healing and growth as the "theater of psychotherapy" (p. 72).

The powerful influence that play and creative/experiential activities can have on client suffering is particularly true when that suffering is the result of trauma, where words are inadequate to express the depth of pain and the lack of perceived meaning. Zappacosta (2011) noted that such activities serve as a means for clients to, "…reconnect with rituals and spiritual practices that supported and helped transform deeply rooted wounds associated with issues of alienation and abandonment" (p. 7). Play and creative/experiential activities further serve as a means to reconnect clients' shattered minds, bodies, and spirits leading to experiences of transcendence, empowerment, and self-nurturance (Leseho and Maxwell, 2010; Williams et al., 1999). Having established the connection between play and creative/experiential activities, and the exploration of spiritual and religious themes, specific examples regarding how to implement these activities with clients will be provided in the following sections.

Play Therapy Activities for Exploring Spiritual and Religious Themes

Given that play therapy aids children with their emotional and psychological development, it can also serve as a valuable opportunity for children and adults to address spirituality and their spiritual development. Spirituality is an abstract concept for some clients. The relationship between the client and therapist allows for a meaningful connection and experiences, which are essential components of spirituality. Additionally, spiritual and religious themes often come up with clients who have experienced loss and trauma with childhood grief, leading to powerful emotions that often require more expressive mediums (Boyd Webb, 2011; Xu and Zhang, 2011). Since play should be natural and spontaneous, the following interventions are broad suggestions for using these expressive modalities, and can be adapted for specific individual and developmental needs.

Using Art to Find Meaning

Throughout history, art has been used to depict and convey profound feelings and emotional experiences, and given the clear connections between art and religion/spirituality, it is no wonder that amazing artistic endeavors cover places of worship (Malchiodi, 2007). As such, art-making allows clients the opportunity to process and release deeply held feelings, gain a better understanding of their lives, and create meaning of their experiences (Van Lith, 2014). It is important to have a variety of artistic materials available, as clients may find themselves naturally attracted to drawing, painting, or working with modeling clay.

If a client has experienced loss or another significant event, using art may help him/her to access and express the underlying spiritual and/or religious themes. The counselor may use a nondirective approach and prompt the client with, *"Why don't you take some time and consider how you might express yourself using the materials that we have available here?"* The counselor can also be more directive and provide specific directions for the client to follow. One such example is *"Draw a picture or create symbols of how you view your Higher Power playing a role in your current circumstances. You can choose the type of paper you want to use, as well as what you would like to use to draw. Try to use a variety of colors and make a key of what those colors represent."* While drawing is the most easily accessible form of art making, it should be noted that some clients may prefer other mediums, such as clay, which can provide a more visceral experience as they squeeze and bend and mold their emotions. The important thing is to provide many options for creating art, as well as have the necessary space, lighting, and atmosphere where the art can be created.

Materials. Materials for this activity might include, (a) crayons, colored pencils, markers, pens, pencils, and erasers; (b) water color paints and different size paint brushes (art easel optional); (c) assorted varieties of paper (plain, construction, etc.); (d) dry erase board and markers; (e) modeling clay and/or Play-Doh; (f) scrapbooking paper, stickers, stamps, and inkpads; (g) pipe cleaners, straws, and confetti; and (h) scissors, tape, and glue.

Process. Counselors should engage clients during the artwork creation process as well as once the actual product has been created. The counselor should begin by asking the client to share about the art-making experience. Once the process of art-making has been explored, the counselor can then shift focus to the actual art that was created by asking questions or giving prompts. To note, it is imperative that counselors not make any assumptions but allow clients to label the elements of their work for themselves. Suggestions for questions include, but are not limited to: (a) *"What was it like for you to make this _____?"*; (b) *"How did you feel while you were _____?"*; (c) *"What came up for you while you were creating this _____?"*; (d) *"What does this mean for you?"*; (e) *"Tell me more about _____"*; (f) *"Share with me what _____ represents for you"*; (g) *"Tell me about the colors you chose, do they mean anything specific for you?"*; and (h) *"What is it like for you to share your views about your Higher Power with me?"*

Art can be made at any point in the therapeutic process, as it can serve as a Level II assessment tool (described in Chapter 2) or as an opportunity to explore recurring themes. Asking these processing questions allows clients to find meaning and make connections on a deeper and spiritual level.

Using Music to Connect

Music is another powerful modality and source of healing that has been documented throughout history as a means to connect with the religious/ spiritual realm. Whether it be the rhythm, the melody, the harmony, the instruments, or the lyrics, music has a way of making people *feel*. Music is unique, in that it often evokes strong emotions or associations to significant events in our lives as well as helps us to feel connected to others and our experiences (Avent, 2016). For those who are musically inclined, creating music can be a therapeutic and dynamically personal expression (Gladding, 2016). For those who are not musically gifted, listening to and sharing music can be just as powerful and transcendental. Whereas songs and lyrics may be introduced by the counselor, the songs and lyrics brought into session by the client often have the most powerful therapeutic effects (Gladding, 2016).

One suggestion for using music would be to ask a client to bring in a song/songs that evoke a connection between the current circumstances and his/her belief system. The client could even create a music collage, using parts of a variety of songs to express his/her inner-most feelings, longings, and/or questions to ask the Divine. If the song includes lyrics, have the client bring those in as well. During the next session, play the song(s) one at a time. The counselor should pay attention to the client's nonverbals and body language while listening to the song(s).

Materials. Materials for this activity might include, (a) a music playing device, (b) songs to play, and (c) printed lyrics (if applicable).

Process. After listening to the music, the counselor can use a non-directive or directive approach to process both the experience of listening to the music, as well as what the song(s) means for the client. A non-directive approach may simply involve using silence once the music is over, allowing the client as much time as necessary to bring his/her emotions and thoughts into the space that was created with the music. A more directive approach might have the counselor asking such questions as, *"When was the first time you heard that song?"* followed by an exploration of the client's association to that time in his/her life. Additional prompts could be, *"Share how the various elements of the song (i.e. the instruments, the melody, the lyrics) most impact you."* and *"As you listened to the song, I could see a variety of emotions pass through you. Can you share those with me?"* and *"What most stands out for you from the song and how does it help express what you've been struggling with recently about God's role in your circumstances?"*

As noted, music helps individuals express themselves in ways that simple verbal expressions cannot, so the counselor should be prepared to gather as much data about the client's religious/spiritual themes and allow the time necessary to process the connections that are made.

Using a Sandtray to Bring Awareness

The origins of Sandtray Therapy go back to the 1920s and the approach has been used with children, adolescents, adults, couples, and families. It is expressive and projective, allowing for clients to communicate non-verbally. Sandtray provides opportunities for therapeutic metaphors to emerge from the clients by accessing deeper intrapsychic issues (Homeyer and Sweeney, 2011). The therapeutic use of a sandtray is an appropriate modality to address spiritual concerns with clients across the life span (Mountain, 2016).

If the counselor believes the use of a sandtray to be appropriate with a client who is experiencing religious/spiritually related concerns, the client would be invited to begin by touching the sand in an otherwise empty sandtray and sharing the resulting thoughts/feelings. Afterwards, the counselor should provide a prompt for the client to create or build a scene in the sand using the available miniatures and figurines. This prompt can be brief and non-directive (e.g., *"Create a scene of your world"*) or it can be more detailed and directive (e.g., *"Build a scene that represents your relationship with your spirituality. Be sure to include people, places, and things that have been a part of your spiritual journey."*).

Materials. Materials for this activity might include: (a) a sandtray (ideally 30in x 20in x 3in with the bottom painted blue); (b) sand (play sand; hypoallergenic – contaminant-free); (c) miniatures (e.g., people, animals, buildings, bridges, fences, items, etc.); (d) religious-based miniatures (e.g., deities, angels, demons, tombstones, other religious buildings and symbols; and (e) a camera or device that can take pictures (to record the creation for future reference).

Process. The counselor should silently observe the client as he/she chooses and places items in the sand. After the client has expressed satisfaction and completion of the tray, the counselor invites the client to share the experience (Homeyer and Sweeney, 2011). It is important for the counselor to allow the client to describe and explain the meaning of the items in the tray, as well as the arrangement of the items. The counselor may ask follow-up questions regarding something the client has shared in his/her description. The counselor may also make observations such as *"I noticed that you placed ____, tell me more about that"* or *"I noticed this here, I'm wondering about that"*. As the client and counselor process the tray, the counselor should note when new insights arise for the client. Taking a picture of the completed tray can help with future processing of the experience.

Often, clients create scenes that are chaotic, and which evoke very strong emotions (Homeyer and Sweeney, 2011). If this occurs and the counselor feels it appropriate, he/she could invite the client to change the scene by saying something like, *"How would you like for this to look? What would you change?"* The counselor should silently observe the removal or movement of items, and then invite the client to share afterward and process the altered tray (Homeyer and Sweeney, 2011). Once the processing of the second tray has ended, the counselor should invite the client to take a picture of the tray, if desired, which can be used for future discussions.

Creative and Experiential Activities for Exploring Spiritual and Religious Themes

Exploring Spiritual Desolation Using a Collage

It is not uncommon to encounter clients who are experiencing what St. John of the Cross called the *dark night of the soul* (Brenan, 1973) or what St. Ignatius referred to as *spiritual desolation* (Ignatius, 1849). During such a season, the *source of the Sacred* feels distant and formerly accessible means of spiritual encouragement or comfort feel remote (May, 2004). At these times, words often fail, and it can be helpful to introduce imagery to help explore the client's experience. The process of collaging is one way to help clients explore the emotions associated with this season of desolation, as well as other spiritual themes and experiences.

For many, the idea of making a collage brings up memories of glue sticks, safety scissors, and poster board from childhood, and the simplicity of collage does make it accessible for even the most reluctant artists (Frost, 2010). However, the simplicity of the process does not limit the potential insights generated through the process of collaging.

Materials. Materials for this activity might include images, cardstock, scissors and glue, and a large enough surface on which to create the collage. As for images, the counselor might find it helpful to keep a plastic storage box full of images rather than piles of magazines, though this takes more preparation by the counselor. When searching for images, it is helpful to gather them from a variety of sources, as clients may not find images in *Good Housekeeping* that represent the spiritual themes they want to explore. Look for images that represent a broad array of emotions and experiences, and for those that represent people who are representative of various cultural, ethnic, and racial backgrounds. When it comes to cardstock, rather than using large sheets of poster board, it is often helpful to limit the size of collages to the size of one sheet of cardstock (8 1/2" x 11"), or less. The size limitation forces participants to be more intentional about their choices and can also prevent clients from feeling overwhelmed by the task.

Process. It is often helpful to limit the subject of a collage to a unitary theme (e.g., the client's experience of spiritual darkness) and to remind the client that sometimes fewer images are as profound as a page crowded with images. For example, one client's collage, which was focused on the theme of loss, was simply a picture of a child with a look of terror and sorrow on her face, who was running from a building that was engulfed with flames. Similarly, another client's collage with a theme of hope and rebirth was comprised of a single image of a blooming flower cradled in someone's hands.

Encourage clients to spend time exploring all of the available images and to set aside those that they are drawn to, even if they are not yet sure if or how the image relates to the intended theme of the collage. Collaging is an intuitive process and the layered meanings of certain images may emerge

later or change over time. Some clients will prefer to talk with the counselor throughout the process while others will prefer solitude. If a
conference room or other private space is available, it may be possible to
have clients come an hour before their appointment (or stay late), so that
they have time and space to work on their collage outside of the normal
session time.

When processing this activity with a client, begin by asking what the
creative process was like for him/her. Was there a point where he/she felt
stuck or a time when new clarity emerged? Were there images that he/she
was drawn to at first but ultimately decided to leave out? What were the
limitations (e.g. amount of time, available images, size of the cardstock, etc.)
like for the client? After exploring the creative process together, ask the
client to describe his/her collage and reflect on how it connects to the
intended theme. Be cautious in offering interpretations of the collage,
instead – if the client is unsure of the meaning of certain elements of the
collage – encourage the client to continue reflecting and follow up with
him/her at the next session. It can also be helpful to ask the client to spend
time during the week journaling about the emotions and thoughts that
come up as he/she reflects on the collage.

Seena Frost (2010) has developed a method of collaging, SoulCollage,
that lends itself to exploring spiritual themes with clients, and offers training
workshops to counselors who are interested in incorporating her methods
into their practice (https://www.soulcollage.com/training-for-therapists).

Mapping Spiritual Development through Spiritual Timelines

In *The Critical Journey*, Hagberg and Guelich (2005) developed a model for
describing the spiritual journey in terms of six distinct stages of development, and noted that movement into a new stage of spiritual growth is
often initiated due to a crisis, transition, or significant life event. Similarly,
clients often come into counseling because a crisis or transition has overwhelmed their current ability to cope in one or more life domains or, in the
aftermath of such an event, they are struggling to adjust. Spiritually, they
may be engaging in ways that were appropriate for a prior stage of
development, but which are ineffective in the new stage. Asking clients to
create a spiritual timeline (Curry, 2009), thereby mapping their spiritual
development, can help them to place their current experiences within the
broader context of their spiritual journey.

Materials. Materials for this activity might include, (a) paper, (b) various
writing utensils (e.g. crayons, colored pencils, markers, etc.), and (c) other
client artifacts (e.g., photos, music, etc.).

Process. This activity can be facilitated during a counseling session or
assigned as homework. Ask the client to create a simple timeline that illustrates significant stages or events in his/her spiritual development, or make
the prompt more specific based on material that the client has shared in

session (Dailey et al., 2011) To encourage affective processing, suggest that the client use symbols, images, colors, or shapes to represent these events, rather than words, whenever possible. There is no wrong way for the client to complete this task and timelines generated by clients are as varied as the clients themselves. One alternate option would be to ask the client to create a timeline by compiling a playlist of songs associated with different stages of his/her spiritual journey.

When helping clients explore their timelines, first, have the client explain the timeline using his/her own words. The counselor can respond with reflections of feeling and meaning, as well as by asking open questions, which help clients explore broader themes that may be woven through the stories represented on the timeline. After walking through the timeline together, it may be appropriate to ask questions such as, "What do you wish you could change about your spiritual journey or your relationship with God?" or "What resources from other seasons of your spiritual life could be helpful in your current circumstances?" This activity may be helpful if utilized early in the counseling process, as the exploration of a client's timeline may bring up emotions that can be further explored in future sessions or help to clarify a client's goals for counseling (Curry, 2009).

Expressing Grief through the Poetry of the Psalms of Lament

The Jewish and Christian scriptures are full of poetry, such as the Book of Psalms. Scholars categorize psalms according to content (e.g. thanksgiving, wisdom, etc.) and many psalms fall into the category of *lament* (Gunkel, 1998). In the sacred Hindu text, the Bhagavad Gita, readers are given instructions for addressing lamentation and grief (Easwaran, 2007). Additional scriptures in the book of Zabur from the Quran also address a variety of poetic expressions of emotion (Abdel Haleem, 2015). Lament has been defined as "a spiritual discipline that assists the sufferer to reconstruct meaning after the disorienting effects of the suffering" (Lewis Hall, 2016, p. 219). Most psalms of lament contain similar structural elements such as a complaint to the Divine, a plea for deliverance, and affirmation of trust in one's deity. When clients who are wrestling with existential questions in the face of grief, loss, or disappointment have difficulty finding a voice to express their experiences and emotions, psalms of lament can be useful templates in helping clients write their own lament poems. A noteworthy example of this practice can be found in Ann Weem's (1999) *Psalms of Lament,* written after the death of her son.

Materials. Materials for this activity might include sample psalms of lament, or other poems or sacred texts that express grief, loss, longing, and hope. (Suggested sample psalms of lament include Psalms 22, 54, and 140). A list of sentence stems or prompts may also be provided to the client in order to facilitate the writing process. Examples of prompts include:

- I call out to *(insert term for the Divine here)* and...
- My situation is...
- I feel...
- My soul is...
- I wonder...
- Why, *(insert term for the Divine here),* do...
- Deliver me, *(insert term for the Divine here),* from...
- I ask or plead...
- However, I ... because...
- I will remember...
- I am confident that...

Process

Introduce the concept of spiritual lament to the client, including the function of lament in sacred texts relevant to the client, common elements included in the poetry (e.g. complaint, plea, affirmation, etc.) and examples of lament psalms from relevant texts. Clients who do not identify with a specific tradition may still benefit from understanding the concept of lament and reading examples of psalms or other poems from various texts that express sorrow or grief. If the client connects with the concept, invite him/her to write a lament poem as homework and bring it to the next session. The counselor can then help the client explore what the writing process was like, emotions that were evoked in the process, and insights that may emerge from the lament experience. An example of this intervention is provided in the case study below.

Case Study

Introduction

In the case of Cecily, the use of play and creative/experiential interventions seem very applicable, given her current struggle with depression (see the full client description in the Introduction to this book). Three assumptions are drawn from Cecily's description of this battle that seem ripe for a non-talk-therapy approach:

1   The origins of her depression are unknown, and the more she tries to explore the source with her mind, the more frustrated she becomes. Rather than spending additional time trying to help Cecily explore the origins from a verbal and cognitive perspective, the use of play and creative/experiential techniques can help access awareness hidden in the non-verbal and emotive realms.

2   Cecily has tried to express the depth of her feelings with others, but has been unable to describe them in terms that lead to understanding and empathy. Again, rather than trying to express her feelings with

additional words to the counselor, play and creative/experiential techniques utilize projective media (e.g., music, clay, figures, symbols, images, etc.) that facilitate expressions and emotions in more powerful ways.

3   The interwoven aspects of faith and feeling stuck add to her frustration and desperation. Given that a good portion of Cecily's being "stuck" appears to have a religious/spiritual component, encouraging her to use the abovementioned media to represent how she experiences this struggle can lead to insights and awareness about how her faith is being impacted by, and have an impact on, her current struggles.

Below is an example of an activity that can be helpful in working with clients with struggles similar to Cecily's. We will describe the activity, discuss how it could be implemented during the course of treatment, describe what actually happened, and elaborate on how she responded to the intervention.

Cecily's Psalms of Lament

Cecily continues to state that she feels distant from God and unable to connect with God through prayer due to her depressive feelings and the shame she felt after the responses from some in her faith community. The counselor decides to introduce the concept of lament to Cecily and discusses that the inclusion of the lament psalms in the Bible gives Christians both permission to cry out to God with complaints, sorrows, and fears, as well as a template for how to do so. The counselor then provides a handout to Cecily that includes the text of Psalm 13, as well as the prompts shown in the table. Psalm 13 begins with a question for God that resonates immediately with Cecily: "How long, O Lord? Will You forget me forever?" Cecily states that because of the sense of disconnection she has been feeling from God she has not been praying much anymore; however, realizing that she can simply pray, "How long, O Lord?" is a relief. The counselor then asks Cecily if she would be interested in writing her own psalm of lament using the prompts on the worksheet as a starting place. Cecily agrees.

Psalm 13 (New King James Version)

[1]How long, O Lord? Will You forget me forever?
How long will You hide Your face from me?
[2] How long shall I take counsel in my soul,
Having sorrow in my heart daily?
How long will my enemy be exalted over me?
[3] Consider and hear me, O Lord my God;
Enlighten my eyes, lest I sleep the sleep of death;

[4] Lest my enemy say, "I have prevailed against him";
Lest those who trouble me rejoice when I am moved.
[5] But I have trusted in Your mercy;
My heart shall rejoice in Your salvation.
[6] I will sing to the Lord,
Because He has dealt bountifully with me.

Cecily's Psalm

How long, God, will you leave me out here high and dry?
I feel abandoned and wonder if I will ever feel better again.
My situation is isolating and I am overwhelmed with sorrow.
My friends have abandoned and blamed me in the midst of my trials.
My soul aches for a sense of connection with you and my community.
Why, God, have you let this go on so long?
I desperately want to return to a sense of joy and peace.
Yet, I am confident that you are still there somewhere and
You are in charge, and
You will bring me through this season.

Cecily brings a copy of her lament poem into the next session, and asks if she could read it aloud to the counselor. As she reads, tears appear in her eyes and her voice wavers. The counselor thanks Cecily for sharing such a personal piece of writing and asks what she was feeling as she read the poem aloud. Cecily says that this poem is the most she has prayed in months, and that it feels good to be honest with God about her sadness; while, at the same time, putting words to her situation allows her to feel her sorrow more acutely. After being asked about the writing process, Cecily states that though at first she felt inhibited, it became easier to express herself with time. Cecily remarks that since writing the lament, she has been praying briefly each day, always starting with the words, "How long, God?" and that – because of this simple prayer – she feels more connected to God than she has in a long time.

Cecily also mentions that she had realized while writing the lament just how abandoned she feels by her friends at church and how angry this makes her. The counselor asks if this was something that Cecily would like to explore further, and the next several sessions are spent exploring Cecily's anger at her friend's responses and her desire to connect in meaningful relationships. Cecily is then able to set new goals regarding rebuilding her social support network.

Recommended Supplemental Reading

Homeyer, L. E., and Sweeney, D. S. (2011). *Sandtray therapy: A practical Manual* (2nd ed.). New York: Routledge.
Landreth, G. L. (2012). *Play therapy: The art of the relationship* (3rd ed.). New York: Brunner Routledge.

Knell, S. M. (2009). *Cognitive-behavioral play therapy*. Northvale, NJ: Jason Aronson Inc.

Kottman, T. (2015). *Partners in play: An Adlerian approach to play therapy* (2nd ed.). Alexandria, VA: American Counseling Association.

Malchiodi, C. A. (2007). *The art therapy sourcebook* (2nd ed.). New York, NY: McGraw-Hill.

Wheeler, B. L. (2015). *Music therapy handbook*. New York: Guilford Press.

References

Abdel Haleem, M. A. S. (2015). *The Qur'an: A new translation by M. A. S. Abdel Haleem*. New York: Oxford University Press.

Avent, J. R. (2016). This is my story, this is my song: Using a musical chronology and the emerging life song with African American clients in spiritual bypass. *Journal of Creativity in Mental Health,* 11(1), 39. doi:10.1080/15401383.2015. 1056926.

Boyd Webb, N. (2011). Play therapy for bereaved children: Adapting strategies to community, school, and home settings. *School Psychology International,* 32(2), 132–143. doi:10.1177/0143034311400832.

Brenan, G. (1973). *St. John of the Cross: His life and poetry*. Cambridge: Cambridge University Press.

Cameron, J. (2016). *The artist's way (25th Anniversary Edition)*. New York: Penguin Random House.

Carmichael, K. D. (2006). Legal and ethical issues in play therapy. *International Journal of Play Therapy,* 15(2), 83–99. doi:10.1037/h0088916.

Curry, J. R. (2009). Examining client spiritual history and the construction of meaning: The use of spiritual timelines in counseling. *Journal of Creativity in Mental Health,* 4(2), 113–123. doi:10.1080/15401380902945178.

Dailey, S. F., Curry, J. R., Harper, M. C., Hartwig Moorhead, H. J., and Gill, C. S. (2011). Exploring the spiritual domain: Tools for integrating spirituality and religion in counseling. Retrieved from http://counselingoutfitters.com/ vistas/vista s11/Article_99.pdf.

Doyle, K., and Magor-Blatch, L. E. (2017). 'Even adults need to play': Sandplay therapy with an adult survivor of childhood abuse. *International Journal of Play Therapy,* 26(1), 12–22. doi:10.1037/pla0000042.

Easwaran, E. (2007). *Bhagavad Gita* (2nd ed.). Tomales, CA: The Blue Mountain Center of Meditation.

Evans, M., and Atkins, M. J. (2007). Making meaning using creativity and spirituality. *Journal of Creativity in Mental Health,* 2(1), 35–46. doi:10.1300/J456v02n01_04.

Fitzpatrick, J. G. (2002). Sandplay and women's spirituality. *Women & Therapy,* 24 (3–4), 161–173. doi:10.1300/J015v24n03_10.

Frost, S. B. (2010). *SoulCollage evolving: An intuitive collage process for self-discovery and community*. Santa Cruz, CA: Hanford Mead.

Gendlin, E. T. (1996). *Focusing-oriented psychotherapy: A manual of the experiential method*. New York; London: Guilford Press.

Gentry, J. E. (2014). *Forward facing trauma therapy: Healing the moral wound*. Sarasota, FL: Compassion Unlimited.

Ginicola, M. M., Smith, C., and Trzaska, J. (2012). Counseling through images: Using photography to guide the counseling process and achieve treatment goals.

Journal of Creativity in Mental Health, 7(4), 310–329. doi:10.1080/15401383.2012.739955.

Gladding, S. T. (2011). *The creative arts in counseling* (4th Ed.). Alexandria, VA: American Counseling Association.

Gladding, S. T. (2016). *The creative arts in counseling* (5th ed.). Alexandria, VA: American Counseling Association.

Gunkel, H. (1998). *Introduction to Psalms: The genres of the religious lyric of Israel* (J. D. Nogalski, trans.). Macon, GA: Mercer University Press.

Hagberg, J. O., and Guelich, R. A. (2005). *The critical journey: Stages in the life of faith* (2nd ed.). Salem, WI: Sheffield Publishing.

Henricks, T. S. (2014). Play as self-realization: Toward a general theory of play. *American Journal of Play*, 6(2), 190–213.

Homeyer, L. E., and Sweeney, D. S. (2011). *Sandtray therapy: A practical Manual* (2nd ed.). New York: Routledge.

Ignatius. (1849). *The spiritual exercises of St. Ignatius of Loyola.* Louisville: Webb McGill.

Ivey, A. E., D'Andrea, M. J., and Bradford Ivey, M. (2012). *Theories of counseling and psychotherapy: A multicultural perspective* (7th ed.). Thousand Oaks, CA: Sage.

Kempler, W. (1965). Experiential family therapy. *International Journal of Group Psychotherapy*, 15(1), 57–71.

Kennedy, H., Reed, K., and Wamboldt, M. Z. (2014). Staff perceptions of complementary and alternative therapy integration into a child and adolescent psychiatry program. *The Arts in Psychotherapy*, 41(1), 21–26. doi:10.1016/j.aip.2013.10.007.

Knell, S. M. (2009). *Cognitive-behavioral play therapy.* Northvale, NJ: Jason Aronson, Inc.

Kottman, T. (2001). Adlerian play therapy. *International Journal of Play Therapy*, 10(2), 1–12. doi:10.1037/h0089476

Kottman, T. (2015). *Partners in play: An Adlerian approach to play therapy* (2nd ed.). Alexandria, VA: American Counseling Association.

Landreth, G. L. (2012). *Play therapy: The art of the relationship* (3rd ed.). New York: Brunner Routledge.

Leseho, J., and Maxwell, L. R. (2010). Coming alive: Creative movement as a personal coping strategy on the path to healing and growth. *British Journal of Guidance & Counselling*, 38(1), 17–30.

Lewis Hall, E. (2016). Suffering in God's presence: The role of lament in transformation. *Journal of Spiritual Formation & Soul Care*, 9(1), 219–232.

Lindell, A. K. (2011). Lateral thinkers are not so laterally minded: Hemispheric asymmetry, interaction, and creativity. *Laterality: Asymmetries of Body, Brain and Cognition*, 16(4), 479–498. doi:10.1080/1357650X.2010.497813.

Lord, S. (2015). Meditative dialogue: Cultivating the transformative theater of psychotherapy. *Psychoanalytic Social Work*, 22(1), 71–87. doi:10.1080/15228878.2013.877395.

Malchiodi, C. A. (2007). *The art therapy sourcebook* (2nd ed.). New York, NY: McGraw-Hill.

May, G. G. (2004). *The dark night of the soul: A psychiatrist explores the connection between darkness and spiritual growth.* New York: HarperCollins.

Miller, L. (2011). An experiential approach for exploring spirituality. In J. D. Aten, M. R. McMinn, and E. J. Worthington (Eds.), *Spiritually oriented interventions for counseling and psychotherapy* (pp. 325–343). Washington, DC: American Psychological Association.

Mountain, V. (2016). Play therapy – respecting the spirit of the child. *International Journal of Children's Spirituality*, 21(3/4), 191–200. doi:10.1080/1364436X.2016.1228616.

Newman, M. G., Castonguay, L. G., Borkovec, T. D., and Molnar, C. (2004). Integrative psychotherapy. In R. G. Heimberg, C. L. Turk, and D. S. Mennin (Eds.), *Generalized anxiety disorder: Advances in research and practice* (pp. 320–350). New York: Guilford Press.

Perls, F. S., Hefferline, R. E., and Goodman, P. (1951). *Gestalt therapy: Excitement and growth in the human personality*. New York: Julian Press.

Plutarch (1992). *Plutarch: Essays* (R. Waterfield, Trans.). New York: Penguin Putnam, Inc.

Riordan, R. J. (1996). Scriptotherapy: Therapeutic writing as a counseling adjunct. *Journal of Counseling & Development*, 74(3), 263.

Rosen, C. M., and Atkins, S. S. (2014). Am I doing expressive arts therapy or creativity in counseling? *Journal of Creativity in Mental Health*, 9(2), 292–303. doi:10.1080/15401383.2014.906874.

Satir, V. (1988). *The new peoplemaking*. Palo Alto, CA: Science and Behavior Books.

Schaefer, C. E. (2003). *Play therapy with adults*. New York: J. Wiley.

Schwarz, R., and Braff, E. (2012). *We're no fun anymore: Helping couples cultivate joyful marriages through the power of play*. New York: Routledge.

Shepard Johnson, L. (2003). Facilitating spiritual meaning-making for the individual with a diagnosis of a terminal illness. *Counseling and Values*, 47(3), 230–240. doi:10.1002/j.2161-007X.2003.tb00269.x.

van der Kolk, B. A. (2014). *The body keeps the score: Brain, mind, and body in the healing of trauma*. New York: Penguin Books.

Van Lith, T. (2014). 'Painting to find my spirit': Art making as the vehicle to find meaning and connection in the mental health recovery process. *Journal of Spirituality in Mental Health*, 16(1), 19–36. doi:10.1080/19349637.2013.864542.

Weems, A. (1999). *Psalms of lament*. Louisville, KY: Westminster John Knox.

Wheeler, B. L. (2015). *Music therapy handbook*. New York: Guilford Press.

Whitaker, C. A., and Bumberry, W. (1988). *Dancing with the family: A symbolic experiential approach*. New York: Brumer/Mazel.

Williams, C. B., Wiggins Frame, M., and Green, E. (1999). Counseling groups for African American women: A focus on spirituality. *The Journal for Specialists in Group Work*, 24(3), 260–273. doi:10.1080/01933929908411435.

Xu, J., and Zhang, R. (2011). The theoretical basis and clinical practice of sandplay therapy applied to grief counseling. *Chinese Journal of Clinical Psychology*, 19(3), 419–421.

Yalom, I. D. (1980). *Existential psychotherapy*. New York: Basic Books.

Zappacosta, J. (2011). Standing in the mystery: Sandplay therapy as ritual and ceremony. *Journal of Sandplay Therapy*, 20(2), 7–30.

13 Special Issues and Interventions Related to Spirituality

Elizabeth O'Brien and Carman S. Gill

"Your grief for what you've lost lifts a mirror up to where you're bravely working."

—Rumi

Introduction

The nature of spirituality and religion creates unique issues and interventions in the counseling process. Consistent with trauma responses seen in other domains, spiritual domain reactions to painful events follow the avoidance and arousal patterns for post-traumatic stress, described in the *DSM-5* (APA, 2013; Dailey et al., 2014). This can manifest as spiritual bypass and/or difficulty with forgiveness and shame. It is likely that most readers can recall at least one case that was both challenging and frustrating, because the therapeutic work became stuck in these processes. Toward unlocking the client's pain, this chapter focuses on the aforementioned topics, and describes techniques that move beyond talk therapy and into the realm of creative spiritual expression. These resources for intervention in the spiritual domain include the bridge activity, meditative prayer, sacred materials, mandalas and other ideas that will be explored. The included case study attempts to illustrate this process and follows one client's experiences.

Spirituality is defined as "a search for meaningfulness involving a relationship with an ultimate concern," while religiousness is defined as "ritual, institutional or codified spirituality" (Harris et al., 2016). Pargament hypothesized that everyone experiences adversity, and that individuals can choose to cope with crisis and trauma through spiritual and religious means. In times of emotional distress and trauma, religious and spiritual coping has the potential to be a wonderful resource for clients (Pargament, 1997). Many clients report that their religious or spiritual practices help them make sense of their experiences and feel less alone while in distress. However, there are individuals for whom religious and spiritual coping is ineffective or unavailable during times of emotional distress or trauma.

When a breakdown in a client's spiritual coping occurs, unanticipated consequences include reevaluating the meaning that is made in the face of emotional distress, trauma, and struggles. Clients may choose to interpret their distress through the lens of their existing worldview (including their religious/spiritual values), which allows them to see the struggle as an opportunity for spiritual growth (Park, 2005). However, clients may also see distressing experiences as incongruent with their previously held worldview, and this discrepancy can be a catalyst for them to reexamine their religious/ spiritual beliefs and alter their worldview, in order to make sense of the distress that has occurred. For example, in the face of tragedy, an individual may question their belief in the Divine or the notion of the power of the Divine (Park, 2005). For some clients, the aforementioned discrepancy can render spiritual coping and forgiveness difficult or impossible. When (and if) clients are ready to make sense of their experiences within a spiritual domain, several roadblocks may occur, including spiritual bypass, difficulty with forgiveness, and shame.

Spiritual Bypass, Forgiveness, and Shame

In the previous chapters, authors described a body of research indicating the positive aspects of spiritual and religious coping. Indeed, in times of crisis, spirituality and religion can serve as strong coping resources. As with any resource, overreliance or misuse of spirituality and religion as an avoidant strategy results in negative psychological consequences. Based in transpersonal psychology and trauma literature, Welwood (1984) first introduced the term *spiritual bypass* to explain avoidance of deeply painful emotional and psychological wounds using spiritual- or religious-focused methods and interactions. Also referred to as "premature transcendence," spiritual bypass is defined as "attempts to heal psychological wounds at the spiritual level only and avoids the important (albeit often difficult and painful) work at the other levels, including the cognitive, physical, emotional, and interpersonal" (Cashwell et al., 2007, p. 140). Consistent with much of the trauma response literature on avoidance and arousal, researchers identified psychological avoidance and spiritualizing as the two key factors of spiritual bypass. In other words, psychological avoidance is the "process of sidestepping or avoiding difficult emotions, experiences, or circumstances through spiritual beliefs or assumptions" and spiritualizing as "ways of appraising ordinary scenarios and exaggerating their spiritual significance," respectively (Fox et al., 2017, p. 10).

The notion of spiritual bypass is, to some degree, a very specific version of the psychoanalytic defense process called *reaction formation*, in which an individual manages their anxiety by expressing an emotion or behavior that is diametrically opposed to the individual's reality (Myers, 2010). As it pertains to the counseling process, the result of spiritual bypass is a client's attempt to resolve their "unfinished business" in a superficial manner which manifests in a variety of methods, noticeable through eight patterns that can be grouped into psychological arousal and spiritualizing. Behaviors based in psychological avoidance include: avoidance or denial of painful thoughts or unwanted emotional states, using religious leaders or teachings in mutually complicit ways of avoiding of individuation and responsibility, misappropriation of spiritual teachings to avoid intimacy leading to isolation, and abdicating responsibility through blind faith in leadership. Spiritualizing behaviors may manifest as searching for perfection or compulsive goodness, self-medicating through spiritual addiction, spiritual elitism or narcissism, and over-commitment to humanitarian causes (Cashwell et al., 2007; Sheridan, 2017). Furthermore, unhealed psychological wounds and compartmentalized spirituality are the hallmarks of spiritual bypass.

Clients who engage in spiritual bypass to resolve their issues tend to be unable to make lasting changes in their lives (Welwood, 1984). Whereas short-term coping using these mechanisms may not be problematic, Fox et al. report that "when it becomes a chronic and systematic practice of emotional repression, the actpdelcumulative effect may be detrimental" (2017, p. 11). For our clients, two specific, negative consequences of spiritual bypass exist, including delayed psychosocial developmental and stifled spiritual growth (Welwood, 1984). Ultimately, as clients continue their attempts to resolve these issues, they are susceptible to becoming even more depressed, frustrated, and angry at the reality that their efforts are not successful. When these individuals enter into counseling, it can take a great deal of time to assess the multilayers of defense and cultural messages that contribute to clients' homeostasis.

In response to the challenges resulting from problematic spiritual bypass, assessments for identifying this issue and recommendations for interventions are becoming more prevalent. Assessments include the Spiritual Bypass Scale (SBS), a quantitative measure developed by Fox et al. (2017) and the use of sentence stems as recommended by experts on spiritual bypass in a study conducted by Picciotto and Fox (2017). As counselors assess and conceptualize their clients' affective, behavioral, and cognitive functions, they may find wellness-based models for conceptualizing the impact of clients' spiritual domain on holistic, daily functioning particularly helpful. Originally based on Adler's Five Life tasks, Myers and Sweeney's (2005) Indivisible Self Model of Wellness (IS-WEL) proposes that spirituality is a key component of wellness, and states that spirituality is the central mechanism by which individuals create meaning out of other aspects of their life, such as relationships, nutritional and physical health, etc. Based on the IS-WEL model, multiple qualitative methods of assessment are available to facilitate the counseling process, as is the 5F-Wel, a quantitative measure of holistic wellness (Myers and Sweeney, 2005). The Indivisible Self Model of Wellness represents one way that counselors and clients can work together to assess and conceptualize the part that spirituality plays in the clients' self-concept, as well as other parts of functioning that can provide personal identity and meaning.

As with most trauma work, interventions should address the unique expression of distress. Following Fox et al.'s (2017) work on the SBS, we recommend interventions based on the client's presentation in terms of psychological avoidance or spiritualizing. Specifically, we recommend working from a wellness based approach, using creative and expressive arts, and mindfulness based interventions. Additional interventions for addressing spiritual bypass include, Developmental Counseling and Therapy (DCT: Cashwell et al., 2004), and the use of motivational interviewing (Clarke et al., 2013). This chapter also describes specific examples in the intervention section, including the bridge, bibliotherapy, and the use of mandalas.

From bypass to forgiveness, the themes of trauma and pain appear consistent. Based in the idea that lack of forgiveness is demonstrated through the desire for avoidance or revenge, Worthington defines forgiveness as "a motivation to reduce the avoidance of and withdraw from a person who has hurt us, as well as the anger, desire for revenge, and urge to retaliate against that person" (1998, p. 108). In the therapeutic sense, some researchers have defined forgiveness as "the intraindividual, prosocial change towards a perceived transgressor that is situated within a specific interpersonal context" (McCullough et al., 2000, p. 9). Davis and colleagues (2013) have further elucidated that forgiveness can be measured as both a state and a trait. *State forgiveness* refers to the client's ability to forgive a specific offense, whereas *trait forgiveness* refers to a client's ability to forgive in their relationships, across situations, and over time. When taken as a whole, these definitions point to the underlying psychological and emotional reactions to a hurtful event, as well as positive aspects of forgiveness for those involved. In fact, the positive consequences of forgiving are well-documented. For example, a study conducted by Lawler, Younger, Piferi, Billington, Jobe, Edmondson, and Jones (2003) demonstrated that state forgiveness is related to lower blood pressure levels and a lower heart rate. Further, they found that trait forgiveness is associated with lower blood pressure levels and increased blood pressure recovery after stress, reinforcing the idea that forgiveness is, indeed, a matter of the heart. A meta-analysis conducted by Baskin and Enright (2004) demonstrated that explicit forgiveness interventions result in reduced symptoms of depression and anxiety, as well as an increase in hope and self-esteem.

Because of the transactional nature of forgiveness, there is no one specific roadmap for helping clients working toward forgiveness (Davis et al., 2013). Large transgressions are often not easily forgiven, and more severe offenses may yield even less forgiveness (Wade et al., 2014), resulting in lingering emotional experiences as consequences of the initial event. To embrace forgiveness requires an individual to embrace relational grief that comes from unmet expectations, broken promises, and/or betrayals (Brown, 2015). As a result, the reality is that forgiveness usually takes time, like any other second-order change (Wade et al. 2014). A second-order change involves altering the perspectives, worldview, and ultimately disrupting the status quo of old behavioral and cognitive patterns. In his writings on this subject, Patton postulates that it takes the distance of time and realization that, "human forgiveness is not doing something but discovering something – that I am more like those who have hurt me than different from them" (Patton, 1985, p. 16). In fact, empirically based models of forgiveness, such as Worthington's (Worthington and Drinkard, 2000) REACH pyramid, are based in the idea that this journey includes a process of building empathy toward the transgressor and offering an altruistic gift of forgiveness for the betterment of society. However, for this kind of generosity to take place, a forgiver must process the discrepancy between the relationship before the injury, and the new relationship that can develop after forgiveness. The pre-offense relationship must be grieved and laid to rest, while a commitment is made to a new, redefined relationship in forgiveness (Brown, 2015.) Worthington and Drinkard (2000) demonstrated that explicit forgiveness interventions are particularly efficacious when delivered individually and with plenty of time to build empathy for the offender. These theorists underscore the idea that forgiveness is very different from reconciling, condoning, excusing or forgetting (Wade et al., 2014; Brown, 2015). To the opposite effect, it is a process of reclaiming one's life from a painful event, in order to heal and live more fully (Brown, 2015.)

To that end, there are some cautions in forgiveness work. For example, over-forgiveness, or the often-subjugating idea that all offenses must be instantly forgiven and forgotten, may be a strong indication that the client is experiencing spiritual bypass in the form of "compulsive goodness." Researchers continue to demonstrate that personality factors, such as Agreeableness and Neuroticism, play a strong role in the individual's ability to forgive (Bellah et al., 2003; Moorhead et al., 2012). As it pertains to survivors of abuse and violence, suggesting that an individual must forgive, in order to move toward self-reconciliation may be, in and of itself, abuse. For example, Brudholm and Rosoux (2009) provide two survivors' reflections after major human rights atrocities alluding that these survivors were considered "ill" or "pathologized," because they were unable to forgive. The reality is that they may not be in a place of forgiveness for a long time and the notion that they are, somehow, diminished or less than as a result is not ethical. The client's road to forgiveness involves untangling complicated and confounded emotions and messages. The counselor is tasked with coupling this temporal distance from the event with reflective questions and reframing to aid the client in altering their perspective of the narrative and the players. Creative interventions, such as the ones described in this chapter, are a powerful mechanism for moving the counseling process into forgiveness work, when used to engage the client's spiritual/ religious perspective on their issues.

Often tied to painful or traumatic events, *shame* can be an embodied experience for clients, with their affect, behavior, and cognition personifying it in ways that can be observed by themselves and others. Author and researcher Brené Brown defines shame as, "… the intensely painful feeling or experience of believing that we are flawed and therefore unworthy of love and belonging" (2010, p. 39). Indeed, many clinicians can recall a time when clients came to the session heavily carrying the burden of shame and guilt. These two experiences, often used interchangeably, are vastly different in their effect on self-esteem, self-efficacy, and interpersonal functioning. While guilt is often situationally specific (i.e. "I made a mistake") shame is felt globally and intimately (i.e. "I am a mistake") (Brown, 2010). As such, shame is a deeply personal experience in which individuals fear that they may be "discovered" or "exposed" for not meeting specific values that are important. Often, individuals will attempt to hide their shame so that they can remain emotionally safe from themselves and others; the unfortunate side effect of this is that as shame is hidden, it controls behavior, limiting healing and vulnerability (Brown, 2010).

Not unlike spiritual bypass, shame is also a defense mechanism that can help individuals manage their negative experiences while attempting to stay congruent with their strongly held religious/spiritual values. In his work, Kaufman (1989) discussed eight defense mechanisms for shame: rage, contempt, striving for perfection, striving for power, withdrawal, humor, denial, and internal withdrawal. One example of this could be an individual who has religious doubts, but portrays himself as devout. During moments of religious worship or conversation with other parishioners, this individual may internally register questions or feelings of doubt that arise from topics related to the interaction. Feeling shame, and afraid that he may be discovered as 'unfaithful,' this individual may become dogmatically defensive of his faith, and attempt to more explicitly conform to the religious culture.

Brown (2010) writes that for shame to thrive, three elements must be present: secrecy, silence, and judgment. In counseling, clients may protect each of these elements, in order to avoid being 'discovered' or having to confront their feelings of unworthiness. When these defenses manifest, counselors may find themselves becoming stuck with clients and unable to help them move through these experiences by utilizing talk therapy alone. This impasse is frustrating for both the client and counselor, and ultimately does not aid in moving the individual through the quagmire that they are experiencing. Creative interventions, combined with empathy, nonjudgment, and validation can provide clients with a safe, but catalytic space that allows them to experience their emotions and cognitions in transformative ways. This transformation and insight can be enacted in clients' lives to develop forgiveness, vulnerability, authenticity, and new meaning out of lived experiences (Brown, 2010).

Expressive Arts and Creative Interventions

Expressive arts and creative interventions allow clients to engage with their cognitive, behavioral, and emotional worlds in a way that is substantially different from traditional talk therapy. Utilizing a medium or mediums beyond verbal expression allows clients the freedom to experience their worldview and specific issues, while engaging their brains in a different way, making new meanings and neural connections around the experience. An additional benefit is that creating an externalized representation of the issues creates a sense of distance from the event or events; thereby, giving a client a sense of safety regarding their experiences (Moon, 2007). The neuroscience behind this begins in the limbic system, between the cortex and the brainstem, referred to by MacLean (1990) as the "emotional brain." This area of the brain contains the majority of the neural networks responsible for our attachment schemas, implicit memories, and automatic patterns. Unwanted patterns can have origins in painful or traumatic events and responses to those events that have spiritual and religious origins or themes, such as those discussed in this chapter. Patterns are central to therapy, and understanding that patterns stored in the emotional brain are learned experientially and activated unconsciously provides insight into the reason that creative interventions are so powerful. They can help individuals make new meanings out of past experiences, create new neural pathways to begin changing behavioral patterns, and help clients gain insight into their lived-in experiences (Armstrong, 2015).

Creative interventions and expressive arts take many forms in therapy, including visual arts, music therapy, drama therapy, expressive writing, and dance/movement therapy (Degges-White, 2011). These interventions are a powerful addition to the therapeutic process, and are adaptable to the counselor's theoretical orientation. Additionally, expressive and creative techniques are readily accessible for all clients, including clients from diverse cultural backgrounds, as these interventions provide an opportunity for clients to express aspects of their culture, worldview, and life experiences in ways that words may not convey.

There is limited research literature on the use of creative interventions with individuals struggling with religious and/or spiritual issues. However, the research that does exist offers compelling evidence that utilizing a modified empty chair technique (drama therapy), letter writing (expressive writing), and relaxation/visualization techniques can help clients in their relationship with God (Hoffman, 2010). Additional research that supports the link between experiential interventions and spirituality/religion comes from counseling supervision research. Using the bridge activity, spiritual life maps, and sandtray interventions with counseling interns have been seen as a helpful and non-threatening interventions to begin dialogues around spirituality and religion, both in the supervisory relationship and in the counselor/client relationship (Buser et al., 2013; O'Brien and Slater, 2013). For the purposes of this chapter and the case study below, the bridge activity, frequently used in the counseling setting, is explained in detail.

Bridge. The bridge activity consists of creating three "panels," created by folding a piece of paper into a "z" shape. In the first panel, the participant creates a metaphorical drawing of her current religious/spiritual experience or struggle. In the third panel, the participant creates another metaphorical drawing that represents how she would like her religious/spiritual experience to be. After the participant has completed her drawings, she is asked to utilize the middle panel to build a "bridge" from one image to another, either drawing or writing words that may help her move from one image to another. As with other projective techniques, counselors can ask questions around the use of certain images, colors, etc., but interpretation of meanings should be in the hands of the participant. In working through the images and bridge, counselors and clients work together to make meanings, gain insights into the client's experience of the world, and create bridges, or agentic steps, that can move the participant from the current experience into their perceived desired experience. Although this tool can be used for a variety of purposes, it will be used in the case study below as a technique to help a client begin conceptualizing where she is on her spiritual path, and where she may wish to go, moving forward.

Bibliotherapy, Spiritual/Religious Readings and Sacred Texts. Utilizing spiritual/religious readings and sacred texts can be a powerful form of bibliotherapy for individuals interested in engaging in religious/spiritual coping. Sacred texts convey the practices and values of a particular religions' beliefs; they have played an integral role in the course of history, and influence the way many individuals live (Young and Cashwell, 2011). Some examples of the most famous sacred texts include the Bible (Christian text), the Qur'an (Islamic text), the Talmud (Jewish text), and the Vedas (Hindu text). These writings convey a religion's truth, can provide a deeper meaning and purpose for individuals and their life experiences, and elicit a stronger connection to the Divine. It must be clarified that the terms spiritual/religious readings and sacred texts are not interchangeable; some texts are sacred because they are believed to have been revealed by the Divine; whereas, texts that discuss religious themes and values are important, but not sacred.

However, spiritual/religious readings can help individuals further clarify the intent of sacred texts and may be more accessible for use in everyday life. These readings can range from specific religious devotionals or daily readings, to less religious and more inspirational books such as the popular "Chicken Soup for the Soul" series. In particular, when clients are experiencing hardships that are challenging their beliefs, books which frankly discuss struggles can be normalizing in a way in which talking with counselors or religious leaders may not. Books that address the philosophical struggle of the *dark night of the soul*, as originally described by St. John of the Cross (Brenan, 1973) and discussed in Ekhart Tolle's (2004) *The Power of Now*, can resonate with clients regarding the depth of existential crisis in the modern age. Regardless of the text a client chooses, bibliotherapy offers a way to take the work out of the room and into clients' lives when they have the time to reflect.

Meditative Prayer. Prayer has been defined as "communion or conversation with the power recognized as divine" and has been observed as one way that individuals can communicate with God (James, 1978, p. 352). This communion with God is one of the ways that individuals can enter states of meditative and receptive prayer. Meditation, as defined and described in Chapter 6, is viewed historically as a spiritual exercise, but in a Westernized context is often viewed as complementary therapeutic strategy, and may be particularly effective when incorporated into prayer. Meditative prayer is defined as experiencing quietude, listening, and experiencing the presence of the Divine. Receptive prayer is an individual's experience of entering a dialogue or conversation with God which can result in feeling the Divine presence in one's life and/or perceiving direct messages from God (Poloma and Pendleton, 1989; Poloma and Lee, 2011). Research literature shows that utilizing prayer as a contemplative practice can be beneficial to an individual's abilities to accept his or her life experiences, maintain a temporal presence in experiences, and promote an increased closeness to God (Jankowski and Sandage, 2014a; Poloma and Pendleton, 1989).

If a client has an established prayer or meditation practice already, it may be beneficial to engage him in a conversation or provide psychoeducation regarding the overarching psychological benefits that prayer can bring to his life, of which he may have been unaware. For individuals who are not engaged in these practices, discussing the psychological and health-related benefits of both prayer and meditation is a way to help clients alleviate symptoms in a manner that is less threatening than more aggressive interventions, such as psychopharmacology. As with any intervention, counselors should complete a full spiritual/religious assessment with clients, in order to ascertain their openness to either of these practices. In particular, individuals who identify as agnostic or atheist may believe that meditation involves religious undertones which may make them uncomfortable. Conversely, individuals from more conservative religions may experience meditation as a practice that is diametrically opposed to their religious beliefs and prefer to maintain a prayer regime, instead.

Mandalas. Based in transpersonal theory and Jungian ideology (Miller, 2005), mandalas represent a unique method for integrating the whole of the self and increasing client awareness, potentially as related to spiritual bypass, forgiveness and shame, as well as other issues impacting the spiritual domain. This cylindrical art form is visible throughout Eastern spirituality, from Buddhism and Hinduism to Tibetan cultures, and is noted as far back as Paleolithic era (Miller, 2005). Mandalas are visible throughout Native American spirituality, including the medicine wheel and Navajo sand paintings (Brown, 2001). Researchers have linked the creation and interpretation of mandalas to improved mental health outcomes including increasing attention abilities and decreasing impulsive behaviors for children diagnosed with ADHD (Smitheman-Brown and Church, 2013 and decreased post-traumatic symptoms in trauma populations (Henderson et al., 2007).

Characterized as sacred art, the word mandala is based in Sanskrit and means circle (Miller, 2005; Pisark and Larson, 2011). Often used in spiritual and therapeutic settings, mandalas assist individuals in understanding the unconscious self and engaging more thoroughly in the meditative process. Because Jungian theory compares the center of the created mandala as a representation of the center of the self, the interpretation will, inevitably, include themes related to spirituality and religion. The creation of a mandala typically begins with the formation of a sacred, meditative space. The mandala is not limited to a specific medium and usually begins by forming a circle, typically by drawing or painting on an object. Brown states that "[a] circle must be drawn lightly on a sheet of paper or on a canvas. It can be filled in spontaneously, letting the drawing emerge step-by-step in a creatively unpredictable way, similar to doodling" (2001, p. 110). A representation of the inner self, the freeform projections are unconscious thoughts as images, transferred in a holistic manner. According to Jung, interpretation of the created mandala is key to bringing forth the internal messages, wholeness and integrating the self (Miller, 2005). The counselor should not interpret the mandala for the client, rather assist the client in forming his or her own interpretations (Pisark and Larson, 2011).

Brown (2001) created a 12-step program for working with clients that integrates transpersonal psychology, psychosynthesis and mandalas, which he calls the CEIS model or "Creative Explorations of Inner Space." The CEIS model is "designed to prepare participants for the inward adventure, guide them in an in-depth exploration, and lead them to integrate the discoveries made through inspired action in the world" (Brown, 2001, p. 112). The preparation steps focus inward and include solitude, meditation, reflective process and receptive thinking. This is followed by the exploration steps which focus on visualization, mandala art, cognitive process, inner dialogue, psychodrama or symbol identification, integration, closure and sharing (Brown, 2001). For clients experiencing spiritual bypass through the compartmentalizing of the spiritual domain, this represents a powerful method for integrating the whole of the self and bringing to awareness negative behavior patterns, toward the goal of healing of psychological wounds. Further, counselors can address the intrapersonal pain associated with lack of forgiveness and with shame, as these arise in the interpretive process.

Case Study

Cecily is a 45-year-old African-American female in individual counseling, having been referred by her pastor. For a full description of Cecily's presenting concerns, please reference her full profile in the Introduction to this book.

The counselor may take many avenues in working with Cecily, noting that sessions are often complicated by other life issues that are going on at a given time. However, the first goal is to lessen the immediate symptoms of depression and anxiety. Cecily and her counselor will work on this in several ways, initially by requiring that she make an appointment with her primary care doctor for medication evaluation and determining if additional medications might be necessary for her heightened symptoms, before returning to counseling. Further evaluation may be needed, focusing on her current routines, including sleep hygiene and general activity level; and evaluating the frequency of her engagement with both trusted and toxic relationships in her life, as well as whether to continue certain relationships. In her initial presentation, Cecily reports some suicidal ideation (SI) and the counselor works with her in creating a safety plan. As Cecily makes doctors' appointments, creates journals for the aforementioned health issues, and examines the nature of her relationships, the suicidal ideation symptoms began to lessen. Early intervention gives her an action-oriented plan by which she can gain a greater internal locus of control, and utilize autonomy in making decisions about how she wanted to manage her depression and anxiety symptoms.

Once she begins to experience greater emotional stability, the counselor engages Cecily in an exploration of her experiences of shame surrounding the idea that she was not "spiritually devout enough to trust God to make her better." At this point in the counseling process, the exploration centers on specific messages that she received in her early years regarding faith, spirituality, and God's presence in her life. Although her worldview is painted by many experiences and beliefs, Cecily holds the internalized messages that, rather than addressing doubts, these should be given to God, in order to gain patience and guidance. This form of spiritual bypass has not only kept her from growing spiritually, but now that it no longer works for coping, it has propelled her to Fowler's individuative-reflective faith stage (see Chapter 3), leaving her frustrated and bitter. As she explores her religious upbringing, Cecily acknowledges that she was raised in a devout family, attended private religious school, and came of age in a small community in the late 1970s and 1980s, which was still a conservative time for young women. In exploring her mental health history, Cecily reveals to the counselor that she and other family members did experience depression, but this was not something discussed outside of the family. Moreover, individuals who displayed symptoms of mental illness were shunned by the family and church community as having "given in to the devil." In Cecily's early experiences of depression, she turned to her church upbringing and prayers to God to help her cope, which worked for many years.

In Cecily's family and community, "keeping up appearances" is very important. Because of this belief, she has spent many years sublimating her shame and pain regarding her depression, in order to look "perfect" from the outside. However, at this point, her previous coping style no longer works. In her counseling sessions she expresses that she feels angry both at God and her church, as she has spent a lifetime trying to push away her depression, in order to belong. Cecily states in counseling, "I go to church, but I don't want to be there. It feels fake to me, all the years that I've participated in various groups, asked for guidance from my minister, and nothing has changed. For the first time in years I decided last month to stop going, I've put my Bible away and I've stopped praying. It's like I can't even talk to God." Themes of difficulty with forgiving God and her father continue throughout the assessment and counseling process.

At this point, Cecily begins to experience a heightened level of anger, as well as a level of liberation. She expresses feelings of hurt and betrayal by her religious family, that they had not been supportive of her and that they had made her the subject of church gossip. Specifically, she asks, "Why am I working so hard to maintain an appearance of love and acceptance for all of God's children, when my brothers and sisters in Christ didn't appear to love and accept me despite my struggles?" Cecily oscillates between these thoughts and her general relief that she can experience depression without the judgement of others – that she is free to explore her experiences through individual counseling, support group, and accepting friends, without the pressure of keeping up a façade that she felt normal. Many counseling sessions, at this time, center on keeping Cecily on track with her treatment for her depression, exploring feelings of shame, loss and lack of forgiveness surrounding her estrangement from her spiritual community, and engaging her to consider other resources within her spiritual life that could help her when she faced the darkness of her depression.

Once Cecily becomes emotionally stable and feels comfortable with her decision to distance herself from her church family for a few months, work will center on exploring how her religion has played a central role in her life, and how it can, again, be part of her life. Treatment will begin with the bridge activity, with the first panel being a representation of her current religious/spiritual experience and the third panel a projection of what she believed she needed in her life. Cecily's first panel is monochromatic, with a great deal of darkness and grays, showing clouds and a figure curled up, seeming to hide. As a result, the counselor's questions to Cecily center around the meaning she made from the lack of color and her feelings for the figure, which she stated represented her. Consistent with this, she replies she feels that she has abandoned God and he, in turn, has disappeared from her life. She feels misunderstood by her family and her church, because in her withdrawal from them, she believes they think she is not worthy of God's love and care. The feelings of pain and isolation that emanate from both the drawing and Cecily's description are profound.

In the third panel, Cecily infuses some warm colors into a similar drawing. The figure is unfurled, but still depicted in black and grays. There are weak rays of sunlight and a general feeling of increasing warmth in this picture. Cecily expresses this drawing as, "I feel like I'm in the dead of winter right now, if things were to change it would be like spring is slowly starting to come." In the middle panel, Cecily lists goals or ways that she could move toward her "spiritual spring," as we refer to it in counseling. Two items at the top of her list were, "to not feel alone" and "to figure out how to talk to God again." Cecily and the counselor discuss issues of forgiveness and how difficult this process can be, particularly when it comes to the reconciliation of decisions.

Although Cecily's symptoms of depression have lessened through her therapeutic work, she still feels betrayed by her church family. She now comes to counseling to discuss how she can manage her depression, anger, and sadness, as she attempts to work toward forgiving the church family. It is challenging when a client wants to feel less alone or "normal," but does not wish to discuss their issues with others. So, for Cecily, bibliotherapy became the mechanism for normalization. Cecily is open to reading many different books that might help her understand her estrangement from God, as well as open to books that might help her to be more caring toward herself. The books that may resonate with her the most were those authored by Thomas Moore (such as *A Religion of One's Own*) and Sharon Salzberg's loving kindness books (particularly *The Kindness Handbook*).

Cecily is beginning to realize that, through her counseling, she is doing the work that she needs to keep herself emotionally healthy, and through her reading appreciates that themes of betrayal and forgiveness were not unique to her. Through further reflection, she realizes that God wants her to forgive herself and her brothers and sisters in Christ, as He forgives. Cecily found grace, defined as "unmerited divine assistance given to humans for their regeneration or sanctification" (Merriam-Webster, 1999) through her trials and the perspective that her experiences have given her. Although Cecily's story isn't a roadmap for forgiveness, perhaps it gives some insights into trails that others might take with their clients to move them forward.

References

American Association for Marriage and Family Therapy (2015). *AAMFT Code of Ethics*. Alexandria, VA: Author.

American Counseling Association (2014). *ACA Code of Ethics*. Alexandria, VA: Author.

American Psychiatric Association (2013). Diagnostic and Statistical Manual of Mental Disorders (5th ed.). Alexandria, VA: Author.

Arias, A. J., Steinberg, K., Banga, A., and Trestman, R. L. (2006). Systematic review of the efficacy of meditation techniques as treatments for medical illness. *Journal of Alternative and Complementary Medicine*, 12, 817–832.

Armstrong, C. (2015). *The therapeutic "aha!": 10 strategies for getting your clients unstuck*. New York: Norton Publishers.

Baskin, T. W., and Enright, R. D. (2004). Intervention studies on forgiveness: A meta-analysis. *Journal of Counseling & Development*, 82, 79–90. doi:10.1002/j.1556-6678.2004.tb00288.x.

Bellah, C. G., Bellah, L. D., and Johnson, J. L. (2003). A look at dispositional vengefulness from the three and five-factor models of personality. *Individual Differences Research*, 1(1), 6–16.

Bond, K., Ospina, M. B., Hooton, N., Baily, L., Dryden, D. M., Buscemi, N., and Carlson, L. E. (2009). Defining a complex intervention: The development of a demarcation criteria for "meditation". *Psychology of Religion and Spirituality*, 1(2), 129–137.

Brenan, G. (1973). *St. John of the Cross: His life and poetry*. Cambridge: Cambridge University Press.

Brown, B. (2010). *The gifts of imperfection: Let go of who you think you're supposed to be and embrace who you are*. Center City, MN: Hazelden.

Brown, B. (2015). *Daring greatly: How the courage to be vulnerable transforms the way we live, love, parent, and lead*. New York: Avery.

Brown, M. H. (2001). A psychosynthesis twelve step program for transforming consciousness: Creative explorations of inner space. *Counseling and Values*, 45, 103–117.

Brudholm, T., and Rosoux, V. (2009). The unforgiving: Reflections of the resistance to forgiveness after atrocity. *Law & Contemporary Problems*, 72(2), 33–49.

Buser, J. K., Buser, T. J., and Peterson, C. H. (2013). Counselor training in the use of spiritual lifemaps: Creative interventions for depicting spiritual/religious stories. *Journal of Creativity in Mental Health*, 8, 363–380.

Cashwell, C. S. (2005). Spirituality and wellness. In J. E. Myers and T. J. Sweeney (Eds.), *Counseling for wellness: Theory, research, and practice* (pp. 197–206). Alexandria, VA: American Counseling Association.

Cashwell, C. S., Bentley, P. B., and Yarborough, J. P. (2007). The only way out is through: The peril of spiritual bypass. *Counseling and Values*, 51, 139–148.

Cashwell, C. S., Myers, J. E., and Shurts, M. (2004). Using the developmental counseling and therapy model to work with a client in spiritual bypass: Some preliminary considerations. *Journal of Counseling & Development*, 82, 403–409.

Clarke, P. B., Giordano, A. L., Cashwell, C. S., and Lewis, T. F. (2013). The straight path to healing: Using motivational interviewing to address spiritual bypass. *Journal of Counseling & Development*, 91, 87–94.

Dailey, S. F., Gill, C. S., Karl, S., and Barrio Minton, C. (2014). *DSM-5 Learning Companion: A guide for counselors*. Alexandria, VA: American Counseling Association.

Davis, D. E., Worthington, E. L., Hook, J. N., and Hill, P. C. (2013). Research on religion/spirituality and forgiveness: A meta-analytic review. *Psychology of Religion and Spirituality*, 5(4), 233–241. doi:10.1037/a0033637.

Degges-White, S. (2011). Introduction to the use of expressive arts in counseling. In S. Degges-White and N. L. Davis (Eds.), *Integrating the expressive arts into counseling practice: Theory-based interventions* (pp. 1–6). New York: Springer.

forgive. (2017). In Merriam-Webster.com. Retrieved June 1, 2017, from https://www.merriam-webster.com/dictionary/forgive.

Fox, J., Cashwell, C. S., and Picciotto, G. (2017). The Opiate of the Masses: Measuring Spiritual Bypass and Its Relationship to Spirituality, Religion, Mindfulness, Psychological Distress, and Personality. *Spirituality in Clinical Practice*. Advance online publication. http://dx.doi.org/10.1037/scp0000141.

Henderson, P., Rosen, D., and Mascaro, N. (2007). Empirical study on the healing nature of mandalas. *Psychology of Aesthetics*, 1, 148–154.

Moorhead, H. J. H., Gill, C. S., Barrio, C., and Myers, J. E. (2012). Forgive and forget?: Forgiveness as an indicator of wellness among counselors-in-training. *Counseling and Values*, 57(1), 81–95. doi:10.1002/j.2161-007X.2012.00010.x.

Harris, K. A., Randolph, B. E., and Gordon, T. D. (2016). What do clients want? Assessing spiritual needs in counseling: A literature review. *Spirituality in Clinical Practice*, 3(4), 250–275.

Hoffman, L. (2010). Working with the God image in therapy: An experiential approach. *Journal of Psychology and Christianity*, 29(3), 268–271.

Jalāl, D. R. (1995). *The essential Rumi* (C. Barks, Trans.). New York: Harper Collins.

James, W. (1978). *The varieties of religious experience.* New York: Image Books.

Jankowski, P. J., and Sandage, S. J. (2014a). Meditative prayer, gratitude, and intercultural competence: Empirical test of a differential-based model. *Mindfulness*, 5, 360–372.

Kabat-Zinn, J. (2013). *Full catastrophe living: Using the wisdom of your body and mind to face stress, pain, and illness.* New York: Bantam Books.

Kaufman, G. (1989). *The psychology of shame: Theory and treatment of shame-based syndromes.* New York: Springer.

Lawler, K. A., Younger, J. W., Piferi, R. L., Billington, E., Jobe, R., Edmondson, K., and Jones, W. H. (2003). A change of heart cardiovascular correlates of forgiveness in response to interpersonal conflict. *Journal of Behavioral Medicine*, 26, 373–393.

MacLean, P. (1990). *The triune brain in evolution: Role in paleocerebral functions.* New York: Plenum Press.

McCullough, M. E., Pargament, K. I., and Thoresen, C. E. (2000). *Forgiveness: Theory, research, and practice.* New York: Guilford Press.

Merriam-Webster's collegiate dictionary (10th ed.). (1999). Springfield, MA: Merriam-Webster Incorporated.

Miller, D. (2005). Mandalas symbolism in psychotherapy: The potential utility of the Lowenfeld mosaic technique for enhancing the individuation process. *Journal of Transpersonal Psychology*, 37, 164–175.

Moon, B. L. (2007). *The role of metaphor in art therapy: Theory, method, and experience.* Springfield, IL: Charles C. Thomas Publisher Ltd.

Myers, D. G. (2010). *Psychology* (9th ed.). New York: Worth.

Myers, J. E., and Sweeney, T. J. (2004). The indivisible self: An evidenced-based model of wellness. *Journal of Individual Psychology*, 60(3), 234–245.

Myers, J. E., and Sweeney, T. J. (Eds.). (2005). *Wellness in counseling: Theory, research, and practice.* Alexandria, VA: American Counseling Association.

O'Brien, E. R., and Slater, L. B. (2013). Utilizing creative interventions to explore spirituality. CSWE Religion and Spirituality Clearinghouse. http://www.cswe.org/CentersInitiatives/CurriculumResources/50777/58508.aspx

Pargament, K. I. (1997). *The psychology of religion and coping: Theory, research, practice.* New York: Guilford Press.

Pargament, K. I., Desai, K. M., McConnell, K. M., and Calhoun, L. G. (2006). Spirituality: A pathway to posttraumatic growth or decline? In R. G. Tadeschi (Ed.), *Handbook of posttraumatic growth: Research and practice* (pp. 121–137). Mahwah, NJ: Erlbaum Publishers.

Park, C. L. (2005). Religion as a meaning-making framework in coping with life stress. *Journal of Social Issues*, 61, 707–729.

Patton, J. (1985). *Is human forgiveness possible? A pastoral perspective.* Nashville, TN: Abingdon Press.

Patton, J. (2000). Forgiveness in pastoral care and counseling. In M. E. McCullough, K. I. Pargament, and C. E. Thoresen (Eds.), *Forgiveness: Theory, research, and practice.* New York: Guilford Press.

Perez de Albeniz, A., and Homes, J. (2000). Meditation: Concepts, effects and uses in therapy. *International Journal of Psychotherapy*, 5, 49–58.

Picciotto, G., and Fox, J. (2018). Exploring experts' perspectives on spiritual bypass: A conventional content analysis. *Pastoral Psychology*, 67(1), 65–84.

Pisark, C. T., and Larson, K. R. (2011). Facilitating college students' authenticity and psychological wellbeing through the use of mandalas: An empirical study. *The Journal of Humanistic Counseling*, 50(1), 84–98.

Poloma, M. M., and Lee, M. T. (2011). From prayer activities to receptive prayer: Godly love and the knowledge that surpasses understanding. *Journal of Psychology and Theology*, 39(2), 143–154.

Poloma, M. M., and Pendleton, B. F. (1989). Exploring types of prayer and quality of life: A research note. *Journal for the Scientific Study of Religion*, 31(1), 46–53.

Sheridan, M. J. (2017). Addressing spiritual bypassing: Issues and guidelines for spiritually sensitive practice. In B. R. Crisp (Ed.), *The Routledge handbook of religion, spirituality and social work* (pp. 358–367). London: Routledge.

Smitheman-Brown, V., and Church, R. R. (2013). Mandala drawing: Facilitating creative growth in children with ADD or ADHD. *Art Therapy*, 13(4), 252–260. doi:10.1080/07421656.1996.10759233.

Tolle, E. (2004). *The power of now: A guide to spiritual enlightenment*. Vancouver, BC: Namaste Pub.

Wade, N. G., Hoyt, W. T., Kidwell, J. E. M., and Worthington Jr, E. L.. (2014). Efficacy of psychotherapeutic interventions to promote forgiveness: A meta-analysis. *Journal of Consulting and Clinical Psychology*, 82(1), 154–170. doi:10.1037/a0035268.

Welwood, J. (1984). Principles of inner work: Psychological and spiritual. *Journal of Transpersonal Psychology*, 16, 63–73.

Worthington, E. L. (1998). *Dimensions of forgiveness*. Radnor, PA: Templeton Press.

Worthington, E. L., and Drinkard, D. T. (2000). Promoting reconciliation through psychoeducational and therapeutic interventions. *Journal of Marriage and Family Therapy*, 26(1), 93–101.

Young, J. S., and Cashwell, C. S. (2011). Integrating Spirituality and Religion into Counseling: An introduction. In C. S. Cashwell and J. S. Young (Eds.), *Integrating spirituality and religion into counseling: A guide to competent practice*. Alexandria, VA: American Counseling Association.

Index

Acceptance and Commitment Therapy
   (ACT) 138–41; case study (Susanna)
   141–4
acceptance and sensitivity 20–1
acculturation and acculturative stress 75,
   78–9
acting as if 122
Adler, A. 34–5, 71
Adlerian individual psychology: case
   study (Cecily) 123–9; focus and
   phases 116–19; interventions
   120–3; and spirituality
   119–20
Adlerian play therapy (AdPT) 191–2
adolescence 53–4
Alcoholics Anonymous (AA) see 12-step
   model
altered states of consciousness (ASCs)
   101, 107
American Counseling Association
   (ACA): Code of Ethics 10–11, 23, 25
American Psychiatric Association (APA)
   see Diagnostic and Statistical Manual
   (DSM) (APA)
"anomalous experiences" 100–1, 103
AQAL matrix 60, 101
art therapy see creative and experiential
   therapies
assessment xvii, 41–6, 118–19; case
   studies 46–7, 125–8; family systems
   182–6; process 42–3; rationale 42;
   types 43–6
Association for Spiritual, Ethical,
   and Religious Values in
   Counseling (ASERVIC)
   xv–xvi, 1, 36;
   competencies xvi–xix, 1–2,
   11, 20, 21, 32, 41
assumptions 22

belief systems 37–41
bibliotherapy 214, 219
biosocial theory of emotional
   dysregulation 136
bridge activity 213–14, 218–19
Brief Acculturation Scale 75
broaching xviii, 22–3, 25
Brown, A. E. et al. 163, 167–9
Brown, B. 210, 211–12
Brown, M. H. 215, 216
Buber, M. 89, 92
Buchanan, M. et al. 155, 156
Buddhism 132, 134, 139, 140; Eastern
   philosophy and religion 101, 133–4,
   136–7, 138, 215–16

Carlson, J. et al. 116, 117, 118, 119,
   120, 121, 122, 123
cartography 100
case conceptualisation 64–5; clinical
   formulation 72–4; cultural
   formulation 74–7; and diagnosis
   65–8; and diagnostic formulation
   68–72; treatment formulation: case
   study (Susanna) 77–9
Cashwell, C. et al. xv, 160, 162, 163,
   208, 209
Cashwell, C. S.: and Young, J. S. xvi,
   13, 19, 20, 21, 24; Young, J. S. and
   35, 41, 51, 89, 214
child-centered play therapy
   (CCPT) 191
childhood: development theories 52–3,
   57; and family beliefs 176, 177–8;
   memories 121; play and play therapy
   190–2
Christian Orthodoxy Scale 72
Christianity 21, 22, 139, 176; models of
   mindfulness 134

client communication *see*
    communication
client coping *see* coping
client culture *see* culture
client profiles and case studies 3–6;
    Cecily 5–6, 61–3, 123–9, 201–3,
    216–19; Lin, Paul, Adam, and John
    5, 181–6; Marian 4, 91–4, 110–12;
    Nassir 4–5, 169–71; Susanna 3–4,
    46–7, 77–9, 141–4, 153–7
clinical formulation 72–4
cognitive behavioral play therapy
    (CBTP) 192
cognitive behavioral therapies *see* "third
    wave" cognitive behavioral therapies
collaborative style of problem-solving 69
collage 198–9
Collins, S. and Arthur, N. 10, 13, 23,
    24; et al. 10, 12–13
communication xvii, 19–26; acceptance
    and sensitivity 20–1; and belief
    systems 39; identifying therapeutically
    relevant practices and beliefs 24–6;
    social behavior and culture 33–4;
    strategies 21–4; tips 26
community feeling 116–17
competencies xvi–xix, 1–2, 11, 20, 21,
    32, 41
conjunctive faith 55
consciousness: levels of 137;
    non-ordinary states of 106–8;
    "spectrum of human
    consciousness" 104
continuously monitor assumptions 22
coping, client 40–1, 45
"Core Values Lifemap" 91
Cottone, R. R. 148–9, 150; et al. 14
counselor self-awareness xvi, 9–12;
    beginning the journey 15–17;
    continuing the journey 18–19; as
    core value 10–11; cultivating 14–15;
    definitions 9–10; gains of 11–14; *see
    also* communication
countertransference 13
creative and experiential therapies 90–1,
    189–90, 192–3; case study (Cecily)
    201–3; exploring spiritual and
    religious themes 198–201; expressive
    arts 91, 194–5, 212–16; role of
    spirituality and religion 193–4
"Creative Explorations of Inner Space"
    (CEIS) model 216
"crises of faith" 70
cultural explanation 75–6, 79

cultural formulation 74–7
cultural identity 74–5, 78–9
culture, client 32–4; versus personality
    76–7, 79; and worldview xvi, 15
Curry, J. R. 16, 199, 200; and Simpson,
    L. R. 20, 21, 24, 25

Daniels, M. 99, 100, 102, 104
Day-Vines, N. L. et al. xviii, 22–3, 25
death: as given of existentialism 85–6
deferring style of problem-solving 69
delusion, definition of 67
developmental theories 51; application:
    case study (Cecily) 61–3; Fowler's
    stages of faith 51–6, 61–2, 70; Genia's
    psychospiritual development 57–60,
    62; Wilber's integral psychology
    60–1, 62–3
diagnosis 65–8; and treatment xvii
diagnostic formulation 68–72
Diagnostic and Statistical Manual (*DSM*)
    (APA) 65, 66–7, 207; *DSM-5* 67–8
dialectic behavior therapy (DBT) 135–8
Dinkmeyer, D. C. et al. 116–17, 119,
    120, 121, 122, 123
discussions, existential 89–90
Divine *see* God/Divine/Higher Power
divine struggles 70
dogmatic faith 58, 62, 74
"Dropping Anchor" technique 141
drug addiction: case study (Nassir)
    169–71

Eastern philosophy and religion 101,
    133–4, 136–7, 138, 215–16;
    Buddhism 132, 134, 139, 140
egocentric faith 57–8
Ellis, A. 66
"emotional brain" 213
emotional dysregulation, biosocial
    theory of 136
encouragement 123
existentialism 85; case study (Marian)
    91–4; givens of 85–6, 87–8, 89–90,
    91; interventions 88–91; logotherapy
    86–7; and spirituality 87–8
experiential exercises 17
expressive arts 91, 194–5, 212–16; *see
    also* creative and experiential therapies
externalizing 150–1, 155

faith: and belief, comparative definitions
    37–8; Fowler's stages of 51–6,
    61–2, 70

family: Adlerian individual psychology 117, 118–19
family systems: case study (Lin and Paul) 181–6; genograms 180–1, 182–6; and socio-metric techniques 175–6, 178–81; and spirituality 176–8
forgiveness 210–11
Fowler's stages of faith 51–6, 61–2, 70
Fox, J. et al. 208, 209–10
Frankel, V. 86–7, 88
freedom: as given of existentialism 86
Freud, S. xiv, 66, 116

Genia's psychospiritual development 57–60, 62
genograms 180–1; case study (Lin and Paul) 182–6
Gill, C. S. et al. 16, 20, 21, 24, 42, 44, 45
God Image Inventory 71, 79
God/Divine/Higher Power 35–6, 40, 45, 46; Acceptance and Commitment Therapy (ACT) 140; Adlerian theory 119–20; belief and mental health 66, 67, 68–9; Christianity 22; developmental stages 52–3, 54, 55, 57–9, 61–2, 70; and divine punishment 76; logotherapy 87; meditative prayer 214–15; *Psalms of Lament* 200–1, 202–3; questioning belief in 208; representation/image 71, 79; spiritual/religious readings and sacred texts 214; 12 step model 162, 163, 164, 166, 167, 169
grief: *Psalms of Lament* 200–1, 202–3
Grof, S. 100, 104; and Grof, C. 104, 106, 109

Higher Power *see* God/Divine/Higher Power
Hodge, D. R. 41–2, 44, 87, 90–1
holotropic breath work 100, 104, 106
Humanistic Model of Spirituality 36
hypnosis and hypnotic states 108

I-thou relationship 89, 92
implicit assumptions 22
individual psychology *see* Adlerian individual psychology
individuated-reflective faith 54, 62, 70
individuation 99

Indivisible Self Model of Wellness (IS-WEL) 209
inferiority/superiority 117
Ingersoll, R. 87, 88, 89
inner experiences in practice 13
insight phase 119, 128–9
integral psychology, Wilber's 60–1, 62–3
interpersonal spiritual struggles 70
intrapersonal spiritual struggles 70
intuitive-projective faith 52–3
Islam: case study (Nassir) 169–71
isolation: as given of existentialism 86

James, W. xiv, 11, 99
Jung, C. xiv–xv, 11, 99, 159, 162, 215, 216

Kabat-Zinn, J. 19, 133
Kasprow, M. C. and Scotton, B. W. 106, 107
Krippner, S. 100–1, 102, 103, 104, 105
kundalini experience (case study) 110–12

levels of consciousness 137
"Life Meaning Map" 91
lifestyle and style of life 117–18, 119
Linehan, M. 135–6, 137–8
logotherapy 86–7
LSD-25 (lysergic acid diethylamide) 100

maladaptive behavior; functioning 74; private logic 117, 119, 123; and religious belief 25
mandalas 215–16
Maslow, A. 11, 99–100
McAdams, D. P. 15–16
meaning-making: and art 91, 194–5; and logotherapy 86–7; *see also* existentialism
meaninglessness: as given of existentialism 86
meditation 107–8, 167, 214–15
midlife and advanced age 55
mindfulness 19, 107
mindfulness-based cognitive-behavioral therapy (MCBT) 133–5
multiculturalism 12–13, 34
music therapy 196
Myers, J. E.et al. 35, 36; and Sweeney, T. J. 209
mythic-literal faith 53

narrative identity 15–16
narrative therapy 147–9; case study
    (Susanna) 153–7; and spirituality 149;
    and techniques 150–3
non-substance-induced altered states of
    consciousness (ASCs) 101, 107

open and closed belief systems
    39–40, 41
orthodoxy 71–2
Oshodi Sentence Completion Index
    (OSCI) 46

Pargament, K. I. 36–7, 43, 45, 70, 207;
    et al. 40–1, 45, 69; and Krumrei, E. J.
    42–3, 46
patterns 70–1, 78
perpetuants 74, 78
personality versus culture 76–7, 79
Pew Research Center 176
Piedmont, R. L. et al. 35, 36
play therapy 190–1; exploring spiritual
    themes 194–7; theories 191–2; *see
    also* creative and experiential therapies
poetry 200–1
Pompeo, A. M. and Levitt, D. H. 10,
    14, 16, 17
Positive Psychology 99, 169
prayer 167, 214–15
precipitants 69–70, 78
predispositions 72–4, 78
presentation 68–9, 78
private logic 117, 119, 123
Psalms of Lament 200–1, 202–3
psilocybin 101
psychological predisposition 72–3
psychospiritual development, Genia's
    57–60, 62
psychospiritual integration 99
push button technique 122

qualitative assessment 43–4
quantitative assessment 44–6
Question, The: Adlerian individual
    psychology 120

RCOPE (Model of Religious
    Coping) 45
re-authoring/re-storying 151–3, 156–7
re-membering conversations 153, 156–7
REACH pyramid 211
reaction formation 208–9
reconstructed internalized faith 58–9, 62
Reflecting As If 122

reflective exercises 17
reflective practice 18–19
religion, defining 36–7
Religious Problem-Solving Scale 69
reorientation phase 119, 123, 129
Richards, K. et al. 14, 19, 35, 45,
    68–9, 72
Rogers, C. 11, 12
Rokeach, M. 38–9, 41, 56, 59
Rollins, J. 20, 21, 23, 24

sacred texts 214
sandtray therapy 196–7
scaffolding conversations 151–3
Schön, D A. 18
self-actualization 99
self-awareness *see* counselor
    self-awareness
self-care, counselor 19
self-concept 140–1
self-directing style of
    problem-solving 69
self-disclosure, counselor 23–4
self-forgetting 100
sensitivity and acceptance 20–1
shame 211–12
Silkwood, W. D. 162
social rules, violation of 178
socio-grams 180
socio-metric (interviewing) techniques
    175–6, 178–81
sociocultural predisposition 73
SoulCollage 199
special issues and interventions 207–8;
    case study (Cecily) 216–19;
    expressive arts and creative
    interventions 212–16; spiritual
    bypass, forgiveness, and shame
    208–12
"spectrum of human consciousness" 104
Sperry, L. 64, 65, 68, 70, 71, 72, 74,
    103–4; and Sperry, J. 34, 65, 68, 69,
    70, 71, 74, 75, 76
Spiritual Assessment Scale (SAS) 45
spiritual autobiography 16
spiritual bypass 208–10
Spiritual Bypass Scale (SBS) 209–10
spiritual ecomaps 44; case study
    (Susanna) 46–7
spiritual emergency 109
Spiritual Health Inventory (SHI) 45–6
spiritual lifemaps 90–1
spiritual struggles 70, 88, 140–1
spiritual timelines 199–200

Spiritual Well-being Model/Scale 35–6
spiritual wellness dimensions 87, 88, 89
Spiritual Wellness model 45
spiritual/religious readings 214
spirituality, defining 35–6, 87, 207
spitting in the soup 121
stages of faith, Fowler's 51–6, 61–2, 70
state forgiveness 210
states of consciousness 106–8
substance-induced states of
  consciousness 106–7
superiority/inferiority 117
synthetic-conventional faith 53–4, 61

therapeutic alliance 12; Adlerian 118,
  123–5; existentialism 89
"third wave" cognitive behavioral
  therapies 132–3; case study
  (Susanna) 141–4; types 133–41
three-phased approach to self-awareness
  16–17
trait forgiveness 210
transcendent function 99
transcendental faith 59
transference and countertransference 13
transitional faith 58, 62
transpersonal theory 98, 102–3;
  case study (Marian) 110–12; client
  reports of transpersonal experiences
  109–10; CEIS model 216;
  interventions

106–8; and spirituality 104–6;
  theoretical development 98–102;
  transpersonal counseling 103–4
12-step model 159–60; case study
  (Nassir) 169–71; historical context
  161–2; interventions (facilitation and
  practice) 166–9; process 164–6; and
  spirituality 162–4

"unhealthy beliefs" 25
universalizing faith 55–6

V-code for religious or spiritual
  problem 67–8
values conflicts 23
Views of Suffering Scale (VOSS) 76

well-being, counselor 13–14
White, M. 148, 149, 150, 151,
  152–4; and Epston, D.
  147–8, 151
Wickramasekera II, I. E. 108
Wilber, K. 101–2, 104
Wilber's integral psychology 60–1,
  62–3
worldview 34–5; and culture xvi, 15;
  dialectic 136

Yalom, I. 85, 86, 88, 89–90, 91
Young, J. S. *see* Cashwell, C. S.
young adulthood 54

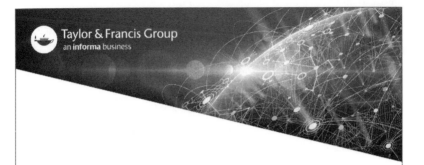